HOW TO SELL YOUR IDEA, OVERCOME ROADBLOCKS, AND LOVE YOUR JOB

KAREN HOLST & DOUGLAS FERGUSON

An imprint of Baring Street LLC
info@baringstreet.com
www.baringstreet.com

Ordering information:
Special discounts are available on quantity purchases by corporations, associations, companies, organizations, and anyone that wants lots of copies of this great book.
For details, email info@baringstreeet.com.

Written by Karen Holst & Douglas Ferguson
Edited by Kellie McGann and Ana Joldes
Designed by Shawn Bueche

Library of Congress Cataloging-in-Publication Data
Names: Holst, Karen, author | Ferguson, Douglas, author
Title: Start Within: How to sell your idea, overcome roadblocks, and love your job / Karen Holst and Douglas Ferguson.
Description: First Edition. | Arizona : Baring Street, 2020.
Identifiers: LCCN 2020905629 | ISBN 978-1-7347518-0-2 (paperback) | 978-1-7347518-1-9 (ebook) | 978-1-7347518-2-6 (audio book)
Subjects: LCSH: Success in Business. | Decision-Making & Problem Solving. | Career Development. | Organizational Change. | Strategic Planning. | Innovation. | Business Communications. | Entrepreneurship. | Intrapreneurship. | Strategic Planning.
LC record available at http://lccn.loc.gov/2020905629

To my husband, Ryan, my favorite person to launch new ideas with and our greatest creation yet, Bear.

— Karen

To my dad who showed me the importance of modesty and my mom who taught me to lead with compassion.

— Douglas

CONTENTS

GET READY

GET SET

GO

INDEX OF SECTIONS

GET

READY

YOUR BIG IDEA

Introduction

Everything changed the day I walked into the lobby of the state agency's headquarters.

Weeks before, my partners and I sold our edtech company to Blackboard. I was ready for a break from the entrepreneur/startup roller coaster and signed up for the opposite—a year-long innovation fellowship with the California Department of Education.

As I wandered the glossy hallways of the marbled government building that first day on the job, I noticed how different it was from my bustling startup. Everyone was wearing a suit; this was going to be a serious shift. In my new role, I was tasked to lead an innovative effort that would change the way the government agency implemented educational technology tools.

Technology was changing faster than the California Department of Education could adapt to it. The regulations and processes in place were there for good reason—they deal with billions of taxpayer dollars and every penny must be thoughtfully accounted for. Which meant I was going to need to learn a new way of working. Suddenly, my entrepreneurial mind had to fit within the mindset of a bureaucratic agency.

Brian, a member of my newfound team, offered to give me a tour of the office. As we wandered from department to department, he filled me in on the "stuff I should know."

"Bill in accounting sits over there. He's who you *really* need to talk to for budget approval—get on his good side. Oh and over there in IT is Julia. If you're going to be changing anything in the portal—she's the one you'll be dealing with."

Almost everyone he pointed out had a specific role with an even more specific skill. I was starting to realize that if I wanted to implement something new, I was going to have to involve a lot of people, who were comfortable in their ways, to embrace change. But who doesn't love change?

Using my entrepreneurial mindset, I quickly set out to shift the way things were done in the middle of a big government agency. It wasn't long before I was stuck in red tape, confused about who I needed to talk to next, what meeting I was supposed to attend, or why everything seemed to take so long. I was used to being able to drive the car and do things the way I wanted them done—so how was I going to make this my own and *Start Within?*

My instinct kicked in. I began sharing ideas, asking questions, and getting buy-in from the people around me. I used the same tools I did to create a company but inside of an organization that desperately needed the innovation. While wading through the bureaucracy, red tape, and hundreds of "nos" to get each idea off the ground, I recognized that I needed to call in support. I sought out mentors and confidants who had done this kind of work before to test out my theories and talk through my work. I was hungry for guidance, but it became clear that there was no manual for how to do this. (Until now, of course.)

I started to wonder, why do some people get through the red tape while others seem stuck? I asked people who had created change in a large organization, "What worked for you? How did you succeed?" And to the people who hadn't, "Where did you get lost?"

It was clear there was a gap between people who wanted to create change and the knowledge of how to do it. A lot of those bright people with ideas start to think, "Well, maybe this just isn't for me..."

There's a myth that you need a certain job title or salary to do the work you want to do. That you need to wait for someone to tell you it's okay or to hand you the keys. But the secret to launching your idea is to just take one step. (Don't worry—you'll learn how.)

THE DOERS

These are the people who see problems and want to fix them. They're the ones who always seem to get things done. Often seen as the persons who always gets things done, the frustrating thing for doers when they're in the middle of big organizations is the tension between an idea and taking action. In some cases, they might not know how to move their idea forward, or they're buried in a sea of their own responsibilities. But when doers have the right tools to bring their ideas to the next level, the potential is endless.

The doers are in a unique position; they're the ones on the ground, close to the problems that plague the customers and the company. And as soon as doers are empowered, problems will start getting solved and new ideas implemented.

The doers don't have a specific title, they're the project managers, engineers, product leaders, customer service representatives, marketing interns, or anyone else waiting to launch their ideas inside a company. They're driven by a desire to solve problems but lack the resources and tools to help them get there. Now there's a step-by-step guide on how to bridge the gap.

This book provides a framework for the doers to identify where opportunities for their ideas exist and understand how to push those ideas forward in a way that won't get rejected by the corporate hierarchy.

Rather than wait for the perfect corporate culture budding with opportunities for innovative new ideas, or a brand-new title bestowing authority or permission, there's a way forward now. A way that motivates doers to move toward more meaningful work, and empowers them to take that work on themselves.

It's the escape from the workday that starts to feel just like the day before. The alarm goes off, check email on your phone, coffee, commute, work, coffee, commute, home, repeat. Cue Bill Murray's character in the movie *Groundhog Day*, reliving the same thing, over and over again.

For the doers reading this, who want to explore new challenges, develop your own ideas, and find real purpose in your work—you are ready to *Start Within*.

FIND JOY IN SOLVING PROBLEMS

The key to truly fulfilling work is spending time on what brings you purpose. It's the kind of work that unlocks the excitement of learning something new, gives you ownership of the project, and allows you to build something you care about.

Pause to think about some of your happiest memories.

As a kid, that might have been working like mad on your soccer skills, and then seeing an opening by the goal to kick in the final tie-breaking score in the season's final game. For me, it was nailing the backflip I'd been practicing all summer off the diving board at my neighborhood pool. With each try, a new lesson was learned. Open my tuck position too soon and I have water blast up my nose. Or push off the diving board at a more horizontal angle and slap my back atop the water. With each mistake, a lesson was learned. And then, dangling my heels over the edge of the diving board for what felt like the millionth time, all of a sudden, I launched and pulled off my first backflip! The hard work and dedication to tweaking my method paid off, the pain a distant memory; I was a proud backflipping 7-year-old.

Or as an adult, it might look like the time you worked on a difficult project launch that your boss told you wouldn't work and after many months of ups and downs, you ended up with record-breaking results.

The path toward happiness, upon reflection, was paved with problems. The challenges and obstacles only made it a bigger reward in the end. Joy often comes from overcoming the problems you face.

So often we think that these problems get in the way of our happiness, but for people like you and me, much of our happiness actually comes from solving problems.

When we work toward solving problems and launching ideas, we gain a renewed sense of autonomy. Very few people proclaim, "Man, do I wish I had excessive supervision. I sure do love it when my boss watches over me closely and provides constant criticism of my work and process." Of course we don't say that. What we seek in our work is the opportunity to own a project and solve a problem we believe in.

According to a report by the *Journal of Personality and Social Psychology*,[1] the number one contributor to our happiness is autonomy, or "the feeling that your life—its activities and habits—are self-chosen and self-endorsed."

It's true, launching your idea will bring you happiness. You will get to roll up your sleeves and start solving problems left and right. You will believe in the projects you are working toward and you will have some autonomy over your work.

Maybe you want to create a sustainable work-from-home program, launch a new fundraising event, institute a new process for green-lighting budget approvals, or any other exciting idea you want to see take off in your company. Launching your idea will be hard and difficult work, riddled with challenges and complexity. It will be a struggle, but with perseverance, you will get to the finish line.

A CHANGE AGENT PLAYBOOK

Start Within will be your playbook to begin navigating these challenges, providing you the tools and resources that you need to bring your idea from start to finish. It will guide you through the process of launching an idea within a company and help you get around the inevitable obstacles that will come along the way.

Here's a preview of the journey ahead:

[1]Barsh, Capozzi, and Davidson. "McKinsey Quarterly: Leadership and innovation." McKinsey.com

PART ONE: GET READY

First up on the journey you'll need to get ready. This section focuses on you. We'll cover the moment of truth—knowing your idea is ready to pursue, assumptions and mindsets that might get in your way, and getting organized to move forward.

PART TWO: GET SET

Our second section will focus on getting you set to launch. This means looking at the environment around you and evaluating the best way to get where you want to go. We'll help you build a process forward that works with your organization, figure out your organization's business strategies and objectives and how to align your idea to them, and show you how to get buy-in from important people who shape the outcome.

PART THREE: GO

You're finally prepared and ready to go—this section is all about making moves. You'll learn to build your idea in stages and how to prototype, how to turn a "no" into a "yes" when you run into naysaying bosses or colleagues, and more about forming and supporting your team to launch your idea.

Each chapter is packed with a one-two punch, starting with stories from the trenches and ending with activities for you to roll up your sleeves and apply the lessons to your own work.

The stories come from people like you—doers from different types of organizations, across various industries providing inspiration and insights from their success and failures. The activities will take what you learned and help you launch your big idea.

There's a lot of work to grow that idea from a personal aspiration into a living, breathing, thriving project within your organization. Bureaucracies are hard to navigate and red tape slows you down. Complicated reporting structures are a tangled web, making it challenging to find a thread and identify a way forward. Or business-as-usual is encouraged and despite the talk of having an "innovative culture," employees are encouraged to "swim in their own lane" and it's not clear how to buck the status quo.

If you zoom out, getting your idea adopted by your organization will look like a formidable agility test. The size of the course, the difficulty of the obstacles, and the time to completion will all vary based on you, the idea, and the organization where you work.

But there is a way through, and this book will provide the tools you need to map your course, anticipate speed bumps, react to hurdles, and get your idea successfully through to the finish line.

YOUR GUIDES FOR THIS TREK

I'm Karen, and both myself and my co-author, Douglas, have spent the last 20 years in the trenches bringing ideas forward within organizations. Reflecting upon these experiences, we began to notice that while no one company is like the other, there are common patterns that are almost universal.

The *Start Within* framework provides a way to assess your situation, how it relates to the unique nature of your company, and what tools and actions are appropriate for you to move forward.

Having co-founded an educational technology company while a junior at the University of Texas, I stumbled into my career as an entrepreneur and have been launching new ideas ever since.

In 2010, when my company, MyEdu, was acquired by Blackboard, I pivoted from being an entrepreneur to becoming an intrapreneur, where I still launched new ideas but rather than with my startup, within larger organizations. I became a fellow with Fuse Corps, a nonprofit organization that enables government agencies to more effectively address their biggest challenges. The organization takes private sector leaders and puts them smack dab in the middle of a government agency to bring new ways of thinking and approaches to life. Through the year-long fellowship, I was head of Educational Technology for the California Department of Education, in the public education trenches, helping steer the large agency to reimagine edtech and design innovative programs.

It wasn't easy, but flexing the entrepreneurial muscle and launching new ideas within a huge, bureaucratic state agency was a dream job for someone who loves uncovering problems and creating traction toward change—like getting second-grade teachers to try new technology in their classrooms. There, I learned what it takes to wrangle stakeholders from Silicon Valley execs at tech companies to policymakers at the White House Office of Science and Technology, and how to drive innovative approaches within a government organization with many layers of complexity and matrixed stakeholder management.

Upon completing my fellowship, I joined the international design firm IDEO to help launch the education platform IDEO U. I found the constraints of building a new product within the walls of an existing company to be one of the most fulfilling career accomplishments. There, I learned what it takes to leverage cross-company collaboration for innovation and have since run the gamut from incubated tech and AI startups to large public corporations like Autodesk.

In addition to the corporate work, I have been teaching courses on product innovation and launching products as a LinkedIn Learning instructor since 2018. This has given me the opportunity to reach learners globally, and help them apply innovation to their day-to-day work.

A few years ago, while I was coaching people doing innovation work, I was introduced to Douglas Ferguson, who was running workshops that made the ideas I was talking about come to life. After an interview for his innovation series, we realized we were aligned and passionate about the same things—equipping the doer with tools to make innovation happen. Our thoughts and ideas for what we wanted to accomplish integrated seamlessly and where they were different they were complimentary. We quickly joined forces and I roped him into being my co-writer. While this book comes from my point of view, Douglas has been my co-pilot through it all.

Like me, Douglas has 20 years of experience in launching new ventures. As a former CTO, he's focused on people, process, and technology. Through years of curious experimentation, he's discovered best practices and invented novel ways to empower teams to build innovative products.

Starting at Coremetrics, a web analytics firm acquired by IBM, Douglas learned what it takes to be a software engineer inside a large startup, how to lead new initiatives in a large company, and manage problem-solving while leading two teams. After Coremetrics, he led engineering and product teams at numerous Austin, Texas, startups including Famigo, a mobile platform that made devices safe for kids. While at Famigo, Douglas managed a large partnership with AT&T, which involved even more massive change management efforts. His most recent venture, Twyla, was an art marketplace backed by Google Ventures (GV). While at Twyla, Douglas worked closely with the GV Design Team, including Jake Knapp, Braden Kowitz, and John Zeratsky, authors of the book *Sprint*, to apply the design sprint methodology to test and launch new and novel ideas.

In 2017, he launched Voltage Control, a workshop agency, which pulled him into the corporate world, where he applies his startup innovation experience while voraciously exploring and studying the problems of the enterprise innovator, the intrapreneur. Applying insights from this inquiry, he gets to create and implement tools to help these companies and people drive innovation.

While launching and building Voltage Control, Douglas observed teams who were struggling to execute their vision after ideation or exploration sessions. They couldn't find a way to move from the now to the next. He wrote *Beyond the Prototype* to help these teams and many like them avoid these pitfalls. *Beyond the Prototype* is a roadmap for navigating the fuzzy area between ideas and outcomes. Full of stories from companies like Google, Liberty Mutual, and Adobe, his book outlines six steps that every team should take to launch their vision.

Driven by curiosity and storytelling, Douglas and I have identified where doers get stuck, and through years of research and implementation, we've created the tools to forge a path forward.

With our combined experience, failures, wins, and tested approaches, we have designed *Start Within*, a methodology for you to launch a new idea at your company. We will share a roadmap and reference guide with stories of doers who got things done, navigated setbacks, and how they dusted themselves off and got back into the race.

Start Within has helped people from a variety of industries and organizational structures to better understand how to pursue and bring their ideas to life—from launching new products within a government agency to building new departments within a large corporation.

This book will give you a blueprint for moving through this process and will encourage you along the way with exercises to help you reflect and personalize.

You will be able to get started, keep going, and get unstuck when things get hard. *Start Within* will give you the tools to rock out your "day job" while balancing this big idea you want to launch.

GO BEYOND DREAMING TO DOING

You don't have to be a data analysis or research consultant to know that businesses are working at breakneck speed to try to innovate. Organizations are struggling to come up with new, viable ideas that will transform markets and lead them into the future. From big corporations like Amazon, working to have the fastest distribution model, to local school districts stretching to quickly build e-learning solutions—organizations of all sizes are looking to innovate.

And this innovation isn't limited to scientific advances or technological breakthroughs. Everything is in flux—and everything demands innovative thinking. Especially in big companies, where more than 70% of senior executives believe innovation will drive growth, though 65% lack confidence in their decisions to stimulate innovation.[1]

Organizations desperately need you to launch your new idea and drive innovation. So what gives, why isn't it happening?

To date, most books and resources have been focused on building a culture that can create change and other top-down innovation systems that leave the doer wondering where they fit in. A hefty challenge and one that often sits outside of the hands of people like you and me, the doers, the people actually trying to push these ideas forward. Innovation is about action on the ground and up until now, there hasn't been a handbook for the change agent.

Whether you have been mulling over your big idea for a while, just waiting for the right time to make it happen, or recently stumbled on a solution that could be substantial for your organization, this book gives you the tools to start, the way forward, and the tips you need to avoid major obstacles.

And while the process to bring your idea to fruition will take time, the benefits of it bringing you purpose and joy won't. By committing to making your idea happen, you will start to see your work have more meaning and the challenges will make it even more exciting.

Now is the time to make your idea happen. Don't wait for perfection or pretend there will be some ideal time to do so in the future. If you've ever felt you were somehow wasting your time and potential, now is the time to find purpose in your work and *Start Within.*

[1]Barsh, Capozzi, and Davidson. "McKinsey Quarterly: Leadership and innovation." McKinsey.com

THE MOMENT OF TRUTH

Ready to Launch?

There it all was, laid across my basement floor: white slabs of particle board in various sizes with metal rods, corner hinges, and mini plastic bags holding hundreds of candy-sized bits and pieces. It was a Sunday afternoon, and I'd decided at last to assemble the IKEA storage unit I'd bought three months earlier.

I told myself, "I can do this!"

I took an inventory of the tools needed, unpacked all the boxes, and breezed through the instruction packet. Time check—it was 2 p.m. By 2:23 I would be done, with ample time left to binge-watch some TV. Sunday afternoon challenge accepted.

After ten minutes of dragging around some of the frames and shelves, I strained to align the base and sideboards. The instructions said "click," but what I heard was definitely more like a "crack."

A half-hour later, I decided I wasn't meant to follow the simple, 46-step assembly instructions sequentially. The best jumping-off point was clearly page five of the little white booklet.

Voila! By the time I got to page seven, things were starting to come together. Several half-assembled modules were propped against the walls. There was something resembling a drawer, and a leaning shelf that slanted like a slide. But nothing looked like the storage unit pictured on the IKEA website.

Disillusion started to set in.

"Ugh, what on earth made me sign up for this?"

Somewhere along the way, I detached the few pieces I had managed to assemble, and laid everything out again. This time, the floor looked less like an organized plan-of-action and more like evidence at a crime scene.

Close to midnight, after many false starts and restarts, I put the drill down. At last, the *fruktansvärd* storage unit was erect! I made a few modifications to the plan and a few screws may have still been lying on the floor, but the completed project looked great.

To this day, for some strange reason, I've become fairly attached to the storage unit. I found out later that there's something called the IKEA effect, a sort of cognitive bias toward items you've created. There's something about having spent hours screwing that thing together that makes me proudly boast whenever a new guest visits.

Launching a new idea within your company is no different than tackling an IKEA assembly project; it takes confidence, persistence, adaptability—and there will always be screws left over.

It all starts with the confidence that you can take on the challenge of launching your idea. A desire to create something impactful is essential, not only to get the project going, but to fuel your tanks when things get messy—as they invariably will.

The journey will be filled with ups, downs, and twists and turns that will force you to think twice about your idea, and most likely even reshape it. Persistence will be the engine that keeps you moving through the bursts of tension and adversity.

In other moments, you'll feel like a sticky mass of taffy being pulled in every direction, not sure which way to lean. You'll need to be flexible and adaptable enough to change direction along the way. Your idea will most definitely look different at the end from what you imagined at the start.

Once you embrace the process and journey, the ambiguity will be fun rather than scary. (Most of the time.)

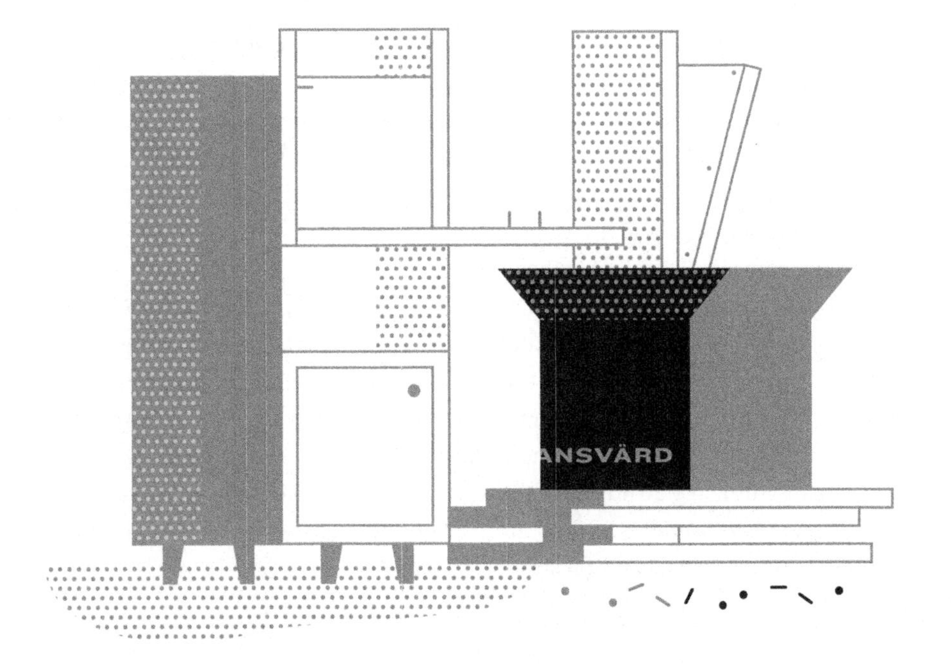

CONFIDENCE: OPTIMISM ROOTED IN REALISM

Would you feel a sense of achievement if your bosses adopted your idea for a new innovation department? Do you believe your product could be the solution your customers desperately need? Do you want to launch a corporate responsibility program that will boost your company's bottom line *and* help the environment?

Good ideas are everywhere, but what's really rare is taking the steps that turn these ideas into reality. That's the hard part.

Instead of taking steps forward, we all too often keep even our most exciting ideas to ourselves, nervous about how others will react to them and unsure of our ability to put them into practice.

Take a moment to think about this. What are the constraints holding you back as you look to launch your big idea?

The first step to overcoming those constraints is to understand exactly what they are, and the best way to do that is to make a list of all the answers you can think of to the question: "Why can't I do this?" Write them out in a notebook or just scribble them down in the margin of this book.

This is the only chance we'll give you to listen to that little voice in your head telling you why this is all too hard. So instead of ignoring it, lean in and take note of what that voice is trying to tell you. This is the time to assess possibilities that are realistic and consider what they really mean for your journey ahead.

Here are some of the questions you should be asking yourself:

- *Why is this hard?*
- *Why won't I do this?*
- *Who and what could get in my way?*
- *How could this affect my job or career?*
- *What else can go wrong?*

When I talked through these questions a few years ago with a senior project manager at PepsiCo, she shared some fears that I have often felt myself:

"I've never done this before. Can I even pull this off?"

"I don't want to get buried in more work. Can I balance the work involved in this new project with the demands of my family?"

"I'm pretty content doing what I'm doing. Why rock the boat and make things complicated?"

You may have listed similar doubts, or maybe you've gone in a different direction. Some long-serving employees, further into their career, may worry that it's too late to take on a new challenge. Conversely, a new hire may fear that a botched idea will be a career-limiting move, or even worse, lead to a pink slip.

Whatever your list of fears and obstacles, take a while to reflect on them. Put each item into one of the following buckets: "I Can Handle This" for problems that are manageable once you identify them; "What If?" for obstacles that come up and are out of your control; and "Showstopper" for challenges that require you to pause and rethink before taking them on.

We're creating these separate buckets because many of the seemingly insurmountable hurdles that keep us from tackling new challenges can be overcome by preemptive and counterattack strategies that will enable us to move forward. Let's go through the three categories one by one.

I CAN HANDLE THIS

Life is full of things we dream of doing and the things that stop us from doing them. Like kicking off a new workout program—we don't have the time, the money, the right food, etc. Realistically, most of the things we think are holding us back can be defeated with just a little thoughtfulness and planning.

These are the "reasons you can't do x" that are within your control that you can address on your own with the right tools in place. (I find that most obstacles will fall into this category. We can generally handle more than we think.)

The first fear listed by Jackie, the senior project manager at PepsiCo, was that she had never managed a project of this size before, and wasn't sure if she could figure it out while still leading her other responsibilities.

She shared that when she first started with the company, she was handed a project to lead a new product within a new market vertical. After learning the ropes along the way, Jackie found that while she was proud of the outcome and work she had done, she had put family and friendships on hold. She had to put in extra hours, week after week, and she lost the work-life balance.

She didn't want to give up her current work-life balance she had worked so hard to achieve. Her fear was that she wouldn't be able to do her job, and her life, well.

To help Jackie identify how she could counterattack this fear, we had to further break it down. Items that fall in the "I Can Handle This" bucket have solutions when you look at the problem and ask, "What tools can I use to make this manageable?"

For Jackie, we started by talking about the "life" side of the balancing act. What tools could help her ensure she still gets quality time with her family?

We talked through lifestyle changes that would help overcome her fear of sacrificing work-life balance, so that she could free up her time at home and focus on her two teenage daughters. She could ease the load by hiring a grocery delivery service and a cleaning service for her home, allowing her to spend more time with her family and less on household chores.

Then we began to unpack the "work" side of the equation. What tools could she leverage to allow her to take on new, challenging work?

Jackie shared that she needed someone to show her how to do this kind of work within the organization. One tool that she identified as being helpful was to have monthly check-ins with a mentor or another trusted colleague who had successfully launched a project at the giant soft drink maker. Jackie decided to do exactly that, and before long had set up a meeting with a more senior project manager, Cole. Cole had been with the company for over ten years and worked in a different product line at PepsiCo. He had launched an internal program that had high visibility and was currently in use.

Besides project management, Jackie was eager to improve her knowledge of business modeling, so she spent her lunch hours for a week watching free online courses and workshops that gave her insights into how to calculate the startup costs of her project and estimate revenues and expenses.

Most fears about taking on a new project fall into the "I Can Handle This" category. While they're valid concerns, you can alleviate them by identifying the tools to make them more manageable.

WHAT IF?

Fear of the unknown is normal. As humans, our fears of the unknown protected us from legitimate threats in life-or-death situations. What if I leave this cave and a bear attacks me?

Though in our modern, working world, the stakes are much lower, we can still find ourselves frozen in fear from various "what ifs."

There will always be unexpected twists and turns in our jobs. What if your competitors hack into your systems, steal your ideas, and beat you to market? Or more realistically, what if a change in management threatens your progress three-fourths of the way through?

These fears have to be combatted head on. You have to accept that sometimes, challenges will come out of left field. That you will do what you can to prevent them, but have to accept that what ifs can unnecessarily paralyze us.

In the summer of 2018, I spoke at an Innov8rs conference in LA about "Quick Wins to Gain Trust and Scale Innovation." After my workshop, one of the participants, a man named Eduardo, came up to the podium. He asked question after question about how he wanted to launch a new process at his company. He had very specific questions and I suggested we dig in and discuss them over lunch.

Over our pasta buffet, Eduardo shared that he was looking for some advice on how to pursue his "big idea" at the global asset management firm where he was a mid-level operations manager.

I learned that Eduardo's job included identifying process improvements and that he had a really exciting idea to improve clients' experience with the firm's financial planning tools. But his idea would require the firm to make a sizable investment in its cloud-based platforms and to move away from existing procedures.

In response to my question about the company's business strategies, Eduardo told me that the firm had recently launched what it described as an "integrated strategic plan" that focused heavily on technology as a competitive advantage and a driver of future growth.

"What's keeping you from moving forward?" I asked him.

He replied, somewhat sheepishly, "I don't want to take the risk in case the company decides to shift direction in the future."

I was confused, everything he had shared in our lunch sounded like the company was going in the right direction for a project like his. His fears sounded like "what if" statements without being rooted in the known realities of his organization.

So I asked him, "Do you have reason to think there would be a radical shift in strategy?"

He paused to think and then said, "No."

"Do you have insight that your idea would be scrapped if there was a radical shift?"

This time he smiled, shaking his head and looking down at his plate, "No, I don't have reason to think that."

Through a few simple questions, he realized that there was little reason that he was aware of today for him to not move ahead.

The trouble with the "what ifs" is that they are, by their very nature, endless and impossible to predict. Rather than giving up, the most effective way of countering such amorphous doubts is to stay connected to players who influence the big decisions, and are in tune with changes at the company and in the marketplace.

Eduardo told me that he reported to a well-respected senior executive who was regularly invited to give presentations at board meetings and strategy planning sessions. In an effort to keep tabs on the company's strategy, Eduardo decided it would make sense to check in with his boss every three months so that he could keep calibrating his idea in light of the firm's overall strategy, minimizing the risk of rejection later down the line.

Make no mistake, "what ifs" can be real threats. It's true, companies do change strategy and ideas can get dumped when the shifts happen. The trouble is, they root us in the unknown rather than in reality. Recognizing when concerns fall into this bucket will help you plan how to deal with them, stop trying to control the fear that comes with them, and focus instead on launching your big idea.

SHOWSTOPPER

While the "Showstopper" is rarer than the "I Can Handle This" and "What If?" buckets, occasionally you do need to stop, evaluate your situation, and get a better plan to move forward.

We cannot ignore the occasional barrier that stops us in our tracks with a loud and clear warning that proceeding any further carries grave risks.

Take the case of Susan, a former colleague at an educational technology company who was in the early stages of a graphic design career. She was super-keen to come up with a creative process that would help her team get their new projects off the ground. The revamped process would require more of her time, but would also give her more authority. Susan was confident that the change would improve productivity and lead to more creative work for our customers.

This was only Susan's second job, and she had spent just under a year in her role as a graphic designer. I knew she felt passionate about her idea, but I also knew she needed to master her current role before she would be ready to lead the transformation that she was proposing.

When I inquired what was holding her back from pushing the idea forward, she confided that she had been discouraged by her manager and team members, and felt that they wouldn't take her seriously. Her team had noticed she had difficulty meeting deadlines and had a hard time staying focused on her work. "I *want* to do this, but my team doesn't trust that I *can* do this," she told me.

We talked about all the positive elements of her idea, but agreed that implementing it would mean more responsibility for her, and less time to do the work she was hired to do—work that was already taxing her to the limit.

Susan had clearly hit a "Showstopper". She needed to focus on her current responsibilities and gain her team's trust before taking on a new challenge. We took some time and identified opportunities for her to put some wins under her belt.

To start, her upcoming project looked as if she would meet the deadline with several days to spare. With that margin, she would invest her time in "getting organized" so that she could both complete her current projects and start planning for the idea she wanted to launch.

We agreed that instead of barging forward, this would be a good moment for her to pause, and to address her colleagues' doubts about her work. She would be able to focus on her transformational idea again when she could point to some successes, proving her capacity to take on more ambitious projects.

Showstoppers are the situations where the best approach is to pause. It doesn't mean stopping forever, and it may just be a moment to consider the best next move. Maybe it's time to plan and wait until next quarter with new priorities, maybe you're getting moved to a new team in the restructuring, or the boss who's always said no takes a new job. Consider your showstoppers whenever there's a change or shift.

Some of the most successful ideas are results of pivots, reframes, and choosing to wait for the right timing.

KNOWING YOU'RE READY

The most challenging part of launching your idea is taking the leap and proceeding forward. There are always a hundred different good reasons why "now" isn't the right time. It's easy to tell yourself you will get to it when you have more time, or when you have your plan perfectly figured out.

But the thing about ideas is that they don't become anything without action. You have to take that first step, trust that you will continue to find ways forward, and embrace the fact that it will never be fully figured out. The world wouldn't be what it is today if the early explorers had "figured everything out" before they set sail.

Your willingness to move on with your idea is the first step toward breathing life into your job and feeling your work has purpose and impact.

And I've been there. Over and over. With this book, it took a few months of conversations with Douglas for us to roll up our sleeves and take pen to paper. Moving from idea to outline, to chapter, to book. We didn't have it figured out in advance, but taking that first step gave us the momentum to take the next one, and the next one, and before we knew it, we were running through editing to publish.

The moment of truth is when you realize you're ready, your idea is ready, and that now is the time. It's when you can run through your list of excuses and recognize that all of them are manageable and you are the only thing standing in your own way. Choose to move forward and own your idea.

ASSUMPTIONS & MINDSETS

Crash Dummies & First-Class Airlines

Count the number of Fs in the following sentence. Read like you would any sentence, but only count once.

The world is full of fearless innovators launching ideas from places of curiosity for the benefit of every one of us.

How many Fs did you see? Feel pretty confident in your number? Think you saw them all?

Most people count six Fs, but there are really nine in the sentence. Because of the way our brain is wired, it doesn't count the "F" in "of"—maybe because the phonetic is similar to "ov" or because during a quick reading, we focus on lexical words like "full" and "fearless" rather than grammatical words like "of."

This exercise is a reminder that we have patterns, beliefs, and backgrounds that help us make sense of the world. While these make up who we are and can give us a unique perspective, they can also create blind spots. For me, I believe I'm good at word puzzles and games so I wrongly assumed that my quick count of Fs would be easy (and correct). But I still missed an "of."

We make the assumption that we can quickly and easily count the number of Fs. Simple task, simple answer. But we have blinders, things that get in the way. We think we have the correct answer, but often, our assumptions get the best of us and we aren't right. There's more to the story, there's more to uncover and learn. If you didn't see all the Fs in this sentence, what might you have missed in a more complex problem?

When it comes to launching an idea in your company, you have to get in front of your assumptions to ensure you aren't blindsided by things you didn't see coming. Getting past your assumptions will help you gain new insights, and understand new possibilities for your vision.

ASSUMPTION-BREAKING IS AN "ART"

In 2014, Douglas accepted an offer to join Twyla, an online art marketplace funded by Google Ventures, as their Chief Technology Officer (CTO). He started in August, with a clear mission: to build up the engineering team with the intent to deliver an initial functioning software product by December in time to launch at Art Basel, an annual art festival in Miami with over 77,000 visitors each year.

The Twyla CEO and chairman had a strong vision and firm belief that online art buyers held the same buying behaviors as high-end art patrons visiting galleries and auctions. Leadership insisted they were sure about the product and directed Douglas to build a platform that would bring an elegant online solution for people to buy art. With a fast approaching deadline, Douglas was laser-focused on building out their vision and got to work right away.

He hired a few key engineering and product roles internally who would build out the systems and work with an outside design agency to do the rest of the design and product development. They were focused on building the software's architecture to support extreme collaboration and rapid iteration. As Douglas's team and the design agency pushed further, they melded into one high-performing agile team.

They were drunk on the elegance of their process and delighted to be building software so quickly. The team built the initial platform, plus a bunch of additional functions and features they were sure customers would love. The rest of the leadership team took note, they were impressed. They not only met but exceeded all the expectations for their Art Basel product launch. They even had time for extra rounds of testing and hardening. They were prepared!

The big launch day finally came. With the product triple-checked and boasting a beautiful customer interface, they released it into the world. The audience was filled with their ideal customers—young people who loved art so much they flew to another city to see the newest emerging art trends. Douglas sat behind the Twyla booth, keeping an eye on the interactions team members were having with customers.

Douglas watched his team members intercept people at the festival to show them the app and website. Everyone he and his team showed it to kindly nodded and left the booth as quickly as possible. Even people who came to the launch party were seemingly more interested in the free booze and sound baths than the software that allowed them to learn more about the artist and story behind the art. Soon, hours had gone by and it had become clear that nobody at Art Basel really cared about the product. The launch was mostly navel-gazing and boasting to their friends. There were no real customer interactions and art patrons showed little interest in what Twyla had to offer. Douglas began to realize he had made a critical mistake.

After getting it into the hands of the real market they were after, the team realized they had made the wrong assumption about buyer behavior. It turned out that people buying art online have a completely different motivation than traditional art buyers and collectors. After more research,

Douglas and his team found that the online buyers didn't care as much about the artist's name or credibility, but instead just wanted a great piece that matched their sofa in the living room.

In an effort to build the most agile product organization and deliver on his Art Basel commitment, the team had focused too much on building things right and had failed to stop and think about building the right thing. Instead, Douglas had *assumed* they were building the right thing. It made sense at first glance, but sometimes the things we assume aren't always right. People are complex.

WE ALL HAVE ASSUMPTIONS

A lot of our assumptions come from the idea that because there's always been a way things are done, it's the best (or only) way to do things. But if we assumed that the best way to travel was by horse and buggy and never questioned if there was a better way to do things, our world would look a lot different than it does today.

Major airlines have almost universally charged for different class services. Economy, first-class, and even seats with a choice of more leg room, all priced differently based on their level of luxury. Selecting your seat and paying for an upgraded class of service became the norm for customers. And so did charging for checked bags. Since most airlines charge a baggage fee, customers became accustomed to it as part of the fee to travel.

But Southwest Airlines, which brought in over $20B in revenue in 2019, has built a company around challenging these industry assumptions. Making business decisions and testing ideas that buck the status quo.

Back in the early days of the company when they were new and struggling, they had to run a four-plane schedule with a three-plane fleet. That meant they had to make sure every second was used as efficiently as possible. They found that one of the most time-consuming parts of flying was trying to board everyone and the time people spent looking for their seats. By eliminating assigned seats, they created much more efficient turnaround times and saw that passengers loaded onto the plane much more quickly. They ditched the idea of class of service, and to date still don't charge for a checked bag. When Southwest let go of the assumptions behind air travel (especially when they were first starting), their business was able to serve customers faster and create their own unique brand of travel.

Assumptions get in the way of the possibilities we could create and what we believe about what we're already creating. When you let go of assumptions, you can start to see new ways of doing things.

YOU KNOW WHAT THEY SAY ABOUT ASSUMPTIONS

A lot of the assumptions we have are actually hidden to us. They're things that have been ingrained in us since childhood through culture or upbringing, or they may be lessons learned from years of career experience, feeding our subconscious without our knowing.

"The best way to work has always been in cubicles."

"Administrators and assistants just juggle schedules."

"People with British accents are smart."

In 1997, crash dummies officially became the industry standard for testing government compliance with frontal impact regulations and airbag safety. GM had developed them 20 years prior in 1977 as a way to understand the impact of a crash.

These first crash dummies were created in the image of the people who were creating them—the all-male engineer team. The height, weight, and body makeup mimicked the build of the average American male. What about the different weights and sizes of the non-average American sized male? What about the anatomy of a female?

Because of the engineering team's hidden assumptions, they built the dummies with their bodies' needs in mind, rather than the variety of body shapes and anatomy we see in males, females, and drivers worldwide.

The assumptions created blind spots and, ultimately, flaws in the safety features of cars. The data from the National Highway Traffic Safety Administration (NHTSA) shows that a female driver or front passenger wearing a seatbelt is 17% more likely than a male to be killed when a crash takes place. Additionally, a 2019 study from the University of Virginia showed that the odds of a female occupant being injured in a frontal car crash are 73% greater than the odds for a male occupant.[1]

While creating crash dummies to test the design of a car in a car accident is helpful, the hidden assumptions that the male designers held kept them from building an all-encompassing solution for varying types of drivers.

What problematic crash dummies might we be creating? Are there things in your work or idea that you can't see because of who you are and how you see the world?

[1]https://www.consumerreports.org/car-safety/crash-test-bias-how-male-focused-testing-puts-female-drivers-at-risk/

THE 5 LAYERS OF ASSUMPTIONS

How can we know the unknown if we don't know what we don't know?

Trying to blindly list our assumptions is a fruitless effort. It could actually falsely lead you to think you've uncovered them all, or when you can't think of any, that you have none, only to further pile up more assumptions upon assumptions.

Instead, it's important to keep in mind that these beliefs will always be present and instead of trying to uncover them all and move on, you are creating the space to explore them and think about how you might address them. Like the men who were designing the crash test dummies, how could they have simply explored their assumptions about the best way to test a car's safety?

When it comes to launching a new idea within a company or organization, there are five layers of assumptions that will affect you. Recognizing these areas and being clued in that assumptions will always lie hidden within them, will begin to prime you to be more thoughtful in how to be open to uncovering them.

The layers of assumptions create a picture that we can explore more fully once we fully understand it. The diagram below shows how assumptions start small, within ourselves, and grow with our teams, organizations, and to the market and world. Give yourself space to explore these assumptions before we delve into strategies to combat them.

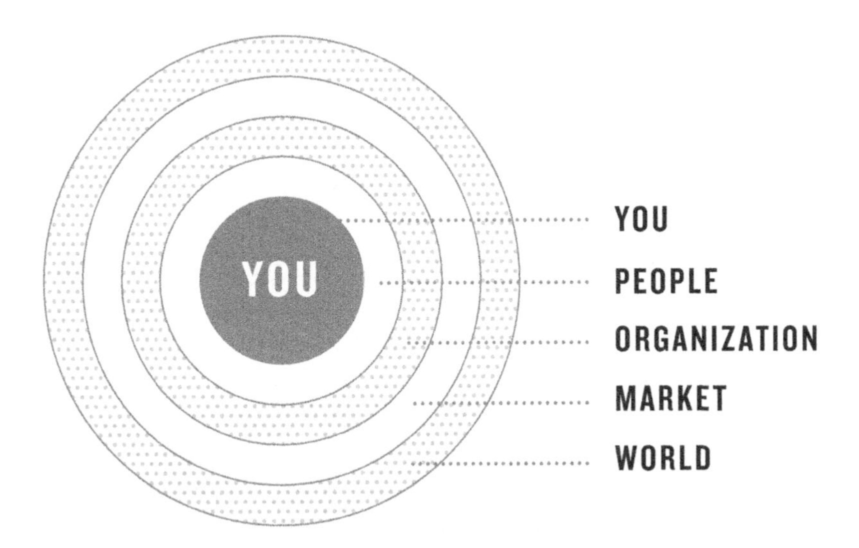

I. Your Assumptions: You Are the Center of Your Universe

I start every morning with coffee. I like it black and without frills. When I arrive at work, I like to watch my coworkers mill about the kitchen, preparing their different coffee concoctions. Some with frothy milk, some with pumps of flavored syrup.

In meetings, I notice the different mugs people carry around with their coffee in it. Most use the standard kitchen-issued mugs. But others have a favorite mug from home.

One day I was hosting a meeting to try to get buy-in and alignment for an event I was proposing. We would need to hold the meeting first thing in the morning in Montreal to allow for people in London to call in as well. In an effort to get people excited and motivated, despite the early start time, I had brought in a to-go coffee carrier with 96 ounces of coffee and brought in the mugs, cream, and sugar. Everything set up in the conference room and ready to kick off the meeting, I looked around and patted myself on the back for being so thoughtful.

Then as people started to arrive, I noticed some weren't going for the coffee. The meeting went well, but why wasn't my gift embraced? What had I done wrong?

I realized later in the morning, when I was actually paying attention, the people that passed on my coffee had mugs that were full of something different. Kombucha, tea, and one with hot lemon water. Not coffee drinkers.

Of course not everyone drinks coffee. If I had thought it all the way through, I would've told you that without needing to be reminded. I just hadn't really thought much about it. I ignored subtle cues like the color of the liquid in the mugs. I saw the mugs and morning ritual around the kitchen and assumed we were all drinking the same thing. It's what I drink. It's not what everyone drinks.

These assumptions we make are deeply ingrained in our subconscious. The opportunity we have with these kinds of assumptions is found in the space between our natural instincts and the critical thinking we use to make decisions. It reminds me of something I've heard different yoga instructors say over the years, "Find space in between the breaths."

In yoga and meditation, you learn that the breath, mind, and nervous system are all linked together. That if the breath is short and shallow then the mind and body will react with a feeling of stress or a fight, flight, or freeze response. When you take longer and deeper breaths, you will bring calm and clarity to your mind and body.

It's the space between breaths that will allow your mind and body to expand.

Our day is filled with moments where we make assumption after assumption, but what if we teach ourselves to find the space between them? What if we give ourselves the gaps between thoughts, and potentially open our minds to a new approach or way of thinking? (As you continue to come across these questions in this section, jot down your thoughts. We'll explore them more in the activity at the end of this chapter.)

2. People Assumptions: Who Thinks What

To launch a new idea with a company, we are tethered to our assumptions as to how the people in the organization will help or hinder the idea. There's a belief that key talent will be available and engaged in the work. Or that certain people will be naysayers and get in the way. Or an even more damaging assumption, stereotyping.

In 2018, through the Stanford Latino Entrepreneurship Initiative housed within the Stanford Graduate School of Business, I mentored an entrepreneur looking to incorporate new, innovative ideas into his brand and design solutions agency.

Francisco was an eager and excited CEO, ready to help his organization scale, grow, and expand into new services and technology. Many of our calls over those months focused on how he might help to inspire and encourage his senior leadership staff to think outside the box and try to come up with new ways of doing business.

He would also share with me his frustrations that he needed to find the right person to step up and fill the role of Chief Operating Officer. A role he badly needed to fill to free up some of his time so he could move from focusing on the daily operations of the business into strategy and big-picture thinking.

He shared with me that the role was between two people: Melissa, a female candidate who was a good fit because of her work ethic and ability to execute on strategic planning but who, according to Francisco, was not a great "people person"; and Antonio, a charismatic, ambitious coworker that reminded Francisco of his younger self but still needed more experience to be able to run the operations of the company.

When we talked about the candidates in more detail, it became clear that some of his beliefs were rooted in assumptions, rather than facts. When I asked questions about how Melissa wasn't as good with people or how Antonio was, I learned that Francisco's ideas may have been more rooted in assumptions based on stereotypes.

"Melissa isn't as warm and friendly as most women in the office. You know the type," he'd shared. He couldn't put his finger on it, but it became clear that he had fallen for the stereotype that women should behave a certain way. That women should be warm and friendly and when they are not, something is "off."

Or when he listed some of the attributes that made Antonio a good fit, I could hear Francisco describing himself. "He's charismatic, people like working with him, and he's quick on his feet."

Francisco had made personal assumptions about what made himself a great leader in the company and then he identified them as being ones Antonio had as well.

During our conversations I asked questions about how we might unlock these assumptions. Does he have facts or examples for the qualities he has identified in each individual? Are they qualities that are needed or necessary for the role? How might he train or mentor either individual to up their game to the level he needs in the COO role?

These assumptions about the people in your organization will directly affect your idea.

Are you assuming that you have buy-in from your team? What if you actually don't, and you go down a path thinking everyone is aligned? Or maybe you have assumptions about a certain team member you see as "difficult," so you don't engage with them on your idea; or if you do, you treat them with disrespect. All of your interactions with this person are tainted by your assumptions or beliefs, but it may turn out that this person could add real value to your idea. Now or later.

Take a look at the people you naturally gravitate to for assistance in a project or work. How might you be making assumptions about them that will affect your idea? Or look at the people you often resist working with because of one reason or another. How might they contribute to the success of your idea?

3. Organizational Assumptions: The State of Affairs

Based on our experiences in our companies or organizations, we all make assumptions about how things get done or what may or may not work. Unintentionally, many of us assume that we know the current state of affairs of our organization. Whether that's based on known revenue or shared strategies from a more transparent company or a perceived knowledge as part of a team that is "in the know," we often assume we know the current state of business.

This includes financial assumptions such as a readily available budget or capital that could be available for launching your idea. Or it may be assuming that your company has the business capabilities and know-how as an organization to execute on your idea.

In 2019, Douglas worked with Liberty Mutual on a project where they were partnering with another company (as of publication this partnership isn't public) to increase the value to their joint customers. Both companies had treasure troves of data they could serve to their customers and if the partnership came through, the resulting data would be groundbreaking in the legal industry.

So Douglas and his team from Voltage Control were hired to help initiate the co-creation of this partnership. They kicked things off and everything was going well. All parties involved were enthusiastic and eager to move things forward.

Then, a few weeks down the line, things started to slow down. The team from Liberty Mutual were left scratching their heads. Why had the partnership slowed down and what should they do?

If the Liberty Mutual team had accepted the silence as a deterrent, the team might have conceded that the partnership went south because the other company found a better opportunity or another partner.

Or if the Liberty Mutual team had relied on previous partnership failures to determine the reasoning for this one, they might have finger-pointed internally about missteps and accepted the partnership failure and moved on.

Instead of succumbing to organizational assumptions, one Liberty Mutual team member, Bob, decided he would try to get to the bottom of what the real issue might be. He reached out to the other company's point-of-contact, and got no response. Days went by and still radio silence.

He found other team members at that company to be a little on edge and difficult to engage. Then Bob went to a senior leader from the C-suite to inquire why the partnership had gone south and fallen apart.

It took some patience but Bob got an answer—the other company was still interested in the partnership, but they were undergoing a major organizational restructure. The nonresponsive team was either in transition to new roles or being let go. So the senior leader Bob spoke with set up a new team to see the partnership through and it reopened the possibility of the project.

Seeing this partnership come through was no easy task and it would have been easier to rely on assumptions to end the opportunity. Instead, the Liberty Mutual team went in with an open mind to uncover what was really happening, rather than what *seemed* to be happening. In doing so, they found a new way forward to make the partnership happen.

When it comes to your idea, are you assuming that you know the current state of work? For many, the behind-the-scenes work coming from executives may not be visible. You may not be aware that a big change is coming up. Feeling frustrated, you may throw in the towel and give up. But assuming that you understand the current state of the business will keep you from seeing the bigger picture, and understanding the right timing for your idea.

4. Market Assumptions: Weed Wacker Meets Supercuts

Market assumptions are the dangerous conclusions that we know something about our idea's customers, competitors, or marketplace. It's our belief that our idea will work because of these factors.

When it comes to our customers, even when we run tests and have strong data, we can make false assumptions about their needs and perceptions that will bite us later down the line. This is especially true when we see ourselves as one of the customers.

As a product leader and advisor to startups, I frequently connect with people who come to me for advice about their great idea for a new product or service.

One Sunday afternoon, I was catching up with my neighbor Penny before my family was to leave for a holiday. She shared her idea for the "next Uber for yard work and haircuts."

Hosing down a newly planted tree in her front yard, Penny explained a problem she was facing. "My 83-year-old mom lives out in the middle of nowhere in Arizona. The nearest grocery store is at least a 40-minute drive, and I have to hire people to help take care of her."

I nodded, remembering how I worried about my grandmother who lived alone in home until she was 92 years old. "Yes, it can be a challenge to find and hire the right people to come and help with our aging loved ones," I said.

Penny continued with excitement, "Well, Ed is the yard guy who helps my mom with her lawn and keeps her pool in shape. He comes once a week to mow the lawn and clean the pool filter. And then once a month, he sets my mom up in her kitchen with a sheet wrapped around her like a smock and trims her hair!"

I had a big smile on my face picturing sweet Ed, covered in lawn trimmings and wearing garden gloves, delicately trimming Penny's mom's hair.

"My idea is to combine the two, and create an app where you could hire a person to come and do yard work and then before leaving, cut your hair. I thought of the name too—Rest A-Sheared. Get it? It's a pun on the saying, 'rest assured' and cutting shears!"

I love wild ideas, and Penny's enthusiasm about her idea made me happy.

"So, what do you think?" she implored.

"What a creative way to help take care of your mom!" I said. I could see she was eager for my feedback, so I continued, "For an idea like this, I would try to understand the market that would be interested in having an all-in-one yard and hair care solution. And what type of people would be able to fulfill both of these services."

While the idea may sound ridiculous, some of the most innovative ideas come from wild spin-offs like Penny's. Rather than shrug it off and tell her it was silly, I encouraged her to do some research.

As our conversation continued, it was obvious that because of Penny's specific need for her mom, she made assumptions that it was a broader need that would be useful to a bigger market.

These assumptions about the market exist as a way forward for our idea. If we didn't make some assumptions, we wouldn't be able to ideate new ways of doing things or would be at a loss for a way forward. Our assumptions give us a way forward. But not always *the* way.

For Penny, she was basing her assumptions off real-world experience and a problem that she had with her mother. This is a common predicament for people with a new idea that solves their specific need. But when it comes to new ideas, we cannot assume our needs represent the needs of others.

When it comes to market assumptions, how might you test and prototype your idea to see if there's a market fit?

5. World Assumptions: From Inside the Fish Bowl

The world assumptions that build around us and through us are the beliefs that certain things are and will be universally true. For instance, that we are building an idea within a stable economy or political environment. Or that laws, regulations, and standards are continuing in the same direction.

As Douglas and I were finalizing this book, the coronavirus pandemic emerged and shattered our world assumptions. Everything changed.

It was just weeks into the pandemic, and we were already seeing major shifts happening across industries. Grocery delivery services went from a nice-to-have luxury to a must-have necessity and were overwhelmed and unable to meet demands. Cruise ship tourism, a once lavish way to travel the world, had ships stranded at sea, a nightmare for quarantined passengers aboard.

Every aspect of our lives had changed and we had to shift our world assumptions. Similarly, opportunities for thinking differently to explore novel solutions were appearing all around us. Big businesses such as Dyson, the iconic vacuum manufacturer, stepped up to design and deliver ventilators to support efforts to treat coronavirus patients. Nonprofits like Mask Maker created an open-source tool that lets you 3D print reusable protective masks at home.

Before the pandemic, people across companies, organizations, and nonprofits were all operating under their own set of world assumptions. Not planning or considering the global shift that was around the corner.

Our world assumptions are built from the limited experiences we have been exposed to. Like a fish in a fish bowl, we have difficulty in understanding the realities outside of our perceived world. Simply put, we cannot see the whole world from inside our own heads.

Think back to the era when taxicabs were the vehicular monopoly. An era where if you wanted a ride home from the airport, you rolled your carry-on through a twisting line of tourists to climb aboard your musty taxi and slide around in the back seat as the driver went through back roads to drop you off at home.

There was little disruption in that industry because there were established protocols to becoming a taxi service. In the U.S., the municipalities controlled the entrance of new taxis and limited the supply on the road through medallions, or licenses, that gave drivers the right to pick up riders where their license was issued. This was the way to become a taxi service, and for decades it was how the established companies and new entrants alike ran their businesses.

Then along came Uber—a company that while disrupting the taxi industry, steadfastly asserted they were not a taxi service. Instead, Uber let go of the assumption that they had to run their business like a taxi service to be one. Instead, they positioned themselves as a communications platform that provides ridesharing. This allowed them to skirt the strict municipal regulations that taxi services had to follow, giving Uber the loophole they needed to scale quickly.

Taxi services were floored. How could Uber just come in and upheave the industry in one swoop? Because they rejected the status quo.

But as the world is ever-changing, so will the need to examine our assumptions. For Uber, their way of doing business became the new status quo and in creeped new world assumptions. Presuming that they could continue expanding globally with the same sidestepping of regulations, Uber later fell short.

Around the world, cities and states were passing new regulations and laws to address the rideshare business model, stalling out the company in their global expansion. Assuming Uber could continue to do business the way they had when they initially launched was a costly endeavor. In the U.S. alone, the company reportedly spent $2.3 million on federal lobbying in 2018 in an effort to help them deal with the regulations.

In the early days, breaking the belief that a transportation solution had to follow the rules of transportation, Uber revolutionized the industry and many others as well. But over time, this assumption that they weren't a transportation application, led them to the incorrect and costly solution that has faced opposition in their expansion.

Be smart about your assumptions and use them to serve your idea. How might your assumptions be wrong? Where can your assumptions be the opportunity for thinking differently about your idea?

ACTIVITY
SHIFTING FROM ASSUMPTIONS TO INSIGHTS

If we all have assumptions, and some are helpful to our idea while others will be detrimental, how do we leverage them to serve us and not bring our idea to a halt?

The key is to question assumptions and be willing and open to changing your mind. If you can expand your thinking to see that perhaps your assumptions are incorrect, or should be challenged, then you will be receptive to new ways of thinking. Solving a problem in a new way. This breakthrough is where new ideas thrive.

So let's get started, let's follow these activities to bust some of your assumptions and uncover insights that will help you in launching your idea within your company.

Option I: Nurture the Naysayers

When it comes to our assumptions, they most often rear their ugly heads when we hear resistance from others to our idea. When we hear opposition, our natural reaction is to point out where the other person's thinking is flawed. Or to explain that you had considered their viewpoint but through some research or other means had come to the final conclusion of your idea. Instead of treating the naysayer like a debate you need to win, consider them the voice pointing out a potential assumption.

I had a student who took my LinkedIn Learning Product Innovation course reach out to me, asking for help in pushing her big idea forward. Surabhi was a product manager at Microsoft in the Hyderabad area of India.

She had a great idea for a product she was heading up but when she shared the idea with her engineers, they all scoffed and pushed back. She didn't feel they had a full understanding of her idea and the implications. Surely if they did, they would be all in.

When her idea was met with resistance from others, rather than the natural inclination to push back and make arguments for the merits, she decided to listen to their concerns. Her idea was to use a tool in their product development that would allow new product features to get to Quality Assurance (QA) faster.

"It would create efficiencies across teams and allow us to learn from QA teams sooner, and thus shorten the time to release the new feature," Surabhi shared over one of our video calls.

So I asked her, "What resistance are you hearing from teammates?"

"The engineers said they don't have the time to take on new work. But my idea, once instituted, won't add more time to the engineers' workload, it will make their life easier." She felt frustrated and indignant. She couldn't understand why something that would help them would be met with such strong opposition.

I encouraged her to think about the pushback she was receiving. What if the engineers didn't have the time? How might her idea be a perceived inconvenience to them?

It didn't happen overnight but with time, Surabhi opened up and tried to see it from the engineers' point of view. Sitting down with the engineers to gain their perspective, she learned that for them, new tools often required onboarding, learning, and slowed down the momentum of progress until fully adopted. Her idea was built on the belief that the tool would solve the problem they had. But with the perceived time it would add to the engineers' current workload, it created hurdles she hadn't considered.

She decided to take the existing way things were done and move just one step in the process, alleviating the QA team's workload. (Relieving the burden of time spent on onboarding and learning something new for the engineers.) The engineers still kept their flow of work and Surabhi got the QA team to try the new tool she was suggesting on the step she had moved. After a few months, they had a breakthrough on both sides. The engineers were happy with their workload and Surabhi enjoyed the chance to try out her idea. By using the naysayers as inspiration she had a major assumption-busting moment that led to new opportunities.

When we run into a contradiction to our beliefs, instead of explaining it away, take it as truth. See where that takes you.

To nurture the naysayers, start by finding the people in your organization that will be against your idea. Who typically points out the flaws to an idea or project? Who is the person that is often skeptical or cynical about things? Sit down with these people and take the time to learn from them.

Start by asking questions about your idea. It won't take long before a naysayer will start to poke holes in the idea. Rather than responding with an explanation or trying to sell them on the idea, instead ask more questions like:

- *What makes you think that?*
- *How would you approach this problem?*
- *Why are you certain it would fail?*

The key to nurturing the naysayer is to truly listen rather than discredit. While their pessimism and opposition to your idea can be frustrating, resist the urge to try to win them over and consider their viewpoint.

The naysayer often uncovers our hidden assumptions when you are willing to listen. It might allow you to make a discovery about a flawed assumption that you were holding on to. This listening will reveal a hidden assumption that is blinding you and the potential of your idea.

Option 2: If-Then Storming

I had a friend in college who while very smart and capable of achieving good grades, only wanted to put in the minimal effort required to pass a class. John saw a means to an end. If he passed his classes, he'd get a degree.

He was so committed to only putting in the required effort that he tracked his grades in an Excel file, so that at any point in the semester he could tell you what he needed to earn on homework, quizzes, and finals in order to pass.

He built complex if-then statements, so that when he entered in each grade he received, his formula would build out the minimum possible scores he needed for the remaining assignments and tests, taking into account the weight of each piece. If he got a 75 on his midterm, he needed to get at least a 65 on his last homework and at least an 80 on his final.

This approach made no sense to me. Why put in all the effort to game the system rather than the work into learning the content?

When I asked John why, he said that he believed in the value of learning the content of a course and passing a class to achieve a degree. But he did not believe that high marks would land him a better job post-graduation. Instead, he saw value in other experiences outside of school. Like hiking with his friends or starting up side hustles through creating new apps. Things that he was able to make more time for, because he had optimized his required study time.

When it comes to breaking assumptions, a great tool to leverage is the if-then statement. In our if-then storming, we start by going through all of the if-then statements to unlock different situations and possible outcomes. Then we take those and combine or remix them to unlock assumptions that may be holding us back.

To start, write out on a post-it an if-statement and then on another post-it, the then-statement. Use one color of post-its for the if-statements and a different color for the then-statements. As you place them on your wall or board, put the if-statements on the left side and the then-statements to the right.

For John, that might include the following:

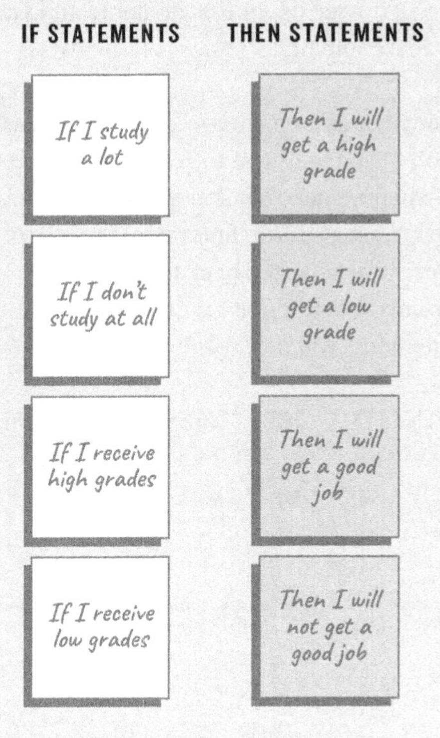

For your big idea, you may land on some if-then statements like the following:

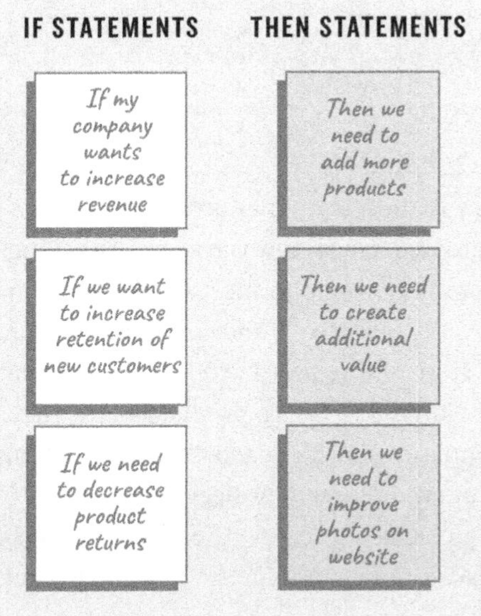

Spend time coming up with as many if-then statements as you can. Now, go back through your list of if-statements and start to add different then-statements that could fit.

For example:

"If my company needs to decrease product returns" may have a new then-statement of, "Then we need to reduce the number of days allowed for returns." Or, "Then we need a better sizing chart for our customers."

When you start to slow down, finding that you can't come up with new if- or then-statements, take a step back from your wall and take some time to combine and remix the statements.

Your new statements will now read:

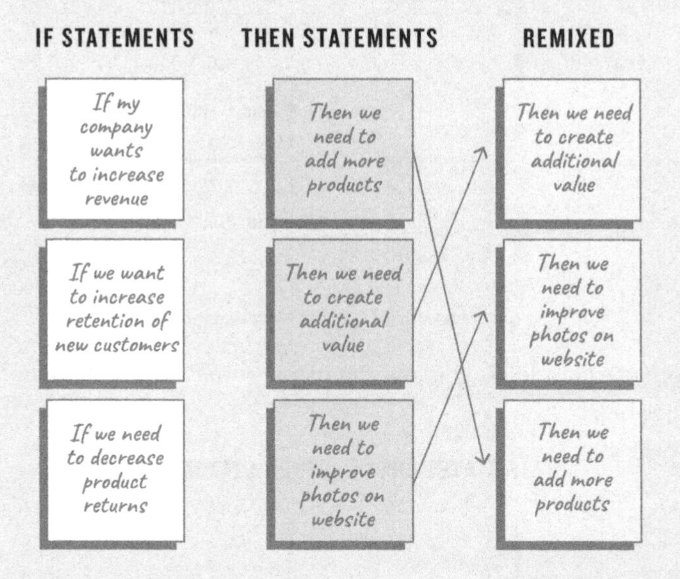
IF STATEMENTS
THEN STATEMENTS
REMIXED
If my company wants to increase revenue
Then we need to add more products
Then we need to create additional value
If we want to increase retention of new customers
Then we need to create additional value
Then we need to improve photos on website
If we need to decrease product returns
Then we need to improve photos on website
Then we need to add more products

When you break these statements from either the "if" or "then" side (or both), you begin to uncover new ways of seeing things.

So, "If the company wants to increase revenue, then we need to add more products" could become, "If the company wants to increase revenue, then we need to stop adding more products." This could lead to thinking about the current products being produced. Are they fully realized? Do they need additional capital to reach their full potential? Would adding new products dilute your current projects?

Or what if you changed it to, "If the company wants to increase revenue, then we need to acquire new products." This tweak could lead you to think about what your customers are doing that may serve your company. Maybe it's not about creating something new but acquiring something that exists?

The if-then storming technique gives you new ideas for considering the problem you are trying to solve. It will break you from being wedded to your assumptions, the things that may be blindsiding you from a new and novel approach you had not considered.

Option 3: Debunk the Truth

Douglas runs Control the Room, a summit for facilitators in Austin and San Francisco with plans to expand to other cities. Their mission is to build and nurture the facilitation community and bust silos that exist around different practices to stitch together a broad community. After running the summits for a few years, it became hard to distinguish the assumptions he had about his event from facts. He needed to debunk the truth.

Debunking the truth will allow you to let go of what you presume as fact and give you a way to move on from tightly held assumptions.

To Debunk the Truth, start by taking inventory of your facts. Write down a list of things that you know to be true. List out all the activities, people, and projects that will affect why your idea will be successful or fail.

In writing this book, Douglas and I created this activity and tested it on ourselves to help him uncover the assumptions he may have around an idea he was launching within his facilitation agency.

Each year, Voltage Control holds a conference in Austin, Texas, converging facilitators from around the world and across different industries. He wanted to make changes to the event that would bring more value to the participants.

When we sat down to go through this exercise, I started by asking Douglas, "What's the big idea? What are you hoping to achieve?"

Douglas replied with a grin, "I want to surprise and delight the people that participate in our event."

"That sounds lovely!" I replied, and followed up with a question, "How do you see that coming together?"

"I'm hoping to create opportunities for more practice time. More space in the meetups and experiences to create richer engagements for the attendees," Douglas shared.

With that information in hand, we got to work.

STEP 1: LIST OUT SELF-EVIDENT STATEMENTS

For step one, we needed to list out all the things that must be true. For Douglas's idea to create new experiences at his event, he wrote down the following:

SELF-EVIDENT STATEMENTS

- *We must host the event.*
- *People attending the event are expecting more than just content.*
- *People attending the event will have time for required pre-work.*
- *People attending the event need more practice.*
- *People attending the event want to practice.*
- *People attending the event will not be surprised and delighted without new experiences added.*
- *My team has the time to implement the idea/experience we come up with.*

This list made up some of the beliefs that Douglas held to be self-evident.

STEP 2: REMOVE 100% ACCURATE FACTS

The second step is to disregard anything on the list that you know with 100% accuracy to be true. Looking at his list, Douglas removed "We must host the event" and "People attending the event are expecting more than just content."

The goal isn't to whittle down the list, it's just to take off the components that are 100% rooted in fact. Something like, "I have a job at this company" or "I am going to be paid for my work" are things you can disregard. While things may shift and you may one day lose or quit your job, as it relates to your idea, it is unlikely there are any assumptions to uncover here.

STEP 3: CREATE STATEMENTS IN OPPOSITION

The third step is to take a look at the remaining list and to put on a different lens. If the statements were false, what would be the impact on your idea?

For Douglas, I asked, "Looking at this list, what if people are not expecting more content? Or what if these people will not have time for any pre-work going into the event?"

Nodding, Douglas turned his list into statements opposing his initial list. His new list came out as follows:

SELF-EVIDENT STATEMENTS	OPPOSITION STATEMENTS
• *People attending the event will have time for required pre-work.*	• *People attending the event do not have time for required pre-work.*
• *People attending the event need more practice.*	• *People attending the event do not need more practice.*
• *People attending the event want to practice.*	• *People attending the event do not want to practice.*
• *People attending the event will not be surprised and delighted without new experiences added.*	• *People attending the event will be surprised and delighted without new experiences added.*
• *My team has the time to implement the idea/experience we come up with.*	• *My team does not have the time to implement the idea/experience we come up with.*

With the new list up on the wall, Douglas paused. He started to talk through different components that stood out to him. "I do think people have time for the pre-work. And I know my team has the bandwidth for creating a new experience for the event. But what if I'm wrong?"

With the opposing statements in hand, Douglas and I went through to the next step, identifying what more Douglas needed to learn. What did he need to do to take an assumption and turn it into a fact?

STEP 4: IDENTIFY OPPORTUNITIES FOR LEARNING

For this step, you want to add post-its to each new opposition statement. For many of them, Douglas wrote, "Interview past attendees." Next to the statement, "People attending the event do not need more practice," Douglas wrote, "How many hours of practice do attendees get from the event?" And then he added another post-it that read, "How many hours of practice do attendees get from outside of the event?"

His work continued as he added post-its around his statements.

With arms crossed and head tilted, Douglas reflected, "I'm pretty sure I know the answer to much of this, but there may be some insights I'm not considering."

OPPOSITION STATEMENTS

- People attending the event do not have time for required pre-work.
- **People attending the event do not need more practice.**
- People attending the event do not want to practice.
- People attending the event will be surprised and delighted without new experiences added.
- My team does not have the time to implement the idea/experience we come up with.

How many hours of practice do attendees get from the event?

Interview past attendees

How many hours of practice do attendees get from outside the event?

STEP 5: VALUE RANK ACTIVITIES

Then Douglas went through the last step of the activity. He needed to evaluate which work would be the most valuable. Looking at your list, rank your activities by impact so that you will be able to prioritize by risk. On a scale of 1-5, which questions or activities would have the greatest impact on your idea? Give those a 5 rating. Which activities are the least risky if ignored and have the least impact? Give those a 1 rating.

For this step, Douglas got to work. For the post-it he wrote, "Ask employees if they have time to design a new experience." He ranked it a 2. He believed they had the time, and saw little value to this assumption being incorrect.

Then he gave a 5 on the post-it, "Interview past attendees." If his wild idea was supported by the expectations of the attendees, then the idea might fall short if the experience they designed didn't address the right problem.

With everything rated, Douglas could go in and prioritize his list as what they needed to take action on today.

Starting this exercise, Douglas and his team were ready to get to work. They had a gut feeling the idea was going to make the event even stronger. But by debunking some assumptions, they uncovered some work that needed to be done.

They were able to think of easy ways to engage the audience and prime them for doing more practice outside the conference. Some of the results informed the team that they could easily get people engaged in their online communications Slack group by creating monthly practice sessions.

Doing this work will get you to ask yourself, "What does my assumption mean, and what would I do if it were false? What would I need to do to prove it as fact?"

In most cases, there will be assumptions. Dropping them as the "truth" will require you to take action and learn more, uncovering insights along the way.

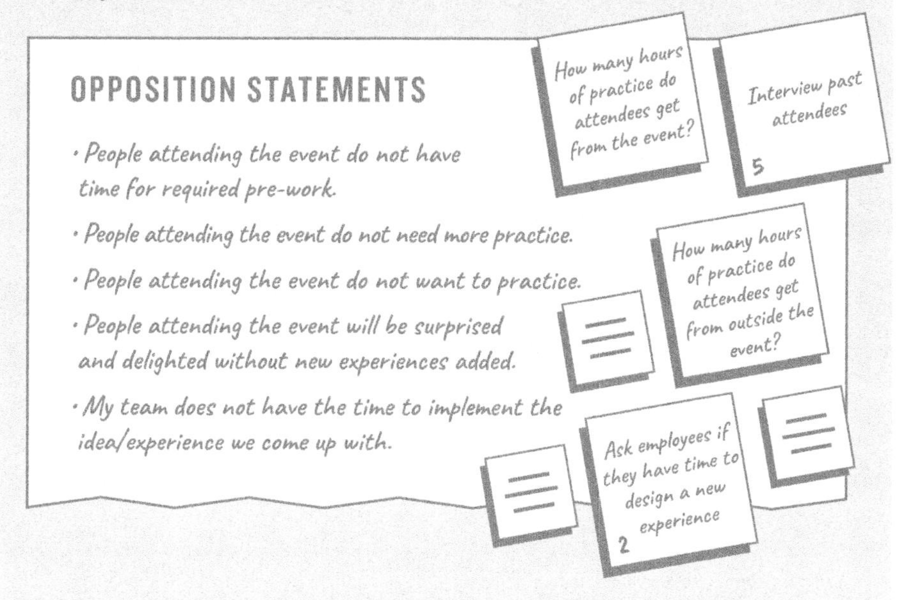
OPPOSITION STATEMENTS
• People attending the event do not have time for required pre-work.
• People attending the event do not need more practice.
• People attending the event do not want to practice.
• People attending the event will be surprised and delighted without new experiences added.
• My team does not have the time to implement the idea/experience we come up with.
How many hours of practice do attendees get from the event?
Interview past attendees
5
How many hours of practice do attendees get from outside the event?
Ask employees if they have time to design a new experience
2

ASSUMPTIONS ARE LIKE BLIND SPOTS

If you went through the above exercise, you undoubtedly uncovered some assumptions that you can address and ensure that your idea is better equipped to move forward.

Assumptions will always be present and will always require you to check in on them. Like your shadow, your assumptions will follow you everywhere. You can try to ignore them or they will be hidden depending on the light, but they will appear eventually and could affect the success of your idea.

It's like when you're driving your car and looking to switch lanes. You will always check your rear view mirrors each time you change lanes. New people will be driving in the lane next to you. In the same way, you have to continue to evaluate new or evolving assumptions. This is true because new assumptions will always be born, evolve, or be replaced. (Don't assume just because someone wasn't in your blind spot a minute ago that there isn't someone there now.)

The assumptions we have can change our lives. If we assume we're stuck in a situation, or aren't capable of pushing a big idea through, we'll stop ourselves before we even try. And if we're assuming the people around us don't want to be a part of what we're doing, we'll limit their involvement before we know the truth. Don't let assumptions stop you from pursuing big things.

You add value to your company and the work that you do will make a difference. Some assumptions will serve you and help your idea along and others can slow down or stall out the best of ideas.

When we check our assumptions, we create a space between decisions. Take a breath, reflect on how your assumptions are at play, challenge them, and uncover new insights.

YOUR ORGANIZATION IS READY

Or Is It?

Can a light bulb light up underwater? Not if it's in a standard lamp plugged into a wall. Submerged underwater, the light bulb wouldn't turn on, it wouldn't illuminate, and in most cases, the lamp would be damaged. But a special encasing around a bulb, something that protects the bulb and source of power from the water? Now that could work.

Maybe you're not trying to light a light bulb underwater, but if you're trying to push an idea through a company—it might feel that way. Conditions for innovation can be tricky, and you might even feel like you're trying to accomplish an impossible task.

You have a great idea, you're ready to go forward with it, but is your company or organization ready?

The environment you're working with indicates how well your idea will be received and supported. Ideas equal change. Ideas will change everything within the organization, from processes to roles and everything in between. Your idea can't flourish inside a vacuum. It will both require and create change.

When trying to launch a new idea, you need to understand how to manage the idea within the setting of your company. This is rooted in the realities of your organization's readiness for change.

To assess organizational preparedness, ask, "Is my organization ready to support an idea like mine? Is it ready AND resilient enough to withstand the change?"

Rather than focusing on changing the environment, we want to focus on what needs to be in place for the idea to work. So how do you get a light bulb to light up underwater?

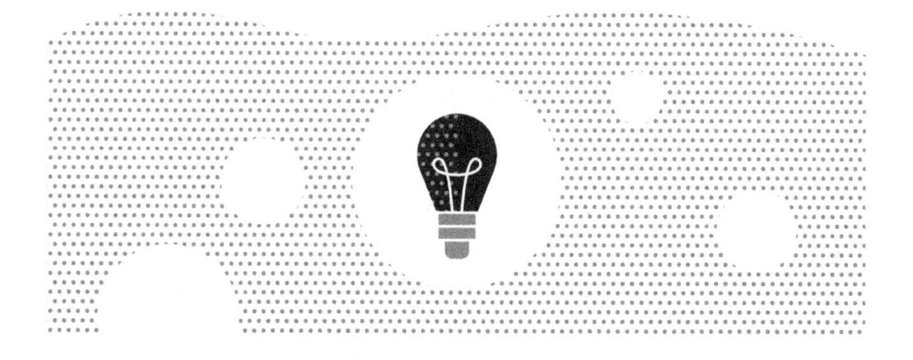

SIZE UP YOUR ENVIRONMENT

Most people, when asked if their company or organization is ready for new ideas, provide a binary answer. Yes, it is. Or no, it is not. Based on experience and gut, we have a cut and dry answer.

If only it were that simple.

Even change consultants, people who are hired to help companies manage this challenging work of assessing organizational preparedness, will share that preparedness can be more, or less, present at the individual, group, team, department, or company level.

Your department may be ready for a big idea at the very same time that the rest of the organization may be struggling to shift cultural values and unable to take on any additional changes.

Between changes in leadership, market forces, and what the idea itself requires, there will be different levels of readiness and it may look different in each situation.

The first piece of the puzzle is understanding your organization's readiness. Knowing this will help you map a way forward. Understanding how ready your organization is (or isn't) will enable you to chart out the unknown territory of launching your idea. With the "readiness" knowledge in hand, you'll have a new perspective. You'll see where you're starting and the potential paths forward as you create a "you are here" sticker on the map.

Keep in mind that because of the ever-shifting landscape of organizational readiness, the map will never be fully drawn. Some areas will be well defined. When you see a person in your company who gets new ideas through, you will see an opportunity to leverage them as a champion.

Other areas will look fuzzy. The ones that are less "ready" are under construction and it will be your job to figure out the way forward. These are areas where good ideas go to die.

Warning: It is your job to figure out the way forward! There won't be a defined set of steps to take or a map assistant to give you the best route. Your map will guide you as you go along, helping you to identify new paths when the one you are on takes a detour.

You will build out your map while you are traveling, and have to trust that with time and perseverance, you will find your way.

Organizational preparedness is the level at which a company is prepared and ready for an idea to be accepted and supported. (Even if that means they're not ready at all.)

Considering their readiness will help you to answer:

- *Can my organization support what needs to happen for my idea to flourish?*
- *Is it resilient enough to withstand the changes required?*
- *Does my organization have a record of supporting new ideas?*

That means identifying how ready your organization is for your idea, and later, identifying the activities and resources you will have to institute that will allow your idea to grow, whatever that environment might look like.

Most people have the ability to create change within their organization, regardless of the phase of readiness the company is in. In the work Douglas and I have done personally, and through coaching and leading others, time and time again we have seen people succeed *despite* the environment, not because of it.

For your idea to succeed, you have to consider the readiness of your organization and use that knowledge as you're pressing forward.

Some organizations are too big to consider every moving piece. To narrow your search, think of it like this: If you go to the doctor with a throbbing toe, they're probably not going to check your eyesight. They'll probably look at the muscles in your foot and leg, ask you some questions, and give you an x-ray or MRI. They'll look at everything relevant to your problem—not every bone or muscle in your body. At the same time, look at the parts of the organization that are relevant to your idea. Bodies and organizations are complex—but you still need to consider the relevant parts to make progress on the problem.

THE 4 "READINESS" FACTORS

Assessing your organization's readiness is a little like preparing to go on a family road trip. There's zero chance of a perfect vacation if you just strapped the kids in and hit the road without some pre-planning. No, you would make sure you and your family were ready for the trip before you left. You might realize that the kids need a new suitcase, the dog sitter will need more dog food and medicine, and the car needs the oil changed. For your organization, you'll need to make sure that everyone's ready and has what they need for the journey ahead.

When looking at your organization, you have to go deeper into the who, what, where, when, and how to begin to name the unruly beast you are hoping to tame.

When you think about your idea, and how it ranks within each component, you have an idea of pitfalls to avoid, and will identify where you might need to spend more time thinking strategically to implement your idea.

1. Who + What: The People & Culture

There's a reason so many academic and business books focus on helping leaders to develop the people and the culture within an organization—it's the heart that pumps the blood and makes the whole organization thrive, or not.

The people, whether we'd like to admit it or not, are the driving force for so many decisions that the organization makes. Even one manager's "gut feeling" that they don't like your idea could throw you completely off course.

I have a friend, Jessica, working as head of product at a global e-commerce company where the company is solely focused on revenue. The strategies, structure, and mission are all anchored to the short-term growth of the bottom line. Jessica has never been driven by numbers, but 40% of her salary depends on her ability to sell products no matter what. (Even when she didn't believe the customer needed the upsell.)

Jessica had always been a people person. Long-term, she wanted to create a branch within the company that solely focused on customer care and quality improvement. To start, she shared an idea where she wanted to introduce a new relationship-based consulting and sales business model. It would help the company to scale and grow in new markets, and over time the investment would pay off by increasing revenue.

In looking at the people and the culture at her company, Jessica recognized that the organization wouldn't be receptive to her idea in its current state. People were focused on the transactional volume versus the lifetime value of a customer. Would the sales team be open to forgoing sales to a later date when they made half their salary on commission? Probably not.

She needed to assess the readiness of the people that would be most affected by her idea.

Think about the people within your team and beyond, throughout your organization who will similarly be affected by your idea. Are they supportive of new ideas? Do they lean in with lots of curiosity and questions? Or do they wag their finger with naysaying and doubt?

Think about your "silent dissenter," the colleague that seems to go along with an idea, sitting silent meeting after meeting, only to speak up toward the end of a project listing out the reasons it won't work. (More on how to deal with the naysayers in the Getting Buy-In From the Right

People and Turning a "No" Into a "Yes" chapters.)

When it comes to your idea, you will have to take into account the different teams and people that may be affected, and reflect on how they react to change. It's critical that the company culture and people involved are on-board for innovation and change. But what if they aren't?

Where people and culture fall short, grit and perseverance can come to the rescue.

For Jessica, she knew her idea for cultivating a customer-first approach would be met with resistance within the company. To combat this, she started by talking with the people that would be most resistant—the sales team.

She sat down with David, head of the sales team, and shared her idea to learn about what would and wouldn't work.

Over time, and many conversations, she started to build her model out based on current and projected sales numbers. He shared ideas like how the company could increase salaries to compensate for the drop in commission.

Within a few months, she started to share her idea and have conversations with others in the sales department. The CFO learned of her idea and asked her to pitch it to the senior staff to consider.

Pitching the idea out of the gate as a "customer-first" initiative would probably have killed her idea. But because she had the patience and fortitude to have difficult conversations with many people throughout the organization, she was able to create a model that was eventually tested.

Understanding the readiness of the people and culture will help you go far in bringing your idea to your organization.

2. Where: The Capital & Resources

If the culture and people make up the heart of an organization, the capital and resources are the lifeblood that pumps throughout.

Most ideas will require resources for them to launch and succeed. Whether that's your free time to see it through, or a large monetary investment to make things run, your company will have to invest in your idea at some point.

You will need to identify your company's readiness to support new projects. If your company displays willingness and ability to invest resources, and the different places that may come from.

Assessing your organization's ability to provide resources will help you identify the right places to turn to for investment.

I was doing consulting work for a startup company that created a mobile app that connects people within their company based on topics, position, and interests.

In my work, I was helping them to identify new revenue sources. I was holding interviews across the company to learn more and gather insights. In one conversation, I met an eager engineer, Fatimah, who was four years into her career. After my interview with her ended, she asked if she could pick my brain on an idea she had.

Intrigued, I responded with an enthusiastic, “Yes! How about now?”

With the afternoon buzz of people grabbing coffee and snacks around us, she leaned in and shared that she wanted to implement a feature that she believed would increase the time customers spent on the app and wondered how she would go about getting the money and team in place to build it out.

“My idea is to create more opportunities for early-career people in the company to get ongoing mentorship from more senior or advanced employees throughout the company,” she shared. “When I was fresh out of school, I was at a company that had a program similar to this and it changed the trajectory of my career. I was headed down the traditional path and would have hated it. It also gave me so many opportunities just because people further along knew who I was and what I was doing.”

I asked, “Has your company ever invested in projects like this?”

She leaned back in her chair and thought a bit and then said, “I’m not sure, I’ve only been with the company for a year. I can’t really think of an example.”

We continued to chat about how she might ask her manager and teammates about projects that have been funded in the past.

We ended our chat with her taking on some homework to learn more and then to come back to me for check-ins each week to discuss.

She spent time talking to colleagues across the company, to see where she could find the resources to fund her idea. She learned that the startup was going through another round of funding. Her colleagues and manager liked the idea, but at the moment resources were focused on keeping the current business running. She hit a roadblock and wasn’t sure how to move forward with her idea if she didn’t have the capital to make it happen.

She felt stuck.

That’s the thing about an organization’s readiness to invest in ideas; it’s where the rubber meets the road. When you turn up short, it becomes default to assume the idea can't happen.

Resources are the fuel to push the idea forward and have the same power to stall them out. It may feel insurmountable to move forward without resources to give you permission. How in the world will you do the work you want to do without the money you need to make it happen?

Identifying the readiness of your organization to invest in new ideas will help you to understand if you have to get creative in finding other ways forward.

After a couple weeks, Fatimah got back to her idea and took the roadblock as an opportunity to find a different way forward. She went down other paths to seek funding. After hitting a few dead ends, she learned of a potential grant that her city was doing for the public libraries. They wanted a solution to connect unemployed people seeking work with others in different industries to get mentoring for job placement.

Fatimah found a possible resource solution—she could build and test her idea to solve this issue and this could be funded externally to develop and use internally as well.

With a funding option in hand, she had what she needed to make the pitch to move forward with her idea. Knowing that the organization wasn't ready to fund her idea helped her to get scrappy and creative as to where she might find the resources.

It's hard to push forward if you don't have a sense for where resources could come from. Investigating this in advance will give you insight for the challenges ahead to get the financial permission to launch your idea.

3. When: Timing

Can my organization handle this right now? Historically, have we made big changes or done things like these? If so, has it been around certain times of the year or after specific activities? If not, when do I introduce my idea to people in my organization?

Before you embark on trying to launch your idea, you need to assess the timing of things. Some companies have cycles for when new ideas are introduced and pushed forward. Other organizations are undergoing major changes and time will be better spent finding advocates for the idea until the dust settles.

Being aware of the timing often dictates how you behave and what steps you'll take to further your idea. Timing really can be everything.

In my role as senior director of innovation at a large corporate software company, I had the opportunity to sit down with people across the organization to ask, "How do you launch new ideas within the company?"

I learned from people with different backgrounds and positions, from product leaders and engineers to marketing and software developers. For the more tenured employees, I learned of a history of hackathons, innovation labs, and other opportunities that they were able to leverage. I also learned from more recently hired employees that they didn't know of any formal department-wide programs. They shared more organic opportunities like "free-time Fridays" where twice a month on Fridays, a product's development team was given the freedom to explore new work.

What stood out was that because of a recent organizational change, restructuring people and processes, the timing for where new ideas would fit was unclear. Tenured employees remember an era when there were specific times throughout the year that allowed for new ideas to surface. More recently hired employees weren't aware of those activities.

One of the newer hires, a software developer named Brent, shared with me that he felt there was freedom to ideate and autonomy to work solo on new ideas but he didn't know when it was the right time to take his idea to the next level.

Brent was hired when his department was still feeling its way forward from the major organizational changes it had recently undergone. The group was regaining its footing and he didn't have personal knowledge of the right time to propose his idea.

We created a group of people across the department and started to talk about how you know the timing of getting an idea through the organization. Clarity on the "when" helped Brent find his moment—the right moment.

Some organizations have a timeline to introduce new ideas. Retail and grocery chains often start their "ideation" time during the slower summer months. Then, during the peak shopping time of the holidays, the businesses are focused on distribution and execution and it generally isn't a great time for new ideas (unless your new idea is related to solving the chaos around holiday shopping).

When you are looking to assess the readiness of your company's "when," look at new processes, ideas, or roles. When has a change occurred? Was it cyclical? Was it around certain times of the year or certain times of the product-life cycle?

The right timing can also be tied to people's emotions and energy levels. An apathetic group or people overwhelmed with full plates can both be telling about the opportunity for the right timing.

Spend time learning from others that have successfully launched a new idea as well as people that have seen their ideas fall short. In both cases, there's an opportunity to learn where things are working and where they're not, to identify the right timing for your idea.

4. How: The Way Work Is Done

Understanding how new ideas move from inception to launch within your organization will help you identify the work you need to do to make your idea come to life.

For many, we leave the formal process of getting work done up to our intuition. Rather than understanding the ins and outs of an organization's process upfront, we allow it to unfold in front of us while we move our idea forward. Reacting to the different phases as we go along.

The problem with this approach is that you don't know what lies ahead. Like a treasure map, you know you want to reach the northeast corner of your map with a giant X for the buried treasure. But without understanding the process, you will miss marked landmines along the way. You will fall trap to avoidable pitfalls and risk your idea ever taking off.

Assessing your organization's readiness will ensure the operating environment of whether your organization is prepared to support and accept the changes that will result from your idea. It will also help you understand what tasks you will need to perform and the deliverables needed throughout your idea's life cycle.

In March 2018, I attended an event during SXSW EDU, sponsored by Stanford Life Design Lab and online education provider, CreativeLive. Attended by people across many industries, the event was an interesting gathering of designers, design educators, and learning and development experts.

The mixer was held at a local Tex Mex restaurant bar in downtown Austin. Sometime between the pork shoulder tacos and craft tequila cocktails, I had a fascinating conversation with a director of digital learning, Olivia, who was trying to launch technology solutions within one of the largest school districts in the U.S.

Olivia had spent seven years working in the district and when we first met we spent hours exchanging stories from the trenches, where we each had spent time leveraging design thinking approaches to try to breathe innovation into a school system.

She was on the tail-end of a project that as she described it, sounded like a slam-dunk idea. Her team had identified a new tool that would replace the work done across four systems currently in operation, all to better track student performance and persistence across the district's programs. It would create a more unified data set to identify the challenges the district was facing and provide an affordable alternative to running the older systems currently in place.

Olivia and her team had done their homework to bring the project together. They developed a rigorous requirements document, selected a vendor after a thoughtful procurement process, and embarked on forming a project plan to move the idea forward. All seemed to line up and the project was met with wild enthusiasm from district leaders, teachers, and even parents across the district.

But her team failed to properly assess the readiness of the organization for such a change. Her team didn't fully understand how the end-user, enrollment administrators, would be crucial to the process of this system being used and taking off.

Olivia and her team had a great idea. They followed all the steps to make it happen but a blind spot of how the work would get done stalled out their project. They didn't realize that the process required buy-in and use from a very resistant-to-change group.

The enrollment administrators weren't open to the new workflow created by the tool and, ultimately, the project was terminated.

This group of administrators was deeply connected to the process of how students move through the system. They weren't ready to change this process as it would have a direct impact on the way they work.

During our conversation, Olivia was shaking her head with remorse, still at a loss for what a waste it was to see such a great idea fall short.

When it comes to assessing organizational preparedness, it is difficult and time-consuming to think through the organization's process to identify the steps that are required to get new ideas through.

But the process of how work is done is part of the organization's DNA. Organizations can't thrive without process and things don't happen without it. It's the only way anything gets done. So you must first understand your organization's process, rather than blindly pushing your idea forward—it's the rule book to follow as you develop new ideas within the organization.

When assessing the organization's process, ask yourself what are the important steps to take to get my idea to work? What needs to happen for my idea to flourish?

As an organization with a multitude of moving pieces, how must we behave? What processes do different teams and people take on?

After SXSW EDU, I kept up with Olivia and learned that while her original project had failed, it taught her a valuable lesson in understanding the readiness of an organization when it comes to process.

She and her team had refocused their time and efforts on trying to identify the right opportunities that would bring change to the process.

YOU'RE NOT READY

Most people presume that their company is ready. The reality is—there are plenty of reasons it might not be. Resources may be scarce, timing may be wrong, processes may be broken, or, gasp, all three!

When you start by assuming your organization is not ready, you can take steps to address the gaps. Now, what does that mean? Where are there gaps in readiness? Why would your company not be ready? How can you help make components more ready?

As a mentor for startups and formal startup incubation programs through Stanford and Techstars, I am often approached by budding entrepreneurs with the next brilliant, Uber-like idea that will disrupt a new market.

In 2019, through the Montreal Techstars AI cohort, I had the opportunity to mentor a cohort of startups leveraging artificial intelligence across all industries and markets.

Early in the process, the founders are put through a rigorous round of "mentor madness" where over a week-long period they sit down with over 80 mentors. All day, each day, they are pitching their idea and then sitting through round after round of questions and concerns with these mentors, hearing where their idea needs work.

You don't have to be on the receiving end to see that it's hard work and exhausting. One mentor may complement an approach a founder is taking and the very next mentor will go against it telling them why it's wrong. I call it mentor whiplash, and all the feedback comes at you like a fire hose. To the founders, all of this "you're not ready because" feedback can be overwhelming.

And so very beneficial.

Over that week-long period, every single founder walked out more confused, less sure of themselves, and ready to rebuild. For every idea, there's a benefit to assuming something isn't ready. Take on the mindset of "prove it to me." (The model that Techstars uses.)

- *Think your organization is ready for your idea? Prove it.*
- *How will the people and culture get in the way?*
- *Where will funding and resources be a burden?*
- *When will timing be a problem?*
- *How will the process create roadblocks?*

Don't solely focus on the opportunity your idea will create for your organization. Consider the readiness of your company and assume there is work that will need to be done. This is the exciting part, the challenge of finding where there are holes in your organization's readiness and where there is work to be done.

ACTIVITY
CHART YOUR READINESS

When you travel by airplane, you will notice as you step through the door to board that the flight crew are busy readying the plane. Outside, maintenance workers are inspecting the aircraft for damage or defects. The flight attendant is at the front of the cabin, ensuring all safety equipment is ready. To your left, you see inside the cockpit that the pilots are running through the aircraft checklist to ensure the plane is ready and able to take on the different stages of flight from take-off to landing.

Before you take off to your destination, there is a meticulous process in place.

As seemingly mundane as a checklist may sound, it's a critical component to preparing to launch your idea. It gives you insight into where there are weaknesses in your organization to help you identify how others might react to your idea. It will also require you to think through things that you may otherwise miss. A "prove it" mindset to break you of any blind spots.

In this exercise, you will assess your organization's four readiness factors:

- *Who/What: People and Culture*
- *Where: Capital and Resources*
- *When: Market and Timing*
- *How: The Process and the Way Work Is Done*

The assessment of each section is a key to identifying your organization's readiness, and your moment of "all systems go." For each of the above, you will gauge the readiness, rating your organization on a scale of 1 to 5. (Half points are okay too.)

1 = Crash and Burn

2 = Not Ready

3 = Could Go Either Way

4 = Have a Good Feeling

5 = Locked and Loaded—Ready to Go

Keep your grades handy. We're going to have you map your overall readiness on a spider graph at the end. From there, you can take a critical look at your organization's ability, fit, and capacity to deliver on your idea, identifying the actions you need to take to address the state of readiness for each factor.

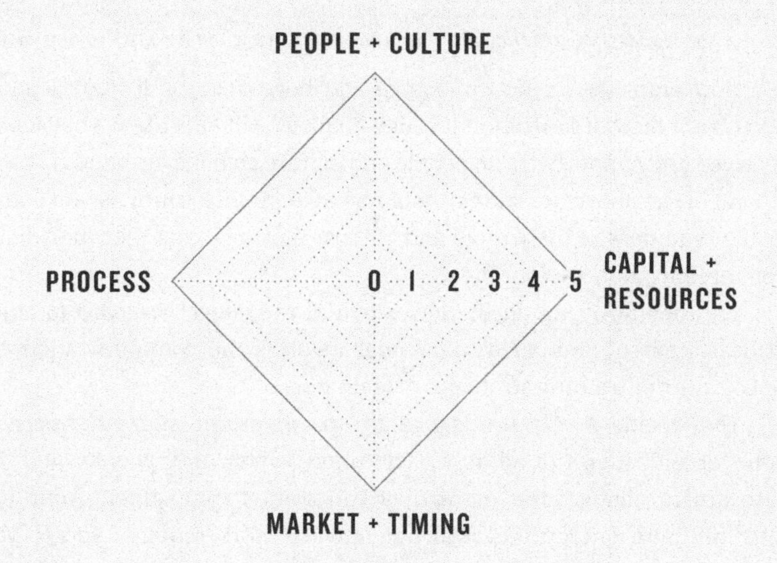

So let's get started on your idea within your organization!

STEP 1: PEOPLE & CULTURE

Look around your organization and take an assessment of the people and culture. Where does the organization stand in terms of its people and culture's ability to handle change?

Consider the teams and types of people that will be directly or indirectly affected by your idea. In general, do people in your company value change? For example, do they see your idea as needed, important, or worthwhile?

Think about each group of stakeholders that your idea will affect. This will include your team, a larger department, a functional group, and leadership. On a scale of 1 to 5, how ready and willing are the people toward change? Ask questions like:

- *How innovative are we, or when it comes to new ideas, what do we value?*
- *For colleagues, are they optimistic, engaged, or excited about new ideas, or are they pessimistic, burned out, or apathetic?*
- *For leadership, are they indifferent or defensive when it comes to new ideas?*

How employees react to change and how business leaders lead (or don't lead) their organization through changes will affect how your idea is received and supported. The people and culture go hand-in-hand.

All of the above questions should be taken into account as you consider the readiness of the people and culture—how ready is the who/what of your organization for your idea?

Are they hovering on the lower end of the gauge? Prepare to adjust critical areas of your idea's plan that involves the communication and onboarding or training strategies of your idea.

The People & Culture gauge is an important start in assessing your organization's readiness. The more open the people and culture are to change, the more they will want to implement your idea and the more energy they will put into the work required to see your idea all the way through. (People are important—we'll talk about how to find champions for your idea and get buy-in from stakeholders along the way in the Getting Buy-In From the Right People chapter.)

STEP 2: CAPITAL & RESOURCES

To gauge your organization's readiness to provide the resources you need toward your idea, think about the budget required to make your idea happen. How many people will you need and for how long?

Go beyond the cost and people resources and think about other requirements such as the hardware, software, and technology needed. When you look around your organization, ask questions like:

- *How ready is it to put resources into new ideas, what hurdles do you foresee?*
- *Knowing what investments your idea would require, how ready is your organization to support it?*

The Capital & Resources gauge can act as the go and no-go of a gas tank. When you are at a one or two, you have to get creative to identify funding or do as much work as you can without resources until you have the right capital available to you.

STEP 3: MARKET & TIMING

Understanding your organization's readiness as it relates to the market and timing is crucial to identifying the path forward. Questions to ask include:

- *Are there certain times that change is embraced?*
- *Does it require advanced planning and approvals for quarterly objectives? Or are there market factors driving your organization to take action in one area or another?*
- *What big ideas and changes are already underway in your organization? Does knowing this help you identify when to postpone your idea?*
- *Or, perhaps, identify the small steps that you can take now to build the case for bigger steps to take in the future?*

The market and timing readiness of your organization can be both structural and psychological.

Structurally, you can look internally to understand what policies are in place to help you identify the right timing of new projects. The day-to-day operations of work can be telling. Are you seeing certain times when new ideas are accepted? Are there times when people are overworked or understaffed and new ideas would be a distraction?

Look externally to understand how ready your organization is within the marketplace. Are there external factors affecting your organization's readiness? Are there big changes in your organization's industry, providing insight into what needs to change? Or customer needs that are increasing yet still not met by your organization (but are by competitors)?

Rate your organization's readiness as it relates to the market and timing. Is it primed and ready or do you see some roadblocks that make the company unprepared for challenges?

STEP 4: THE PROCESS & WAY WORK IS DONE

To assess your organization's readiness as it relates to the process, take a look at the current state of how people perform their jobs using the existing systems, tools, and processes. Think about each group throughout your organization and ask:

- *What business procedures are in place? What policies and process guidance do people follow?*
- *Are these "ways work gets done" creating roadblocks to change?*
- *Are people feeling stuck in the status quo? Or are they given a place in their process to innovate and try new things?*

Create the rating for your organization. How do the current processes and systems in place rank?

When you find that your organizational readiness for change is ranking low, it requires you to try to create chunks of small changes. Rather than going big out of the gate, you will need to identify how to slowly effect change within the process.

When you create your own readiness checklist, you will identify gaps in capabilities. Through this activity, you will have additional information to help identify ways you might respond differently to address the gaps.

Whatever your organization, the readiness is multifaceted and multidimensional. Understanding it will be a complex puzzle that will never feel fully developed or complete. But as your assessment is underway, the fuzzy parts of your map will become clearer.

You will begin to have the gratifying *aha* as your map toward launching your idea comes together.

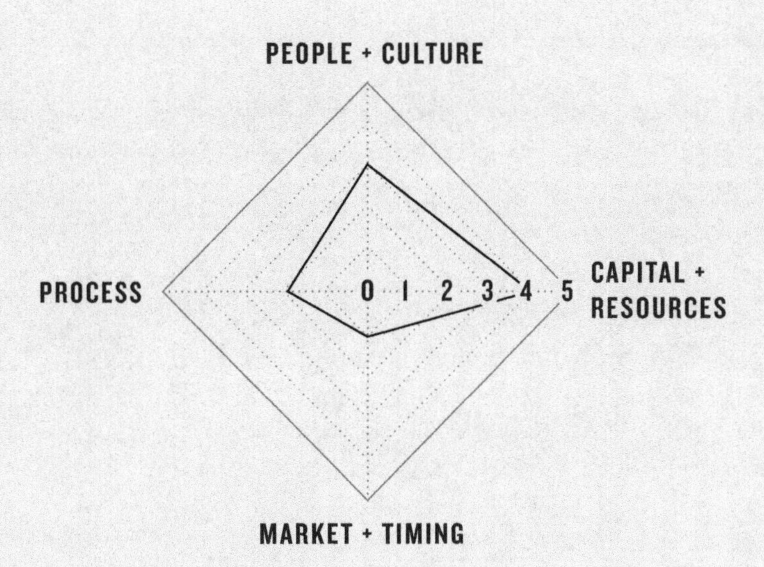
PEOPLE + CULTURE
PROCESS
0 1 2 3 4 5
CAPITAL + RESOURCES
MARKET + TIMING

GET YOUR ACT TOGETHER

Organize Your Idea

For anyone who has ever seen a crime show on TV, there's always a scene with the ubiquitous "crazy wall." The wall where the investigators pin up and plot out all the clues and suspects. Red strings and sharpie lines track connections and relationships between people and clues. The wall is the place to lay it all out, step back, and try to make connections, contemplate different theories.

The idea being that if the investigators stare at this board long enough—bam! Suddenly, they crack the case! Somewhere between the tangled strings connecting the suspects and crime-scene photos pinned to the map, they have a breakthrough and see something they hadn't seen before.

When it comes to working out the kinks of your idea and pushing it through your company, you'll need your own proverbial "crazy wall." Essentially, you need a place to get organized so you can have your own *aha* moments.

Organizational skills exist on a spectrum: On the one end, you have the fly-by-the-seat-of-your-pants person who thrives on chaos and doesn't need the tether of an identifiable system to move through life. It all makes sense, but only to themselves.

At the other end, you have a tightly-wound, always-in-control person who has a Bullet Journal listing out everything from the complex to the mundane and finds peace in order. Being organized is as ingrained as it is to breathe, but creates rigidity and only makes room for things that are "figured out."

The problem with these two extremes is that neither will get an idea to the finish line, gaining buy-in from others on your work. Embark on the journey without structure and you will miss out on a specific activity along the way, one that will make or break buy-in from an important stakeholder. Go too structured and you miss the opportunity to see the bigger picture, swirling in the tactical. In many cases, you'll have to find the right time to lean in to each side of the spectrum. At times you'll be required to pinpoint every detail on your P&L or in your presentation to the tech team, while at other times you will need to explain the big-picture vision to the board of directors. Getting organized helps you wade back and forth between these two sides.

As a person who likes to break the rules and figure it out as I go, I have to find the right balance for getting and staying organized. My natural inclination is to get started and get to work. To altogether skip getting organized so I can start my new idea.

But I make myself pause at the start of a new project and spend the time to get organized. I figure out who I need to work with, project goals, and even create milestones and a timeline to follow.

Once I have a structure in place, I allow myself the freedom to change and update it as I go. Maybe I didn't capture all the right people I need to work with, or my timeline was too aggressive.

I use those moments to evaluate how my organization is serving me and how it is not. Then I make the appropriate changes and get back to work.

As someone who embodies the "embrace ambiguity" mantra, but with a keen eye toward purpose, I work hard to hover somewhere in the middle of organized and flexible. I like to get organized as a place to start and break the structure as I figure things out while moving forward.

I like the guiding light that organization can bring, but I step outside the lines and explore the unknown in an effort to find the best way forward.

EXPLAINING THE UNEXPLAINABLE

Have you ever tried to explain an idea that no one seems to understand? You end up talking in circles, repeating yourself, and asking, "You know what I mean?" to a group of confused listeners.

For a project with a large American sports apparel brand, Douglas utilized a "Story From the Future" exercise to help the team realize how jargon and assumptions prevent the effective and accurate flow of information. Only after realizing the problem were they able to begin to improve how they share new, complex ideas.

In the exercise, the team was divided into pairs. Each pair would decide who would tell the story from the future. The storyteller's jobs were to describe an iPhone to their partner who was to imagine they were living in the 1800s and ask questions as if they only knew of things from that time.

One guy shared, "It's a way to connect to friends via text."

Then his partner pointed out, "But what is a 'text'?"

Another woman shared, "It's a small device that stores all your friends' and family's contact information."

And her partner asked, "What is a 'device' and what do you mean by 'stores'?"

You can see how challenging the exercise can be when you are trying to describe something complex in a simple, easy-for-anyone-to-understand way to someone who lacks the basic context that your explanations rely on. In other words, when they don't know your jargon.

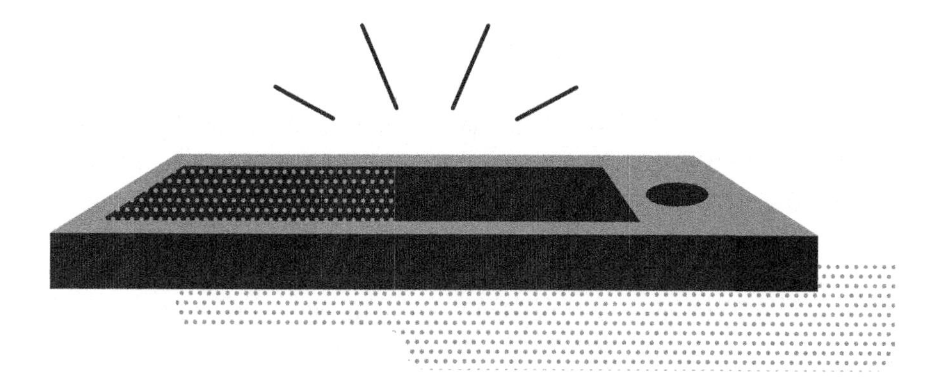

When the team thought about the benefits and features of the iPhone, and then broke it down further based on the knowledge of people from the 1800s, they had organized a very simple way to describe it:

"It's a thing about the size of your hand. If someone else has one of these things you can speak into it and they will be able to hear you even if they are very far away. This all happens through the air, the two things don't have to be touching each other in any way."

There's no right answer to describing the iPhone to someone in the 1800s. The task is almost impossible, at least not in five minutes. The point is to come to a moment of realization that the way we explain things matters. That sometimes you have to boil something down to the most important feature and start from there.

Most new ideas are confusing and foreign. People can't connect to their purpose or value. No one will support an idea that can't be explained simply. Organization is the secret key to being able to explain your idea.

When I was working at Autodesk, a corporation that makes design software, I was hired to help push new ideas forward. I worked in the Media and Entertainment (M&E) products division, where they provided the software used to create content for the world's most popular movies and video games.

My job was to create documentation and experiences that would help the teams and employees within M&E to better connect with a 10-year vision of where their work might be in the future; to make the vision more "real" and relatable to their day-to-day work. The project would require loads of input from people across the organization, many different perspectives on how to get there, and all with high stakes that the output would succeed.

Creating and presenting a 10-year vision is complex work. It's hard to imagine what the world might look like in ten years and even harder to try to articulate it in a way that has meaning across the division and to everyone at the different levels.

Early on, I had to get organized as I didn't have anyone to tell me where to start or what to do. I was hired in June 2019 and had six months to pull off getting the 10-year vision in front of the employees in a way that made sense and inspired them. I needed to come up with a system that would allow me to track the different ideas and conversations while helping to identify the best way forward at any time.

I needed my own version of a "crazy wall." A system that I could refer back to over time and get big-picture snapshots while simultaneously keeping track of details. And maybe I would have my own *aha* moment.

Before I could get started on gaining traction for my project, I needed to get myself organized. I had so many questions swirling in my head that it made "getting started" feel like a daunting task. But getting organized unlocked the chaos and started to create a path forward.

I started by outlining all the different stakeholders involved. From leaders that might help in creating the vision to the different employees within the division that would need to understand it. I outlined the different ways we would have to communicate and the work I needed to do to understand what would resonate and have meaning to help people connect their work to the final 10-year vision we created.

A week into my work, I was at a meeting with senior leadership. The meeting didn't have anything on the agenda related to my project, but unexpectedly the conversation shifted to the work I was taking on.

My boss looked at me and asked, "When can we convene everyone across the division to share the 10-year vision?"

I thought, wait, we want to hold an event to convene 300 people from around the world to discuss a vision yet to be decided on?

Usually, a week into a new project with a new company, a curve-ball question like this from a senior leader could make you sweat and nervously answer, "Ummmm, I don't know. Let me look into that and get back to you."

But because of my faithful work in getting organized, I had a sense for a timeline.

"I still have more to uncover and learn but given what I've put together and with the resources at hand, it looks like we could hold something as early as the second week in December."

That led to a conversation around the best timing for the event and the different pieces that would need to be in place before then. The senior leaders were bought in, and I was off to go start the work I was hired to do.

I walked out of that room thinking I had a lot more organization to do to pull off all the different components required for this project. But I knew that my early work on getting organized paid off in helping me get alignment and buy-in from the senior management team.

CONTAINER STORE YOUR IDEA

It's one thing to have your home office organized, so you can find bills to pay on time and important documents needed for travel. But it's a whole other level to get an idea organized. Your home office is dimensionally constrained. It has a set number of items and is fairly static. Ideas live in your head. They are going to be dynamic and involve emergent phenomena. When you have to work with other people, the complication compounds to account for their behaviors and attitudes that shift and change over time too.

How you organize the moving pieces of your idea will be the difference between success and failure. Not putting in the upfront work of getting organized will cause you to skip steps in a process or miss opportunities for people to buy in. Like the "crazy wall" for investigators, a disorganized idea will prevent you from seeing the whole picture and having your own "I got it!" moments.

When you are doing the work to push an idea through a company, you have to lay out all the different pieces you are working with, and continue to keep up with those pieces as new ones are introduced. Keep in mind that being organized isn't about having everything "perfect." It's just about starting to categorize things and figure out one way forward.

AN IMPROMPTU WEDDING TOAST

Imagine being asked to give a wedding toast ten minutes beforehand. Now imagine the difference if you were given six months to prepare. The stories told would be vastly different, and the organization of thought for most of us would be evident. The difference between putting time and organization into it is clear.

To help your idea evolve, use organizing it as the necessary step to get started, and make improvements along the way. When you get your idea organized, you're unlocking it from your brain. Rather than seeing a spilled mess of an idea, you start to see the pieces and identify ways to categorize them.

Like when you are going grocery shopping. You start with a list of things you have in your head:

> *Pasta, oil, tomatoes, green beans, toothpaste, oh yeah, I need shampoo too, more pepper, something for breakfast, coffee creamer, paper towels, window cleaner.*

As your list is written out, you start to categorize and group the different items:

> *These are in the fruit/veggie section, oh yeah, I need more garlic, and the last items are all in the house/cleaning aisle.*

And sharing your list with a family member or roommate to make sure you get everything you need? They'll be able to follow your thinking and add their own items to your categories.

Before you know it, you are ready to take on the chore of grocery shopping. Organizing yourself in advance so you don't forget items or spend an exorbitant amount of time bouncing around aisles as you remember items you need that you passed ten minutes before.

It's a simple and glorious thing. Ideas are complex but organizing them up front will help your idea evolve and, at the same time, allow you to get buy-in from others along the way.

WHAT DIET WILL YOU FOLLOW?

Many people wait for the right tool or method to follow in order to get their idea organized.

Like a new year's resolution for a healthier diet. What diet will you follow? There's a million resources online guiding you to the number one, fastest way to lose weight. So many options that you can swirl in the choices, keeping you from actually taking a step forward in making progress.

Like New Year's Day, now is the time for you to get started. It's the kick-off moment to organizing your idea—but how will you know what needs to be organized or the best tool to help you on your journey?

To figure out the how, start by understanding the two major components: getting yourself organized, and getting your idea organized. With these considered, you will begin to develop a more complete picture. One that gets into the weeds but still gives you a high-level perspective of the next steps.

READY YOURSELF

When you are pushing a new idea through an organization, you're taking on a second job. There's the job you were hired for, and the job you are doing to get the idea to launch. This second job might be similar or only slightly adjacent to the current work you are doing, but the key distinction is that your boss is still expecting you to do all your *other* work.

You need to make sure that you continue to rock out the job you were hired for, or else you won't be given permission to take on the additional work for your new idea.

There may be a time in the future where you will be given the authority or position to take on your idea as a full-time job. Hooray! But until then, you still have job responsibilities you were hired for that you have to execute against. (Side note, if you're one of the lucky few who were specifically hired to execute on your new idea, that's great. You can skip to step two.)

Organizing yourself will allow you to ensure you are performing your expected job duties and still have space for taking on the work your new idea requires.

What job responsibilities were you hired for? Where can you let some things go to free up your brain and time to tackle the work your new idea will require? People that do not take the time to get both camps in order often find that they start to fail at one (or both) of the jobs.

Getting yourself organized is a three-step process.

Step 1: What Is It You Do Here?

Start the process by identifying the job responsibilities you were hired to accomplish. An easy place to turn to is the job description you applied to (if you can dig that up). You can also refer to reviews with your boss. What are you getting reviewed on? These expectations are part of the work that you are expected to do.

Knowing what you were hired to do also means understanding what success looks like. What metrics or outcomes are expected from your work?

Step 2: How Can You Show Your Value?

Take your list of job responsibilities and connect them to tangible outcomes and metrics. For example, let's say you are a product manager at a big company. You are expected to evaluate market competition and position your product line so that it appeals to customers. There are lots of activities you are doing day-in and day-out related to this work.

One way to highlight that you are getting your job done is your ability to keep customers engaged, so you could track the percentage of customers that use your product and the percentage that stop using your product. Called the "churn," it's a great indicator of your product's health and when the churn percentage is dropping, and fewer customers are leaving your product, it's a win worth highlighting to show your focus and dedication to the work you were hired to do.

Take your job responsibilities, identify where you can track progress and tangible metrics that relate to the role. From there, you can determine how you share your successes and prioritize your efforts.

Step 3: How Can You Share Your Success Stories?

Look, I know self-promotion can seem egotistical and like you aren't a team player. But you need to ensure that your boss and teammates see your work as valuable. Don't rely on someone else to do this for you or assume the work will speak for itself.

In most cases, the daily wins of your work will go unnoticed and it's your job to make sure people continue to see the value that you bring. And if people don't know about your great work, you won't get the opportunity to explore new work like your big idea.

Showing others how you are knocking it out of the park will give you the credibility you need to prove your ability to take on new, more challenging work. Rather than waiting for your successes to surface, be proactive and share them along the way.

Think about how you have met (or better yet, exceeded) the goals and expectations for your role. How can you share it with others in a way that feels authentic?

If you are more introverted or don't feel the need to self-promote, this will be an exercise in stretching your boundaries. For some, self-promotion feels "icky" and reserved for the arrogant know-it-alls you roll your eyes at.

The thing is, when you are self-promoting the right way, sharing your value in a sincere and authentic way, you will find the value without feeling the ick.

In coaching Sandra, a woman that typically excelled at her job behind the scenes, we talked about how she could share her wins with others in a way that felt true to herself.

"I don't like to talk about my work. I'd rather highlight the team's work collectively or another individual's work," Sandra shared with me.

I asked her, "If you were in a performance review, and your boss asked right now, 'Why are you good at your job?' what would you say?"

Without a beat or even blinking, Sandra very matter-of-factly replied, "We've seen an 82% increase in our production this year and without incurring any additional fees or expenses. That is what I do here."

"Wow, Sandra. That's really impressive. Have you had the chance to highlight your part in making this happen with your boss?"

You could see reality settle for her when she plainly responded, "No."

She realized that while she and her team were aware of the huge successes they had achieved, her boss may not be clued in to the magnitude of her contribution.

Sandra decided right there that she would reach out to her boss to schedule a coffee where she could highlight her work and discuss other ways they could improve efficiencies. Her plan was to not only share her value but to focus on what she enjoys about her job. She loved her work and used that as a way to lead the conversation.

The key to authentic self-promoting is to let go of the feeling that it's too egocentric, and instead take action to go out there and share.

Depending on the work you are doing, you should set a cadence for regular check-ins, letting your boss know how you are doing and communicating what you are learning and accomplishing through your work.

When it comes to sharing your value, I like what I call the "80 to 1 Rule." For every 80 hours that you put specifically toward a project (about 2 weeks of work), you take an hour to share back how it's going, focusing on the positive or learning from the negative.

You can plan this out in your calendar. Looking at your weeks, how much of your time is spent on a specific task or job? How many weeks does it take to get to the 80-hour mark? Add to your calendar a one-hour block of time for you to collect what you need to share with your boss.

Schedule a one-on-one with your boss to share. If you have a manager that doesn't allow for these types of conversations, share it in an email.

For Sandra, after she started to have scheduled check-ins with her boss, she saw that she was given more freedom to take on new opportunities. Her boss could see the value she was bringing to her role and gave her a promotion as well as helped connect her to mentors throughout the company that could help her in her work.

The best part of doing this work is that it will hold you accountable. Getting yourself organized will keep you honest, ensuring you don't neglect the work you were hired to do because your idea was more interesting and time-consuming.

You don't want to have your job responsibilities creep up on you, leaving you with a feeling of "Whoa, I forgot I had that deadline because I was busy with the idea that no one is giving me permission to work on!"

For you to succeed in both areas, the job you were hired for and the idea you want to launch, you have to organize, hold it all together, and show the value you bring. By communicating well with your manager and showing that you can get things done, they're going to be more supportive because they know they can trust you.

DECLUTTER YOUR DESKTOP

My friend Zac is an artist with lots of projects going on from writing novels and short stories to playing music and stand-up comedy. He has a creative mind bursting with ideas, but a very disorganized way of keeping track of his many ideas.

I remember one sunny Sunday afternoon, when I was trying to help him organize a project so he could publish and launch one of his books.

Sitting at his kitchen table next to him, he opened up his silver laptop and there before me was a glowing desktop so cluttered with files and icons that some overlapped and it filled the screen.

The chaos was palpable and made my heart race. He could read my disbelief and immediately went into explaining that he had this laptop for years and that he knew where things were even though it looked a mess.

But when I asked him to locate his most recent draft of the story, he started clicking around and mousing over different icons and version histories to try and find it. Five minutes later, when he finally found the correct file, it took what felt like an eternity for it to open because of all the memory being used for the items stored on his desktop.

Zac was overdue for organizing his idea. He had excuses up and down for what was holding him back, but the reality was he needed to roll up his sleeves and take the time to come up with a better system. One that would be organized but still fit his way of flowing through work and projects.

To get your idea organized, the specifics of exactly how you do this are less important than the act of doing it and referring back to it over time. Think about the different apps or tools you have downloaded with the promise to help you organize your life. At first, you download it in the hope that it's finally the solution that helps you keep things in order. Something to make life feel less messy.

You start out by diligently filling out your to-dos, setting everything up so you finally have a way to keep everything in order. And then, time passes, life settles in, and you fall back to your old habits. Sticky notes strewn across a desk or abandoned to-do lists found in coat pockets.

So instead of telling yourself you need to adopt a new app or system, take an inventory of what you already use. What techniques help you stay organized? A file cabinet of folders? A notebook with dividers for different themes of activities? You're already going to be taking on a lot of new work, so use the systems you already naturally gravitate toward. It's not the time to try to change the way you work.

For Zac, that meant creating folders for his projects and moving all the older documents into the right places. Then, for the projects he considered active and wanted quick access to, he created a folder specific for "Active Projects" and then at the first of every month, put into his calendar a reminder to move, rename, organize, and archive projects that have been completed.

He could still track his ideas and this new setup freed his mind from having to navigate through the mess. Like decluttering his desktop, organizing his ideas gave him a clean slate to open his mind to more important tasks, like creating.

The first time I needed to get organized for a new idea, I had a beautiful leather bound notebook that I would take notes into, to use as a way to keep all the tasks, conversations, and to-dos in one place.

While beautiful (and I thought it looked cool and professional when I would meet with people in coffee shops), I learned that writing in that little black Moleskin journal was my way of taking notes, and then never thinking about them or looking at them again.

Notes got lost and didn't follow a system where I could go back and find things to take any actionable steps forward.

I would try learning the Bullet Journal method but that was time-consuming. I then tried creating sections for different components, but that just led to half-used notebooks with blank pages between sections and still didn't lead to a working organization system for me. I even tried one of those new journals that allows you to take photos of the pages and upload to an online journal. Another wasted attempt to try to fit myself into an organizational approach that just didn't work for me.

So then I did some reflecting—what *does* work for me? Why am I failing with this method? When am I most organized and productive?

I realized that what works for me was having things accessible electronically. Most importantly, the ability to take and retrieve notes and files across devices and computers.

I would take notes on my cell. And then need access to them later when I was working on my laptop. Or would remember an email conversation I had that would help a presentation that I was creating and have to dig through email threads to find the file.

This realization allowed me to let go of my urge to use a pretty little journal.

Instead, I started to create a sophisticated system that made my work more efficient and gratifying when I was able to pull a quote I captured from the CEO months before or a random idea I had while on the go.

I made my organization available online, on-demand—in a system that I can drop things into as they pop into my head. I use it to grab inspiration, and keep an eye on it for when I want to jump into work. I start by creating a deck in Google Slides and like a presentation, I have a title slide. I spend time formatting and designing it to be appealing because I know I will be referring back to it frequently, so I may as well enjoy looking at it. I then start creating new slides as different pieces come together. A slide about data would have links to resources or company documents supporting my idea. Or a slide about my different stakeholders may have quotes from conversations. The deck serves as my system to stay organized.

In the beginning of a new idea, there's a lot to take on. Rather than getting hung up and slowing it down until I figure everything out, I come up with a way to organize all my different lines of thought so that I can step back and see a way to take a step forward.

Sleep experts will tell you that if you are a worrier, someone that will lay in bed making lists, keeping yourself from much-needed sleep, then you should keep a notepad and paper by your bed. When all those fleeting thoughts pop in, *need to buy bread, remind Daniel at work to share feedback, check in on Chris to see why you haven't heard back...* you jot them down.

The act of releasing them from your brain, putting them on paper, knowing you will address them later, that's what will lead you to be able to relax and fall asleep.

Organizing your idea is no different. You need a system in place that will allow you to take all that jumbled up mess and get it out of your brain so that you can unlock it for moving forward.

Your idea will thrive when it has organization to back it up. As more and more goes into making it happen, being organized will allow you to take action to move things forward.

Find a strategy that you enjoy and understand through testing what does and doesn't work. Because when you find the system that does work, you'll have the freedom to focus on what matters—your idea.

UNLOCK SURPRISING BREAKTHROUGHS

Once you have found the way that you will organize yourself and your idea, you have enough to get started. You'll begin to see themes emerge and tasks that when done serve multiple purposes.

It's like when you think about batching your work to increase productivity in your workday. You could answer email throughout the day, as it comes in, or you could block off chunks of time to dedicate to responding to emails, distraction-free. Then, create other blocks of time where you can accomplish deep thinking, uninterrupted by the "I just have a quick question" emails. Batching things will allow you to leverage that work you put into organization, making sure it serves you.

When you organize yourself and your idea, you will find your own "crazy wall". It will help bring meaning to your work to unlock surprising breakthroughs and to make your idea stick.

While my writing partner, Douglas, was researching for this particular chapter, he found a quote we both thought rang true:

Clutter is no more than postponed decisions.

—Attributed to Barbara Hemphill, a professional organizer

We postpone making decisions when we're afraid to commit, when we're worried that maybe it won't work, or we'll make a mistake and fail. By now you probably know that making a mistake is inevitable and that it's never going to be perfect.

It's taken me years of stop-and-go to figure out the best way to organize my new ideas. One approach would start out great, but then when it fell apart, I had to evaluate what did and didn't work so I could come up with a better system. This gave me room to learn and think about what could work instead.

Launching an idea and organizing it is an evolution, and will build on itself over time. Whether journaling is your thing, or cleaning your desk, or clearing out your closet, organization declutters the mind and creates the space for the things that matter to surface. So how do you figure out what "works for you" and what doesn't? How do you actually get organized?

ACTIVITY
GET YOURSELF & YOUR IDEA ORGANIZED

STEP 1: WHAT WORKS

Think about your work, home, and personal life, how do you manage all the things that need to get done? To-do lists? Notes on the fridge? Calendar reminders?

Think about the different approaches you take to get things done and how they help. Organization comes in all forms and utilizes tools of all shapes and sizes.

Make a list of what you already use.

Examples:

- *Asana project management tool at work.*
- *Email threads between family members for household chores/tasks.*
- *post-its for listing life to-dos.*

STEP 2: WHAT DOESN'T WORK

Even the King or Queen of Organization doesn't reign over a perfect system. Where are there flaws in your approach?

- *At work, not everyone wanted to use the Asana tool and this caused team members to have to use multiple tools and channels depending on who was involved.*
- *The email lists to family members had no ability to track or keep people accountable.*
- *post-its would get lost or misunderstood with messy handwriting.*

Knowing these flaws in the way you are organized can help bring about ideas that will improve your current organization systems.

Make a list of what's not working and consider how each system can be tweaked. How could you improve your system?

- *At work, content and conversations were getting lost and redundant throughout too many channels. We identified one to two methods that worked to stick to.*
- *The email chain lacked accountability, so I changed my system to nerd out on Asana for household chores, due dates, and reminders for everything.*
- *post-its were relocated to the "notes" app on my phone to eliminate the lost notes and messy handwriting.*

STEP 3: WHAT PIECES ARE YOU ORGANIZING?

It's one thing to get your household to-do list organized, but it's a whole other ball game to organize a complex idea across a diversified team or company to get it launched into the world.

There are a lot of moving pieces, so it's important to brainstorm all the components involved.

If you like to keep things digital, you can use Mural, a post-it board in the cloud tool. For me, I like to use good old-fashioned physical post-its on a wall. An individual post-it to capture a single topic or component that pops in my head.

This system turns my brain on and forces me to dump out its contents without caring about staying too focused or being perfect. I can jump from one component to another and in a stream of consciousness, set free the things that are filling up my mind space.

Ask yourself, "What are the components that make up my idea?"

Capture the ideas and questions that come to mind:

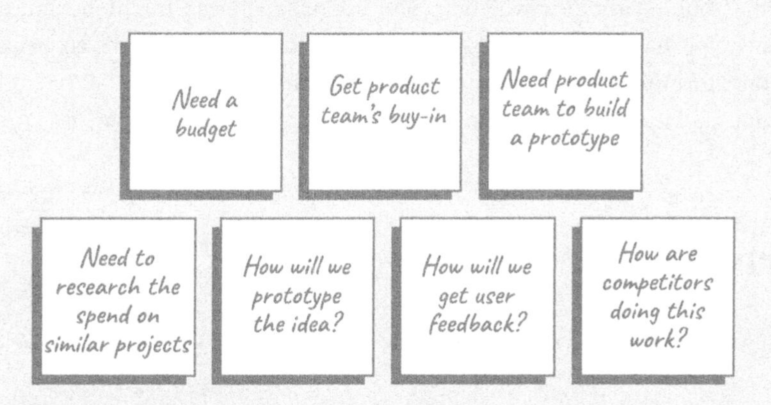

Don't worry about duplicates or perfect wording. Instead, focus on getting everything stored up in your brain out onto the post-its.

Soon the wall will be full of colored square post-its. At this point, you can start to group the post-its by themes: Things like, "Need a budget" and "Need to research the spend for similar projects" get grouped together as they are related to finance.

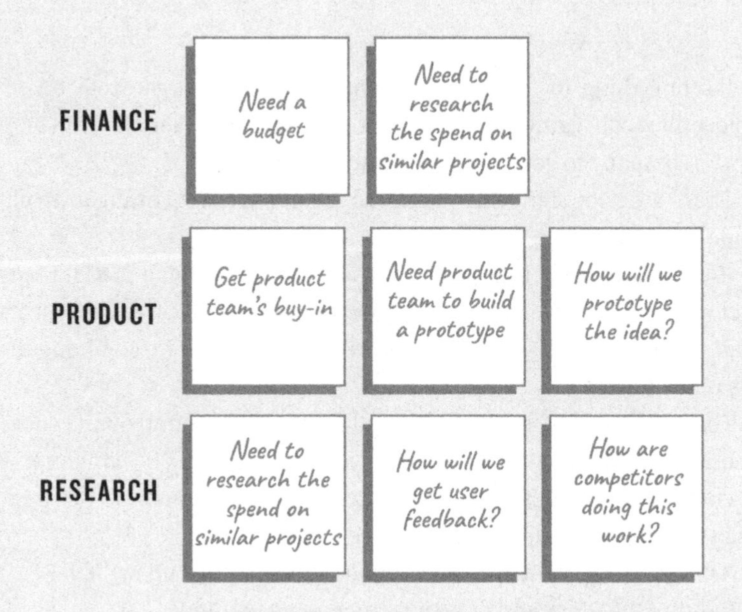

Grouping themes will help you see what pieces might be missing. Once you have some groups and themes surfacing, can you go back to brainstorming to see some components that you missed? What other things fall under the "finance" theme?

A second and third round of brainstorming will allow you to get to many of the pieces that your idea will require. You won't be able to identify every single step, theme, or topic upfront as you plan to organize your idea. New things will unfold as you begin your work.

The initial brainstorming can be done over a two-hour block of time to give you time to pause and reflect, capturing as much as you can.

STEP 4: INCUBATION

Leave room after your brainstorm for "simmer time." This is the opportunity for your subconscious and conscious to catch up. Over time, this space that you allow for will start to create tiny connections and get you closer to a light bulb moment where you feel the solution coming to the surface.

During this incubation step, you keep your organization brainstorm up and available so you can look at it. Go back to it with a cup of coffee. Think and reflect on it during a break.

This time is normally about a week long. A few days in and you'll get past thinking about the problem and solutions the same way. Add to the brainstorm board anything new that comes to mind, but spend most of this time stepping back and thinking.

It will feel like an emergent approach, moving from preconscious processing to conscious awareness. This step is the easiest to do and the easiest to skip. You might be ready to get to work, why deliberate on something as simple as getting organized? Don't succumb to the urge to skip to the good stuff. Ensure you have the time, energy, and space to allow new ways of doing work to emerge.

STEP 5: LANDING ON AN ORGANIZATION SOLUTION

The final step in getting organized is identifying how important something is and who will execute on the different pieces.

To decide "how important" something is, we'll use levels of priority.

- *"Budget approval" will be urgent to the success of your idea.*
- *Other pieces, like "Great design" will be less critical and take a lower priority.*

As it relates to the "Who Will Execute" on the work, we'll use a people meter.

- *Research like "Competitive research" could be done on your own*
- *But the "Need product team to build a prototype" will require work outside of you, landing on the product team.*

Once you weigh in on both the how and the who, it's time to take your individual post-its and map them onto your Priority & People Matrix.

The matrix is made of an x-axis, representing the "who" or people required to do the work. On the left side, you find work that can be done alone and on the right, work that must be done with others. The y-axis displays the "how" or priority of the components. At the bottom will be work that is noncritical and then at the top, the most important work to be done.

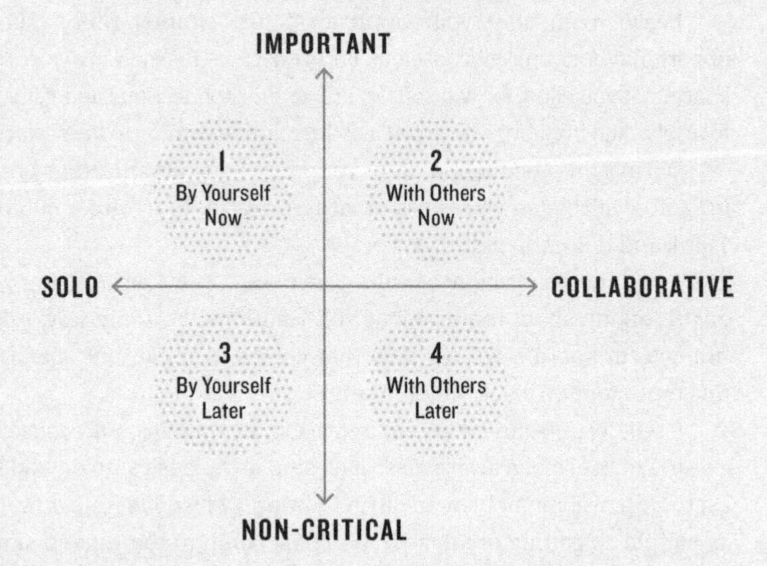

Map your post-its to your matrix by putting the important items that you can do alone in quadrant 1, *By Yourself Now*. For important items that must be done with others, place them in quadrant 2, *With Others Now*.

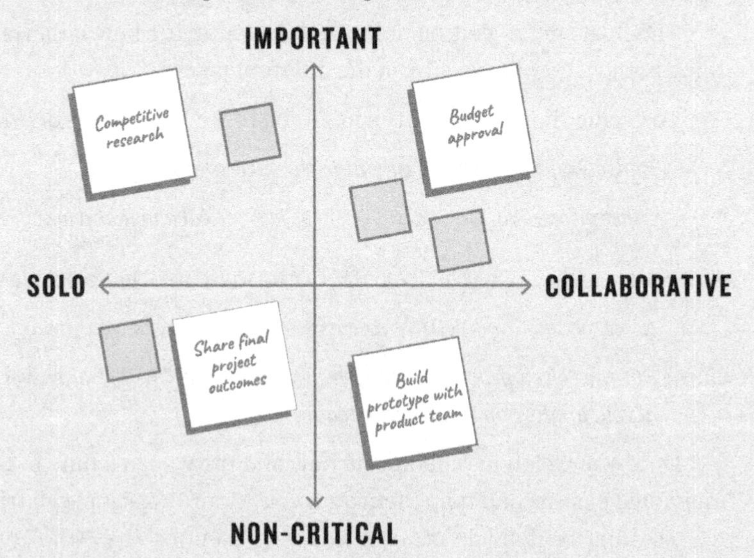

After I get most of my important components mapped, I can start to think about the less important pieces. These remaining post-its will fall into the lower sections. The lower left will be the *By Yourself Later* work. These are things like "Share final project outcomes" that I can do on my own but aren't time-sensitive.

The lower right will be the *With Others Later* work. I find that "Build prototype with product team" can be work that I do later, but will require collaboration from others.

With the post-its living in different quadrants, you'll start to see your brainstorm come together and be ready for the final step in identifying the right solutions to organize your idea.

STEP 6: PICK A SYSTEM & TRANSFER ACTION ITEMS

Go back to your list of "What Works" and "What Doesn't" and choose your organizational system to help you turn these post-its into plans, deadlines, and meetings.

Whether you organize your plan on Asana, email chains, or Mural, make sure you have your organization plan in place. Additionally, because of all the homework you have done, you have some action items in hand that you can start the work on. Things you can do in your own time, the *Now Solo* items, will be a great place to start working on your idea!

With a plan in place for keeping things in order, you have given yourself the permission and steps forward. It will be a journey. A messy one with some moments of one step forward, two steps back. That's to be expected. Getting organized is the start, but it won't be the end. Things will inevitably come up, changing how you do things.

DETECTIVE-IN-TRAINING

In no time, you'll become your own detective—piecing together pieces of your "crazy wall" and organizing your next big *aha* moment. The process of organization takes work upfront but it will benefit you for the rest of the journey.

Getting organized now won't be the perfect plan, you will have to tweak, iterate, and get organized again and again throughout the process. Just like exercising or eating healthily, it's a continuous effort. You'll have moments where you have "cheat days" and fall off the organization wagon. Be sure to check in on what you have set up and make changes or improvements where needed.

Because the organization of your idea is the framework for your idea. With this blueprint in hand, you have the opportunity to really get to work. Start building the pieces that will actually make your idea become a reality.

GET

SET

YOUR PROCESS

Gaming the System

If you've ever played a lively (read: competitive) game of Monopoly, you know there are two categories of rules in playing the game: classic rules and house rules.

The classic rules, dutifully found in the mini instruction pamphlet inside the Monopoly box, outline how players take turns rolling the dice and advancing around the board. Pass the Go space? Collect $200. Land on owned property, pay rent. The rules outline the constraints to playing the game. Following the rules, the players build their strategy to winning the game.

Whether Monopoly takes an hour or stretches over days during a winter holiday break depends on the second type, house rules.

My family followed the informal "Free Parking Jackpot" house rule where all the money collected from Income Tax, Luxury Tax, Chance, and Community Chest all went to the center of the board instead of the bank. When a player landed on the Free Parking space, the payout was all the juicier. A lucky dice roll delivering me to Free Parking caused my older brother to eye roll and groan with me swiping up the colorful cash, saving me from eminent bankruptcy.

Our informal house rule changed the strategy of the game and also increased the time to play it, saving players from bankruptcy along the way.

When I went down the street to my best friend Alison's house, her family had different house rules. One was a fine to the bank to any player who knocked over a house or hotel lining a property space. New players joining their family were inevitably burned by that fine the first go round. I learned as a kid that when playing in a new house, ask about the house rules.

Any suggestion to change their house rule or try to add my own was met with a resistant tension, "That's not the way we do things around here."

Can you imagine the response if I had tried to play by my own rules? "This is how I do it," certainly would not have gone over well.

Pushing ideas through an organization is a similar game of strategy. There are certainly formal rules, like the ones that come written out in the Monopoly box, that will help you move your idea through the right channels. But there are also "house" rules that have to be acknowledged or could cost you the game. Plus, no one will take you seriously if you try to play by your own rules.

JAYWALKING & BUDGET APPROVALS

Rules and processes are the way that work gets done. For those of you who hate rules, I hear you. No one likes getting a ticket for going one mile over the speed limit, just like the process of filing taxes year after year makes us want to pull our hair out. But before you roll your eyes and shrug off the idea of succumbing to the process, let's talk about it.

Everywhere we go, we're surrounded by formal and informal processes. Depending on where you live, there's a process for things as simple as crossing the street. For a busy metro intersection, that would require pushing the "Walk" button, waiting for the signal to change to the walking man, and completing the walk across the street before the light turns to "Do Not Walk." Simple. And you follow it because if you don't, you risk getting hit by a car.

But when you live in a place like New York City, you'll quickly learn that through the hundreds of blocks throughout the city, the informal process for people crossing the street looks more like jaywalking any chance you can get. Because if you followed the rules for every crosswalk signal, it would take hours to traverse the city.

From city to city, crossing the street is the same idea, but the rules and process to do so look very different. On a recent trip to Italy, I stopped in Naples and saw that there were no crosswalks for some of the busiest intersections. Locals ran across when they saw their chance—and sometimes walked casually across while cars suddenly stopped in the middle of the busy road. I took their lead and quickly followed a local to make my way across.

The same kind of processes are followed in an organization to get work done. Identifying the processes your company uses, both formal and informal, will help you strategize your way forward. Looking throughout an organization to find and understand the processes followed can sound daunting to some, or benign to others. The truth is, it's both.

A product design team may follow design thinking, a human-centered approach to innovation that combines the needs of people, the possibility of technology, and the requirements for business success. Or a software development team may follow Agile, an approach where adaptive planning, iterative development, early delivery, and continuous improvement are followed to adapt to rapidly changing requirements.

Informally, an organization may have a chain of command that's not exactly written out on paper. You might have a boss named Chris who you think will love your initiative for the next quarter and you excitedly tell your coworker about your pitch next week.

Your coworker might inform you, "Everyone knows that Jenny has to approve the budget before you can present it to Chris."

Although Chris might be your direct manager, the common knowledge around the office is that Chris hates getting ideas without budget approval, and if you come with a tentatively approved budget already, your project is five times more likely to get approved (or at least heard).

This part of the process isn't written out, but it's something that could make or break the future of your idea.

Start thinking of what formal and informal pieces of the process are standing between you and launching your idea. What steps do people follow to get their idea tested and launched at your company? What steps do you need to take to make sure you get the right people involved, the resources you need, and the permissions to move forward?

DON'T BURN THE CARROTS

We have the process for crossing the street so pedestrians don't get hit by cars and we have jaywalking so we can efficiently get somewhere when it's safe to use our own judgment. An assembly line is an obvious model of efficiency, wherein a mess of parts gets turned into a finished product just by quickly following a set of steps.

Just last week I told myself that I didn't need to follow the "process" for a new recipe of honey-glazed carrots with ginger. How hard is it to cook carrots? I gathered the ingredients and got to work. Trying to cook multiple new dishes at once, I only had time to read the cooking steps as I went along. With the green bean casserole and chicken in the oven, I was well underway in my cooking adventure.

For the carrots, the recipe told me to pour a single layer of the glaze I had made earlier over the carrots and start cooking. There was plenty of glaze so I generously drenched it atop my organic carrots neatly lined up across the foil. With my lavish pour, the carrots popped up and floated atop the maple ginger sauce. It looked perfect.

Twenty minutes later—ding! My timer reminded me to pull the roasting carrots out. With my oven mitt on one hand, I used the other to scroll my laptop for the recipe for the final step.

"After carrots are done cooking, drizzle the remaining honey glaze over them and serve."

I looked in the sink at the empty bowl of glaze and realized my mistake. Something I couldn't have known if I hadn't read all the steps. I pulled the carrots slowly out from the oven and cringed at their wrinkly, burnt appearance. My liberal pour-over escapade had evaporated and burned off in the oven leaving me with naked, dry carrots—not the beautiful side dish I envisioned for our dinner.

We follow recipes so we don't end up with burnt carrots (or burnt ideas) and we follow processes in organizations so that we have a chance at working together, creating the best outcomes. As frustrating as they might seem to go through, processes are a necessary constraint and reliable way forward.

MORE THAN A NAME

Beware, if you think you know the process, you may not. Like playing Monopoly at a friend's house, you establish an understanding of the "house rules" up front—lest you knock over a hotel on the orange block of St. James Place and pay a fine to the bank you weren't expecting.

At a startup, your process for getting a new idea approved may simply involve moving quickly through informal phases; starting with identifying a problem or opportunity, collecting data and insights to support a solution, and presenting the idea to the founder for approval to go after it.

In a large corporation, the process may look similar but require more time, resources, and management approval to proceed. Or it may have additional layers to the process, requiring legal, compliance, and HR to weigh in on the idea.

When searching for the processes around your company, don't be lulled into thinking that because the process has a name, you understand all the layers behind it. The same processes look different in different organizations, dependening on who is spearheading them (the processes), the people on the team, and the different industry rules.

One organization, Leo Burnett, a global advertising agency, adopted the design thinking approach to create an internal professional development program branded as Leo Leaps. The program leverages design thinking to create a learning experience that builds employees' skills to help them develop their careers and solve business problems more creatively. As an employee at Leo Burnett, you may not be aware that Leo Leaps is rooted in design thinking principles and methodology. (Even if it does have a different name.)

Or consider IBM, where they took a step away from the traditional design thinking process to achieve a method that is more suitable for a big enterprise, built upon many complex processes. Rebranded by IBM as Enterprise Design Thinking, their process comes with new principles, techniques, terminology, and jargon. One difference that you will find in Enterprise Design Thinking is the introduction of three "keys" as integral to the process: (1) "hills" to align teams on user outcomes to achieve, (2) "playbacks" for regular exchange of feedback, and (3) "sponsor users" to invite customers into the work to stay connected to the problem. If you are relying on your knowledge of design thinking, you would fall short in understanding all the important principles, process steps, and jargon that make for the process that IBM follows.

Even though both organizations were using design thinking as a process to launch new ideas and initiatives, they used it in different ways. Processes are unique to the company you work within, and the way things are done will be very different from organization to organization.

BEWARE OF THE SHINY NEW PROCESS

Sometimes, when looking at the processes your company follows, you may be tempted to introduce a new approach, thinking, "This would be a lot easier if we just used X."

There may be truth to that thought. Oftentimes, especially in big organizations with unwieldy processes, it can seem unnecessarily bureaucratic and stifling. And turning to the new, popular business-book-of-the-moment as a solution can be enticing.

Douglas shared a story of a friend who works in the tech industry, Jack. He works for a well-funded company based in New York City. He's been with the company for about five years and in that time has seen countless attempts for the company to test out new processes and methods as a way to innovate.

Whatever new business book-of-the-week that the CEO gloms onto becomes the "new way" employees are encouraged to work. Jack has seen formal programs like the lean startup way start and fail because of process-whiplash—the company's inability to stick with a formal way forward.

His company was so enamored with trying the newest "ways to work" that they sometimes took a turn for the absurd. One Monday morning, Jack walked into work to find all the cubicles rearranged. With his to-go coffee in one hand and laptop bag in the other, he zigzagged around the office, in search of his new sitting area. When he ran into the office administrator, he asked where he would find his seat. Flipping through the seating chart on her clipboard, she informed him that he was over by the back corner, with the other Geminis. Apparently, over the weekend the CEO had made the request that to improve the energy in the space, people should be reassigned to sit amongst their astrological signs.

A new process will always come along and sometimes seem like a better way to do things within your organization. But if you want to focus on the idea you have in hand, it will require you to follow accepted processes in place, without overhauling the way work gets done.

The thing is, if you want to overhaul the existing processes, that will complicate your efforts and slow you down. At a certain point, instead of pushing your idea through, you are pushing a new way of doing things through.

WHERE'S THE OWNER'S MANUAL?

No one gives you a manual on how to write an email, but I can tell you right now there's a protocol to follow.

I remember a college student interested in an internship role with my startup. The applicant had a great resume and I was reaching out to him to schedule an interview. His emailed response floored me.

"yo, im home this week. can we talk sunday?"

Yo? No capitalization? And what's this business about scheduling an interview on a Sunday?

Needless to say, I didn't proceed with the interview. I took the time to respond, politely (through gritted teeth) to let the student know that in the future, he should treat communication with potential employers more seriously.

When no one tells you what to do and there's no formal way forward, don't guess and walk into the process blindly. Instead, play the role of an anthropologist, studying and learning the norms and principles of getting work done.

When it comes to your work, what is the etiquette that you have to adhere to if you are going to be taken seriously? What are the social norms? How do you figure out unwritten rules?

Start having one-on-one conversations with people within your organization to learn more. Try to get a diverse perspective by sitting down with people from different departments across the organization.

Schedule a conversation that starts with you sharing more about the work you do and what you are hoping to learn. You want to build trust in the one-on-one, to allow the person the space they need to be vulnerable and speak the truth, rather than the predictable company lines.

Playing the humble card, you can highlight that you are new to this kind of work, and that you want to learn how different parts of the organization work. Questions to help guide the conversation include:

- *"How does work get done around here?"*
- *"Who has done work like this that I should learn from?"*
- *"What ideas have you seen fail? And succeed?"*

Get curious and approach the conversations with humility, ready to learn from whatever is shared. Stay curious and don't jump to conclusions. Allow people to share their perspective. People love being asked what they do and sharing their expertise. In addition to getting the information you need, in most cases you'll gain an ally and friend.

Uncovering and understanding the unwritten rules, the etiquette to getting work done, will save you from missteps along the way. It also builds trust across the organization that you are engaging in conversations to learn the best way forward.

The interviews are your way to understand how things happen within your company—the what people do, how they do it, how long it takes, and what resources they need. With this information in hand, you can identify the process you need to take to move your idea forward.

ACTIVITY

LEARN HOW WORK GETS DONE

When I first started at IDEO, I was hired to help launch a new product. Day one I was in awe of the people, the project, and the awesome office perched on a pier on the Embarcadero in San Francisco.

Day two, I started playing the role of an anthropologist. I needed to know how to get things moving within the organization to ensure our launch was a success. I knew, of course, that IDEO subscribed to design thinking as a process; they live, breathe, and teach it, so I knew I needed to follow it.

But operationally, who did I need to work with to make things happen? How would I get permission to market the new product upon launch? Who would I work with to get creative with our budget?

The only way to follow the formal process in your organization while managing and making space for all the informal "house rules" along the way is by starting with all the steps in one place. And the only way to get all those pieces in one place is through a fact-finding mission I call "Learn How Shit Really Gets Done."

This means you want to learn the method you will take, beyond the jargon and step-by-step processes outlined by your employee handbook. Sure, that's a great place to start, but how does work *really* get done within your organization? Understanding both the formal and informal processes will enable you to navigate the treacherous waters of your company and come to the end of the journey having successfully launched your idea.

"Learn How Shit Really Gets Done" comes from a place of curiosity and inquiry. Going into your interviews, the focus is on discovering and designing the best process for your idea to follow. It is not about being negative or critical about the current state of the organization. The goal is to visualize what you are learning and documenting a way forward.

You will start by interviewing a diverse sampling of people across the organization. From there you will document what you are learning to uncover new insights and confirm what steps to take moving forward. Then you will have identified important steps to take, people to engage, and have the ability to visually layout a strategic process for your idea. So let's get to understanding how to move your idea forward and "Learn How Shit Really Gets Done" in your organization.

STEP 1: CROSS-EXAMINING ACROSS SILOS

To do this investigative work of understanding how to make things happen at IDEO, I needed to interview and observe how people successfully push new ideas within the walls of the company. I started by reaching out to people within different parts of the organization. From finance to marketing and design to legal, I invited people to lunch and coffee meetups in an effort to learn more.

It starts with sharing your goals and expressing appreciation for the interviewee's time. When I sat across the table from Rochael from legal, I knew she had her day stacked with important meetings and that her time with me was a gift.

"Thank you so much for taking the time to meet with me. I know you are aware we will be launching the new IDEO U learning platform in the coming weeks and I've joined the team to help make that happen. Being new to IDEO, I'm still learning the ropes of who I need to work with to ensure this launch is a success and wanted to ask you a few things about what I should be thinking about, who I should be working with, and any lessons you have to share in your experience helping other ideas launch at IDEO."

With a serious nod, Rochael immediately shared some nuggets of wisdom, "Have you updated your Terms and Conditions on the product website?"

"We are working on that right now, is there someone from your team I should be in contact with to help with that? Any advice for how to do this the right way?" I asked. Truthfully, I thought going into this meeting that I had that simple task covered. We would reuse verbiage from other services and call it a day. But rather than claiming to have it all figured out, I really wanted to learn.

"Yes, I'll connect you with Daniel and he can help to make sure we are covered on all fronts. Same for the privacy policy. We want it to be clear to the users how we store data and for what purpose. We don't want to use legal jargon to make it too difficult for people to understand."

Smiling, I nodded in agreement, typing notes of Daniel's contact information in my to-do list. One minute into my meeting and already I had uncovered some new insights. Avoiding legal jargon to help our users better understand our goals and use of their data? Brilliant, and not something I would've come up with on my own.

Here I thought the process was just to present our verbiage for approval, but instead I learned of a new collaborative process that would bring more value to the task. It was refreshing and unexpected to see the human-centered design process applied to approaching legal problems.

This is the voice of human-centered legal practice, emblazoned at the bottom of the IDEO U website:

> We use cookies to improve your browsing experience. And cake to boost morale on Fridays. Find out more about our cookie policy here.
>
> CLOSE

Never underestimate what you can learn from different people across the organization about how work gets done. Through all my meetings, like the one with Rochael, I not only learned about how to do things at IDEO, but I improved the chances for a successful launch of my idea because of their input and guidance.

STEP 2: ACKNOWLEDGING EVERYONE'S NEEDS

The goal of your interview is to learn about the right processes within your company—the steps and guide for you to launch your idea. To get to that knowledge, you need to meet and learn from others through meaningful conversations.

When asking for others' time, we have a habit of getting right to the point. Even after a few minutes of pleasantries, "How was your weekend?" or "What about this weather!?" we dive too quickly into our questions. Of course you want to make the most of the time together, but there is an important piece that comes at the front end of the meetup.

It's about creating the environment where you are open and curious, and the interviewee is able to be vulnerable and candid.

To do this, go into the conversation without trying to predict the value or direct the learning. Sure you should start by describing the goal of the sit-down, but don't try to force the interviewee into following your lead. You don't want them to confirm your approach or proposed method forward. Instead, you want to allow for the interaction to be authentic. That is where you will get the most value and real-life knowledge.

In my work at IDEO, I had the opportunity to speak to another product leader, David. He had recently launched a new service at IDEO and was someone with many years of experience in the company.

Sitting in a room with a view of the bay, I shared what I was trying to do. "Thank you so much for squeezing in the time to sit down with me. I know you have a lot going on and I appreciate you making the time. In a few weeks, we'll be launching IDEO U and given your experience in launching new products at IDEO, I wanted to sit down and learn from you."

"Yeah, how are things going so far? Where can I help?"

"Well, being new to this work here, I don't know what I don't know. I would love to learn more about the steps you took to get from idea to launch. Thinking about the early phases, what did you learn?"

David then spent the next hour sharing a wealth of information that would help me in my work. From his experience in launching products at IDEO, as well as his previous roles in marketing and product development for hardware companies, I learned more about how to leverage IDEO's different design teams to help in our product's launch. As I took notes and listened, David was comfortable to go into details about how work gets done at the company.

You need to get beyond asking, "Tell me about how to do things around here." For your interviews, start by sharing the goal and purpose of your sit-down and express gratitude and openness to learn.

The content is simple: Thank you. And here's why I wanted to meet with you.

Where you will disarm people and allow them to candidly share their lessons is in your ability to stay curious and listen. Don't anticipate your next question. Really soak up what's being shared and take notes.

Your genuine intent to learn will come across, and the interviewee will have the freedom to think back to a time when they were doing the work you will be embarking on. They will be able to share real lessons that will be of value.

Reminding yourself to stay in the moment of learning and gathering insights will ground you throughout every interview. If someone is willing to share their time and knowledge with you, show gratitude and appreciation.

STEP 3: QUESTIONS THAT GET TO REAL LEARNING

To help keep your interviews on track, there's a loose framework to follow for your "Learn How Shit Really Gets Done" fact-finding mission:

1. *Know your goal for the conversation*
2. *Leverage their expertise and experience through questions*
3. *Leave room for the "what else?"*

In my one-on-ones, I let the interview take shape based on both my needs and the expertise of the person sharing. You don't want to have a prescripted list of questions. Instead, let the conversation evolve organically.

In one conversation with someone from the marketing team, I learned that she had previously worked at a startup. With that nugget, the conversation went in a new direction. Rather than solely focusing on how work was done at IDEO, we spent much of our time talking about how it was different at her startup and what worked and didn't work there. This reaffirmed some of my own startup lessons and together we brainstormed how a launch might look different within our company.

Starting with your goals and needs allows the interviewee to know why you scheduled the meeting in the first place. Share the following:

- *I'm trying to identify all the steps people take to get a new idea through our company.*
- *Being new to this work within the company, I don't know what I don't know. What questions do you think I should be asking?*
- *Who else would you recommend I meet with as part of my discovery process?*

From there, you can go into your open-ended questions that will help guide the conversation. Some questions to consider include:

- *Tell me about a time you had an idea to do things differently in our company and how you made it happen.*
- *Describe the process or method you took to get started.*
- *After things were underway, explain how you knew what steps to take next.*
- *Explain the formal process you think people follow around here. How about the informal approaches?*

Notice that with the questions, you are leading with open-ended statements. This allows your interviewee to include more information, feelings, and ideas around your question. It will give you more insight into their true feelings on an issue.

As you conclude your interviews, always end by asking how you can help the person you are meeting with. They just shared their time and insights, what can you do for them?

In one meetup with Molly, another product leader at IDEO, I asked what I could do for her.

"Report back to me what you learn through these interviews so I can apply them to my work and share with my team."

With that request, and knowing that I learned so much through my one-on-ones, I created a monthly meetup where different individuals within IDEO who were launching new products or services could meet and learn from others across the organization.

Each month, in our biggest conference room (stocked with coffee and fresh donuts) we would tackle a different problem that a startup might face. Answering questions like, "How do you track marketing initiatives across products?" We had groups such as our finance team, engineering department, legal, and marketing and communications team come talk to product leaders all at once about the specific processes for operations. The teams were excited and eager to have the chance to talk to everyone, while the product leaders were happy to learn the exact ways to go forward.

They were communal versions of the one-on-one interview process above. Participants had the opportunity to learn from people further on in their journey and avoid potential mistakes along the way. Together, we helped each other understand the right processes to move as quickly as a startup would, but within the walls of a bigger company.

The one-on-ones and group meetings were a continual source of knowledge and inspiration. One that reminded me to make time to listen and of the ongoing value of learning from others.

YOUR EVOLVING PROCESS

Taking all that you learned, start to think about the process that is the best fit for your idea. Visually outline the different steps. For me that starts as post-its of themes on a wall. Eventually, when I move notes around and see something forming, I'll move to my laptop and start using a tracking tool to keep tabs on my process and the steps within them.

The process may evolve over time, but setting out with an approach will guide you on a way forward. Take note when there is a misstep. Did you skip an important task that you overlooked? Or was there a hidden, informal way to do things that you uncovered?

Identifying the process will give you an idea of a way forward. The lessons from your interviews will uncover what worked for others and shed light on how you might want to approach launching your idea.

ALIGN WITH THE BUSINESS

Become the Clever Artist

My first real winter experience was in Montreal in 2018. Growing up in south Texas, later moving to Austin and then eventually San Francisco, I can't say I really knew what it takes to schlep around town through a snowy winter season.

One particular white winter morning in Montreal, I was driving my Jeep downtown on a busy two-lane road, and the car began pulling to the right, with my steering wheel vibrating.

It was subtle, but it was making navigating the wintry roads challenging. I assumed it was par for the course. *This must be what it feels like to drive in snow and ice.*

After a couple of errands, the zigzagging through the city was getting out of hand. I pulled over to a gas station and walked up toward the repair garage.

I could see the repairman sitting behind the counter, shaking his head. He probably thought I was a reckless driver.

I walked in and was going to ask if someone could look at my Jeep as he kept nodding, mumbling something in French. My beginners-level French made the exchange challenging but within a few minutes, I realized he was telling me my tires needed alignment.

It turns out that when I had my winter tires put on the week before, the technician at the shop didn't set them up properly and as a result, my tires were out of alignment. Something that only got worse the more I drove. I needed to get my front two wheels aligned so my car would track correctly.

A couple of hours later, I was waving goodbye to my gas station friends and on the road again. This time, my drive was smooth. I was ready to take on my first real winter, with my car and tires ready to drive safely again.

When the tires are misaligned, the whole car is ineffective. It might not be obvious at first, but over time it can become problematic or, worse, cause an accident.

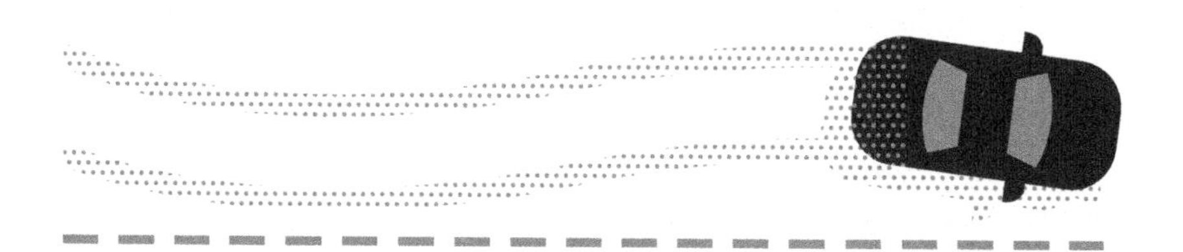

The whole system needs to be aligned. And it's not just an adjustment of the tires themselves. The key to a proper alignment, I've learned, is adjusting the angles of the tires to change how they make contact with the road.

When pushing your idea through your company, it's all about finding this same alignment. How does your idea fit within the business? How does the idea align with the company's goals? And if it doesn't align, how might you adjust your idea to affect the outcomes so that it does fit?

Back when Douglas was working at Twyla, he felt the strain of how an idea that didn't align with their business strategy created tensions within the team, and eventually led to the idea petering out.

As the CTO, Douglas and his product team prioritized customer-facing experiences over internal back office tools. While the internal tools were critical to getting the job done, the customer experience was paramount. His team quickly built a robust but imperfect backend.

When Twyla hired a head of design, she came in ready to make an impression. Having worked in high-end fashion, she had years of experience in conceptualizing, designing, and executing marketing for luxury brand websites. These websites were simple and straightforward e-commerce experiences, unlike the custom complex software that Twyla was building.

When she joined Twyla, and saw the crude backend, she cringed. Admittedly, Douglas agreed, it was messy. Especially by "brand" standards.

She had an idea to completely overhaul the backend. Over and over, she kept telling Douglas that she couldn't have employees looking at that system. That, "we need to be living the brand at all times."

Douglas could see the urge to overhaul the backend from her perspective, but given all the other needs of their resource-strapped startup, like marketing operations integrations, art discovery tools for customers, and support for interior designers, he didn't think it was a place for him and his team to spend time on in that moment.

Finally, after her continuous requests to get the work done, Douglas told her, "None of our business objectives have anything to do with updating the backend."

With each of her requests to try to push this idea, he would ask what business objective it would serve. Finally, she responded with, "Why do you keep harping on business objectives?"

Stunned, Douglas knew it wasn't his place to argue the reasoning. He just knew it was why he needed to focus on other projects. Projects that the business had identified as being key to its success. The objectives that had measurable outcomes that he was responsible to execute on.

Updating the backend would be a nice-to-have, but focusing efforts on that would be at the detriment of the projects the business outlined as being important.

Given that her request didn't align with the business objectives, her idea to overhaul the backend fell short. She may have been right. It may have been a valuable project, but she couldn't articulate why it would matter to the business or the strategic initiatives the business was facing. In this case, the business strategies were clear, her idea wasn't aligning with them.

There are always signs that you either are or aren't aligned with the business.

I had a conversation with a woman I used to mentor through my start-up. Rachel had moved to work as a program manager at Dell. She was telling me about a new idea she wanted to institute with her team and asked for advice on how to move things forward.

After hearing the details of her idea, I got right to the point, "How does your idea align with the business objectives your team has been assigned?"

Nodding, she shared, "The idea would fit a couple of our goals, but I'm not sure if they are the ones my boss really cares about."

I then explained, "When you first talk with your boss about your idea, if it fits with something important to them, they'll usually light up with excitement, or start pointing out all the opportunities that come to mind."

Rachel agreed, she needed to look for signs that the idea aligned to the right business objectives that mattered to her boss. She wasn't sure how, but she was going to feel it out to gauge his temperature and excitement for the idea.

About a month later I checked in on Rachel through a video call, "How's the big idea coming together?"

Her enthusiasm was palpable through my laptop screen, "I ran into him in the elevator and after briefly sharing the idea, he asked that I follow him to his desk so we could chat further about it. By the end of the conversation, he had made a couple of email introductions to people in other departments trying to do a similar project."

"Congrats, sounds like you found the right business objective to align with what matters to him!" I observed.

"That's the funny thing," she continued. "He saw alignment to an objective I wasn't even aware of as it hadn't been announced yet. He went on and on about how my idea could help kick off that work."

For Rachel, she learned right off the bat that she had found alignment to new business objectives that mattered to her boss. His excitement was a telltale she was onto something when he gave her extra time in his morning to chat about it and connect her to others in an effort to help move things along. When he gave her extra time in his morning to chat about her idea and then connected her with others to help move things along, it was obvious she was onto something.

When you're aligned, you'll be given permission to test your idea. Or maybe, less obviously, you won't be prohibited from prototyping your idea.

But if your conversations don't go like this and it feels more like the warning, vibrating the steering wheel, telling you that your idea isn't aligning quite right, you'll need to slow down. Take note if you're not getting permission to move forward with prototyping or testing the idea.

When you find your boss changing the subject, becoming distracted while you talk about your idea, or stop listening altogether, you might be coming up against some red flags. While not as helpful, these nonverbal cues and red flags can help you get back to the drawing board and ask yourself, "How does my idea find alignment?"

NO ROGUE COWBOYS

When you are working at a company, there are constraints in place. Some of them can feel restrictive but they are the guardrails to keep things moving forward. Go too far off track and you'll derail other initiatives and potentially risk losing your job.

But don't confuse the constraints with restraints.

The work of innovation and doing something new requires the innovator to take calculated risks. To go against the grain, but not push so hard against the grain that you're seen as causing unnecessary friction.

Simply put, when your idea aligns with the business strategy, there's room for some risks. The benefits just have to outweigh the potential risk. That's the art.

Go too far into the risky areas and you are a rogue cowboy, off charted course, with your "business alignment" a faint image behind you in the distance.

The clever artist sees the constraints and rather than going off the canvas, brings stakeholders along and uses the business strategy to find areas where they can paint outside the lines. They are aware enough to realize where and when to push the boundaries and when to leave things as they are.

Connect the dots between your idea and business strategies and you will find the excitement, and permission, behind getting your idea through. When you find the alignment between your idea and the business you're in, you will bring people along.

There's a reason the business has certain goals and objectives. It's setting the direction and keeping the company on the right track. Just try to imagine what a football game would look like without end zones, or what a Formula 1 race would look like without a finish line.

Business strategies give your company a goal to run toward. Aligning your idea to those goals will help get team members on board to help push forward with you. The business strategy is like your compass guiding you. You are a bit of an explorer, going forward into uncharted territory, but you have a tool that will help you stay aligned with your company.

TAILOR FIT

Sometimes, when you don't see business alignment with your idea, it means finding a way to modify your idea so it fits the strategies in place.

Let's say you are a chef at a restaurant, and you have a recipe you want to try that you know people would love—kung pao chicken. You think this will bring in new customers and keep current customers coming again and again.

Just the right kind of spicy, interesting textures and flavors, a surefire crowd-pleaser. But your restaurant is a seafood restaurant and the manager has shared that he is interested in increasing the fish and shellfish dishes instead of adding a different type of meat.

Rather than giving up, or worse, forcing an ill-fitting idea through, what about tweaking the idea? What could the chef do to make his new recipe idea fit within his manager's goals? What if instead of kung pao chicken—the new dish was kung pao shrimp?

With a slight modification, you are able to align with the business needs. Now the idea has legs.

The key to modifying your idea is to recognize where there is a real opportunity for it to align with business strategies while still staying true to your original purpose. The modifications may make the idea look different, but it's still effective in achieving the goal.

TALK THE TALK, WALK THE WALK

Before you start to push your idea through, you not only have to possess a clear understanding of your company's business objectives, you need to understand your company's ability to meet those objectives and follow them through.

There are three places to look to get a deeper understanding of your company's ability to perform against the business objectives set: the financial health, development phase, and competitive position.

FINANCIAL HEALTH CHECK

My husband started a visual effects company in 2009 that was acquired by Method Studios in 2018. He had been CEO of his company and upon acquisition, he took on a new role of solely focusing on the creative work and supervision of their VFX work. Almost a year after the acquisition, Ryan could see an opportunity to help the company create efficiencies in their project pipeline.

But in his new role, he no longer had access to the financial documents. He used to have ready access to the profit and loss (P&L) statement, where he could see the summary of the revenues, costs, and expenses incurred. But in his new position, the parent company didn't provide him with the same level of knowledge that he had before. While his idea would require an up-front investment that would yield results bringing value across the company, he didn't have insight into the financial health of the company. He wouldn't be able to gauge whether the company could take on this effort and continuously fund it until full implementation. He needed to understand whether the company had an appetite to invest in his idea. Would they be open to improving the project pipeline?

To align your idea to the business strategies within your company, make sure you understand your company's financial health.

The P&L (or profit and loss) statement is a place to see the revenues, costs, and expenses of your business.

Depending on your seniority, and the culture of your company, you may want to ask your finance or accounting department if you can have access to P&L statements across divisions within the company.

Reviewing the P&Ls can highlight business objectives across the organization and the realities of getting your efforts funded.

For example, if your company is struggling to reach a healthy profit margin, your leadership may resist a radical product innovation. That usually requires a huge investment that they may not be ready for.

So instead, you may consider how to turn your idea into smaller chunks, with an incremental approach to getting a green light, because that won't need a large infusion of cash to test.

Even if you are unable to gain access to the P&L statements, you can learn a lot by interviewing the people in your organization that do have access and control over this information. Reach out to team members in finance and ask questions like:

- *Are we profit positive?*
- *Have we made any recent strategic investments?*
- *What efforts are we investing in?*

Share the purpose behind your questions—that you want to understand the company's financial health in relation to an idea you have.

Your company's financial reports and statements can allow you to read the tea leaves, giving you small signs for how to understand the future. These reports are an important starting point to understand your company's performance against profitability and productivity objectives.

KNOW YOUR PHASE

Another place to understand whether your organization has the ability to execute on your new idea is to identify what development stage your company is in.

I have a friend, Julie, on the co-founding team at a well-funded startup. She's head of product, leading a large global team of engineers and software developers. I asked her how things were going over wine at a happy hour one night in San Francisco, and she shared big news she recently had with her team.

"Well, six months ago things were starting to even out with sales and we needed a big win to get another round of funding."

I nodded in sympathy. Yes, I knew the roller-coaster ride of a startup.

"So I gathered the engineers and product folks, and created an Innovation Fest," she continued. Over a two-day hackathon, I asked them to share their big idea. Something that would blow our business out of the water. Something that would attract customers, media attention, and investors."

On the edge of my seat, I asked, "Two days to innovate? Wow! What did they come up with?"

"That's the thing, the ideas were already there. Some of the team members were just holding on to them, not thinking it was the right time to push the envelope in our thinking. They knew we were trying to get funding but didn't realize that we didn't have to wait for the funding to start testing and pitching the ideas."

"So by having an Innovation Fest, it gave them permission to share their ideas?" I asked.

"Yes, and it reinforced the need to share via our culture—always innovate. They just didn't realize the timing would allow for big ideas. The Innovation Fest provided that insight and they were able to think about pitching and prototyping their ideas."

We clinked our wine glasses and continued to celebrate her success and commiserate on the ups and downs of startups.

For your idea to thrive within your company, you need to evaluate what phase the company is in. For Julie, her team members hadn't considered that being in the startup stage, where they were seeking heavy investment, it was a good time to introduce a big, new radical idea.

Understand the phase of your organization's business growth, and then consider what that means for introducing your new idea. This will inform you as to whether your idea is aligned with the business, or in contrast to it.

THINK DIFFERENT

In the late 1990s, the personal computer industry was ruled by Dell, IBM, and Compaq. If you were around for this era, you likely remember the overplayed, popular "Dude, you're getting a Dell" commercials where the flannel-plaid-wearing teen would say the catchphrase in a chipper surfer accent at the end of the commercials.

At the time, Apple was a shadow of its former self. It was no longer the tech leader in personal computers. Later, Steve Jobs admitted that Apple had been late to the party on writable CD technology, the then-popular way that personal computers could use compact discs to write, read, erase, and rewrite.

In an effort to turn the tides, Apple took a look at its competitors and decided to do something different. To think differently about the opportunity of a personal computer and make the Apple Mac a digital hub that linked and created an "emerging digital lifestyle."

This brought about the radical idea and launch of the iTunes music player software that enabled it to burn CDs as well as the release of the iPod, Apple's first successful handheld device.

It's also where Apple turned the tides and re-established itself as a viable tech giant amid the other companies.

Evaluating the competitive landscape, you will have a sense for where there might be an opportunity for your organization to grow.

Look at your industry, who else is providing the same services or products? For your customers, where else do they go to solve the problems that your company is trying to solve?

Research the players in the same space as your company and understand how they are different, or where they are the same and there is opportunity to do something different.

At the foundation of every good company or organization is a list of business objectives that create the guidelines for business planning and the work that gets done. By understanding your company's current profitability, growth, and competitive alignment, you will be equipped to understand how to fit your idea within your organization.

ACTIVITY
FIND YOUR ALIGNMENT

When it comes to aligning your idea to the business needs, there are three types of objectives that may surface: defined, fuzzy, and idea-focused.

First, some objectives are clearly defined and identifiable like, "improve profitability." These are the explicitly stated and understood goals that are shared by leadership. They are usually quantitative goals, like increasing profits by 20 percent or $250,000.

The second type is made up of objectives that are a bit fuzzy. Informal things you hear about from leadership at an all-hands meeting like, "develop core competencies." What exactly does that mean? These might be more qualitative goals—focusing on intangible outcomes that are harder to measure.

Finally, the third type includes idea-focused goals. These are objectives your idea can solve, but are not strategies expressed by leadership. Your idea may strive toward "going green" or "social change" but if the company isn't focused on corporate responsibility, these are objectives that will fall under idea-focused, not formal or fuzzy.

The following steps will help you identify all of the objectives for your idea and map them out so you can then step back to see where there is overlap. When your fuzzy and idea-focused goals align with defined goals, it will give you the *eureka* moment of what business objectives to prioritize.

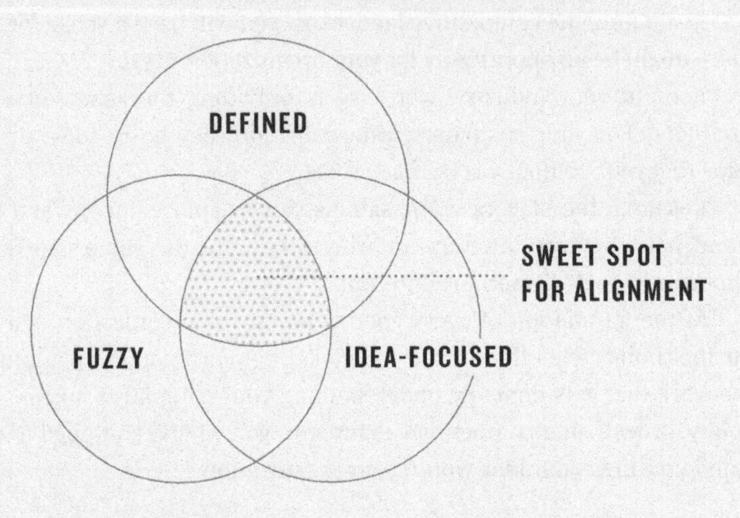

STEP 1: THE WRITING ON THE WALL

Start with a blank board or wall to capture the objectives that fit within the three areas: Defined, Fuzzy, and Idea-Focused. You will start to write down individual goals and strategies onto a post-it and then place it within the right camp.

DEFINED	FUZZY	IDEA-FOCUSED

Let's start with the defined objectives. These are the business goals that are clearly defined by your organization, department, and team. For a smaller company, the objectives may fit across the many layers of the company but for medium- and large-sized companies, it's important to go through all the relevant layers of your organization because as you do your research, you will uncover more insights within different departments and teams. Some organizations will be too big to consider everything—but focus on what would be impacted by your idea.

Starting at the company or organization level, business objectives can usually be found in an internal website outlining strategies that the company is taking on in the short and long term.

As an employee at Autodesk, I had access to our internal website that made finding and understanding the business objectives of the company very easy. Within the pages of the "Our Company" section, I could read the vision and understand what inspires the work at Autodesk. I could also find the mission on what we do, and the strategy of how we will get there.

The internal site shared strategic priorities and clearly listed out the business objectives to get there. Take a look at what you can find shared within your organization. Go deeper to understand the objectives for different departments, product teams, or divisions, that make sense in relation to your idea.

Then, begin to capture the different objectives that you find. Maybe you work at a landscaping company that has listed "cross-sell more services" as one of its business objectives. Capture this on a post-it and add it to your wall. You may start to see themes of objectives, like when adding the goal of "create best-in-class service" you see that your first two post-its are customer-focused goals.

Make note when you see clusters or themes around objectives as it will help you understand the level of importance of the goals.

Joe is an electrical engineer at a large automotive manufacturer. In doing his research for the company's defined objectives, he found through the internal website goals including:

- *Increase share of market*
- *Reduce cost by 18% annually*
- *Reduce error rates*
- *Streamline core business processes*

In capturing these on post-its, he recognized the theme around most of his company's current objectives—operational excellence.

With this insight in hand, he realized that his idea would be well aligned with the company's objectives if it clearly improved the process within his company.

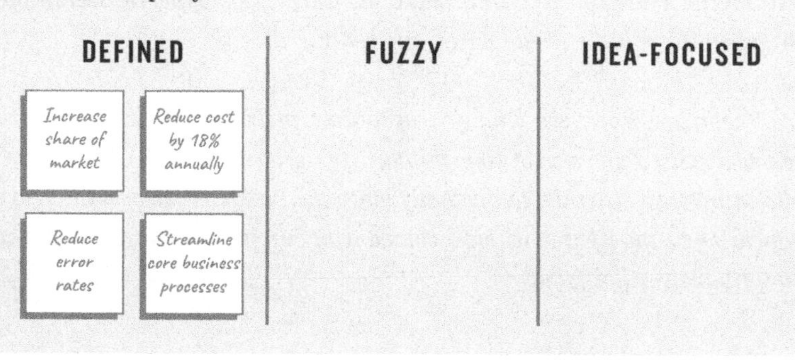

Beyond the goal of launching your big idea, understanding your company's business objectives will help you understand how you can succeed in the company by better understanding core values and beliefs. It will also help you understand the actions and outcomes the company expects to move closer to achieving the mission.

You will want to keep tabs on when the vision, mission, and strategies get updated at the corporate level as well as down to your team. They will evolve and update over time based on company needs, growth, and economic factors.

STEP 2: THE FUZZY INFORMAL

Some organizations have it all figured out—clearly defined goals that are well communicated and understood by every employee throughout the organization. I have yet to work within a company (even the one I co-founded) that has figured out that magical formula.

But with a little sleuthing, you can uncover some of the more "fuzzy" goals and strategies that leadership may be excited about. Start by paying attention to what's said, what's celebrated, and what's ignored. These three are amazing telltale signs for what to align your idea to.

To find what's being said, pay close attention to objectives that are shared via different communication channels that your senior leadership uses.

For Robin, a senior product manager at Amazon, there were very well-defined business objectives on hand. She also went beyond the internal website and team documentation and did some research to find more about "what's said."

She listened in and watched webcasts, podcasts, and interviews where different senior leaders talked about the future of the company. She read internal blogs and paid attention in division meetings where she learned more about her work at Amazon Web Services (AWS) in the mobile space.

She even turned to the annual letter published by CEO Jeff Bezos. From the 2019 letter, she captured some standout "fuzzy" goals that Bezos outlined.

Toward the middle of the letter, she read:

> *"As a company grows, everything needs to scale, including the size of your failed experiments. If the size of your failures isn't growing, you're not going to be inventing at a size that can actually move the needle. Amazon will be experimenting at the right scale for a company of our size if we occasionally have multibillion-dollar failures."*

On a post-it, she added, "Large scale bets." This insight gave her pause. Was her idea big enough to matter at her company? How might she ensure that her idea aligns with these goals shared by Bezos?

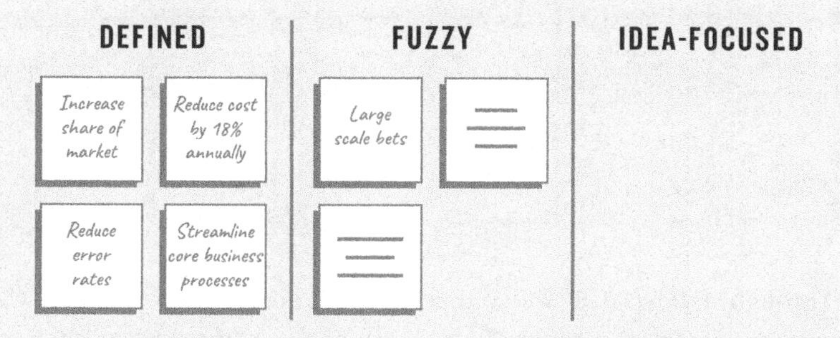

Looking back at her idea, she realized that she may have been thinking too small. Her idea had potential but it wasn't audacious. She went back to her notes and started to rethink how her idea might have a bigger impact, even if it meant bigger risk.

Robin later shared with me that she had a mantra of "Go big, or go home" that she reminded herself as she worked toward her idea. This allowed her to align to the informal, fuzzy goals that the company adheres to.

While uncovering the business objectives that are undefined will take some research, it will pay off later as you pitch your idea and align it to the goals that get leadership excited and your idea the greenlight. What objectives are more qualitative and harder to measure that your company values? Where can you look to find more informal goals the company is working toward? Start brainstorming and writing down informal goals on post-its and begin to add them to the fuzzy section and consider how your idea might align with them.

STEP 3: YOUR IDEA

When you think about your idea, you probably imagine the value it will bring to your customers or how it would make things run more smoothly at your company. These are worthy initiatives but perhaps they aren't business objectives shared formally or informally. For these, you would add them to the idea-focused area.

Capture these objectives and be sure to identify the specific business objectives they would achieve.

Matthew, a product leader at the large gaming company Ubisoft, took my LinkedIn Learning course on product innovation and reached out to me to discuss some of his work.

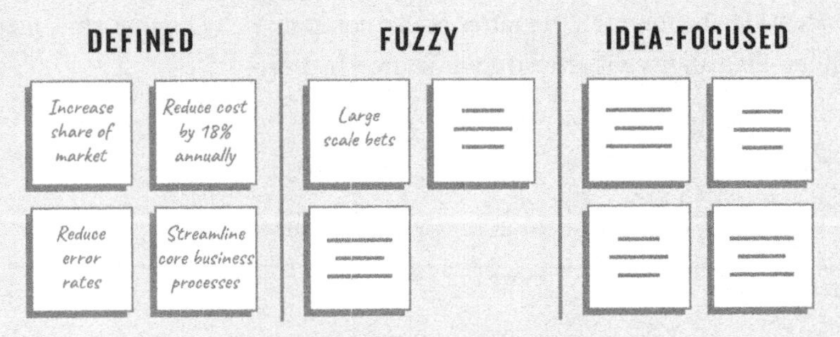

Through a video call, we connected from across time zones. It was 9:00 am in Los Angeles, where I was working from that day, so I had my second cup of coffee in hand and given it was 6:00 pm for Matthew in Paris, he joked it was time for his first beer.

Once we got through pleasantries and introductions, I asked Matthew, "What product innovation project do you have going on right now?"

"Well, my work at Ubisoft has been interesting. I've gotten to work on different projects in production that were all focused on creating efficiencies in how we do work."

With large headphones on his head, he continued to share his plight: "We have over 15,000 employees right now, working from studios around the world. I spent the last year going around to different studios to try and learn how new ideas get done."

"What a great way to get to know the company and travel the world," I shared in awe.

"It is, and it's also sometimes frustrating. I get to see some really amazing ideas getting implemented and the work is either getting duplicated at another studio facing the same issues, or it's not efficiently being shared to bring value to the company more globally."

I nodded as I heard his story unfold. I often hear this story from people trying to innovate within large companies, with siloed studios or departments. Then Matthew got to the juicy part.

"I have an idea. One that would allow innovation to scale. A process for sharing across studios, to allow the work from one team to be usable for another team. But I don't know how to get the permission to focus on this new way of doing things."

Interested in the idea taking off, I asked, "What business objectives would it solve?"

Smart and thoughtful, Matthew quickly shared back, "It would help replicate innovative ideas and reduce overlap of redundant efforts."

"How do you measure that?" I asked.

Matthew thought for a moment and then shared, "How many good ideas get implemented."

We ended the call with him sharing he had some homework to do—to think more about the measurable business objectives that his idea could solve.

In Ubisoft, a company with many different product lines (they create games from Assassin's Creed to Just Dance), he saw his idea as a way to apply across one product line to another. With a streamlined way to innovate, it would create improvements in their R&D efforts as well as make the production of these initiatives more efficient and replicable. Additionally, his idea would improve the quality of an engineer's work because they would have best-practices in hand to follow.

With his idea's objectives identified, Matthew had the information he needed to evaluate where his idea might fit existing business objectives.

With your three areas explored, where do you start to see overlap? Where do the defined and informal objectives overlap with the ones your idea would accomplish?

STEP 4: FIND THE SWEET SPOT

Draw a Venn diagram with defined, fuzzy, and idea-focused. Move your post-its from your lists to the Venn diagram. If the objective on the post-it aligns with multiple categories, place it into appropriate overlap.

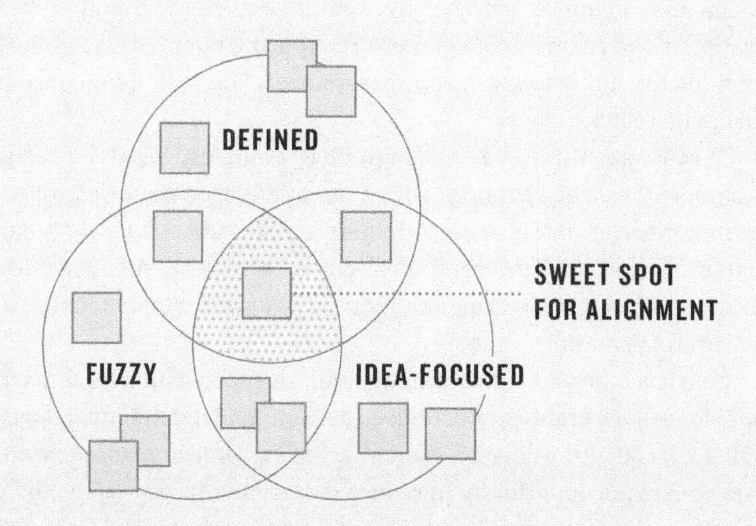

The sweet spot is right in the middle, where the various objectives all meet. Sometimes you will find an overlap between just two of the areas.

It's like playing darts. The inner bullseye has the greatest point value, earning you 50 points when your dart hits the center. But the outer bullseye, just adjacent, still earns you 25 points. Even if you aim for the center and miss slightly, you still see a big payoff.

With your idea, aligning it to the bullseye overlap of the three types of objectives will likely have the best chance of getting buy-in. But don't lose sight of the nearby overlapping alignments as there may be more of those, upping your total value for the company rather than just addressing the one.

ART OF ALIGNING

In 1995, Leslie Ferguson, Douglas's dad, had an idea to help his company, Carolina Power & Light.

Power plants used to have to take down turbines when they were doing maintenance on them. It's like getting your car's oil changed. Except with a power plant, you have to take down huge turbine rotors, each weighing over 50 tons. The process is necessary to create electricity for an entire city.

Turbine inspections are typically scheduled every five years or more often if component inspection or emergency maintenance was required. Couplings between the turbine section were disassembled and separated and the alignment between the rotors were checked and corrected. Rotation of the rotors had to be performed using the overhead crane provided for the unit assembly and disassembly. This was time-consuming and created safety issues.

To overcome this issue, Leslie invented "Campins," which he designed to connect the rotor couplings where the multi-rotor train was rolled via the motor-driven drive system. Leslie's design allowed for 180 degree rotation and negated the need for a crane. While this sounds technical, the short of it is that his plan both reduced costs and eliminated the safety concerns of operating a crane.

Convinced he had a great solution, he consulted with a local machine shop to get accurate production costs and understand final logistics. Armed with all of the details, he approached his project manager with the plan. Seeing the opportunity to reduce costs and improve safety, the project manager approved the production of the first pin.

With the project manager on board and proof of concept in manufacturing, Leslie's idea was well on its way to reality. While he awaited the arrival of the first pin, he continued to share his story with the other plant workers to help them understand the design and why it was important to make this change. Leslie filed a patent on his invention and today is now selling Campins as an independent power plant consultant.

Over and over we hear stories about how people pushed their idea through their company. Wherever they were, they found the time to do this work. Once you understand your idea's alignment with the company, you have landed on the value it will bring to the business's bottom line.

When purpose and passion drive you and your idea's alignment, they give you permission to do the work you long to do. This will open up your work, allowing you to be fully focused on it, because the business has already bought into the value.

The alignment to your company's strategy will show a clear path toward execution. It's the mandate for your idea and goals to strive toward. Alignment is the lighthouse beacon guiding your idea home.

BUILD STAKEHOLDER SUPPORT

Secrets Only Assistants Know

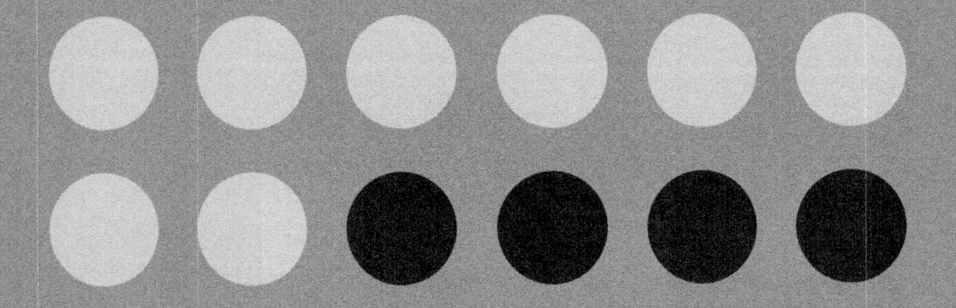

I don't consider myself as someone with a green thumb. I love having plants at home, but I've learned to stick with the hardy ones. The plants that can survive my back and forth over-watering and under-watering. Simple plants that don't require as much effort.

On the other end of the spectrum, there are people like my mother and stepdad. Once they retired and had more time on their hands, they took on some serious gardening. Their large backyard was filled with rows and rows of different vegetables. Something to envy and enjoy season after season.

We harvested tomatoes, carrots, broccoli, zucchini (so many zucchinis!), cabbage, and many other delicious goodnesses. Each season had a different bounty and brought me to further appreciate the effort that goes into the payoff of fresh, tasty meals.

There was a lot of research that went into figuring out the right layout for the garden, what seeds to plant, and when to plant or harvest them. Then there was the trial and error of gardening, like finding the pepper plants failing to produce because of the season's temperature fluctuations. But with tilling and patience, seeing them bloom later, once the temperature evened out.

Every day my mom or stepdad toiled in their garden. Looking at the leaves, identifying soil needs, dealing with pests, and putting their time into whatever the garden needed in the moment to continue to thrive.

Both have since passed away but my memory of their garden and the amount of time and energy that went into it will always be with me. It took a great deal of work and research, patience and grit, to attend to the ever-changing environment and fickle sprouts. The payoff was always worth it when we sat down to a vibrant meal, to see the work come to fruition and nourish our bodies. It was one of the greatest life lessons they could share with me.

Trying to push an idea through an organization will require an incredible amount of effort in tending to it. You will be the gardener of your idea—identifying all the components that will help it thrive and tending to it along the way as it grows.

Just like in a garden, when it comes to your work, there will be problems along the way, things that cause the idea to stall out or slow down in growth. There will be pests that are easy to spot, like a budget constraint announcement, and others that will take research and surface through investigation, like a disgruntled person on your team that doesn't believe in your idea. Or environmental problems like a culture shift or organizational restructure that your idea will have to weather through.

The way past these issues will be the same as my mother and stepfather used in the garden—passion, persistence, patience, grit, and hard work. There are ways forward past issues that may arise by tilling your soil. Keeping your idea healthy and growing requires the right people tending to it and the support of those people throughout the process.

The right people are the ones who will push your idea forward with you, support your work, or even be the gatekeepers standing between you and your budget approval. Getting buy-in from them involves asking the right questions, finding each person's unique motive and perspective, and checking in appropriately. This work is like the meeting-before-the-meeting. It's testing your idea and gathering input and reactions before sharing the big push.

YOU AREN'T WORKING IN A VACUUM

This step of getting buy-in and understanding the important people in the process is indispensable to the success of your idea. In the last chapter we covered how to align with the objectives of the business, but working with people is complex. Because you aren't working in a vacuum, doing whatever you want. You're collaborating and working with others, and you're going to run into differing opinions and motivations. Few people would say they enjoy navigating what feels like "office politics," but the intent here is to gain real support for your project. Getting alignment from others can look like a lot of different things, but in most cases, it starts with a conversation, a way to talk about your idea to feel out the potential responses from the people who matter most.

Throughout this process, you'll want to make sure you understand the perspectives of the people you're trying to include in your idea. Getting buy-in isn't a way to simply sell your idea and get insurance for the journey. You're creating something and garnering people's acceptance as a way to make sure your idea is the right idea, that it benefits the company as a whole, and that it's the right time to pursue it.

Getting acceptance early on helps you avoid the dreaded "idea squash" by your manager or higher-up. There's little hope pursuing a project that your manager is adamant you're not going to do. In some (rare) cases you'll need to go around your manager, but do everything you can to avoid that.

The process of getting buy-in will educate you. It will save you time and resources if you're feeling friction early on. When you slow down to get alignment from the important people around you, you'll be asking questions that will reveal what may need to change, how long you may need to wait, or how to tweak your messaging so it aligns with what the people around you are saying. Even if you get a big fat NO, you'll have a lot of insight into the situation as a whole. (And we'll talk more about turning a "no" into a "yes" in Chapter 9.)

Before you get this magical buy-in, you'll first want to identify who the "right people" are that you'll need to get support from.

UNLIKELY ALLIES

When it comes to your idea, your company is chock-full of people you must convene and convince to help you prune your idea. These people have a lot of names, they're influencers, stakeholders, and even managers. While these people will have varying levels of authority and title, they all hold power over your idea—you will need their support to get your project to move forward.

To brainstorm those "right people," start by thinking about the **titles** of those in your organization. Based on their title alone, your boss will likely be among the people you'll need to communicate your efforts and request resources through. And perhaps there is an executive at your company who has the power to slow things down when not kept in the loop.

Although (hopefully) most of us aren't working for a Meryl Streep-like character from *The Devil Wears Prada*, we all have bosses to contend with. The people with the appropriate titles need to be clued into your idea. Whoever they might be. If you're working at a software company and trying to change a feature in the app, it'll be worthwhile to get someone with the title "engineer" involved in your process.

When thinking about people based on title, ask yourself, who has the authority to make things happen? Who can empower others on the team to get things done?

Then, go beyond titles and think about the **roles** or the job descriptions of what people do.

You can probably brainstorm the traditional roles that you might need, like the people in authority or teams you'll have to interact with, but what about beyond that?

A friend of mine, Suzie, was looking to get the support on her idea from the executive director at the nonprofit where she worked, but his schedule seemed to fill up and last minute donor-meetings kept pushing her meeting back, as the nonprofit was under pressure to fundraise before the end of the year.

Suzie would drop by each day in hopes of finding an opening in his schedule. But his assistant would smile and shrug, unable to find any time he was open. Suzie knew that her idea would need his buy-in and she didn't want to spend too much time chasing after it without getting his thoughts on it.

Rather than wait until the new year, as his assistant had initially suggested, Suzie decided she would check in daily. Annoying, yes? But her perseverance was endearing and she ended up getting to know his assistant over time. One day, when the assistant was shaking her head no as Suzie approached, Suzie joked, "I may have to run into him in the men's room to find the time to chat!"

The assistant suddenly had an idea, "You know, Jack does like early morning breakfast meetings. It's the one time slot he doesn't book because he can meet near his house and let traffic die down before heading in. Want to see if you can meet over breakfast this Friday?"

Jackpot. Suzie had asked early on for creative solutions but it took some time to earn the trust of the assistant. Suzie needed to tend to the garden a little, getting to know the assistant, in order to get on the books.

When you are identifying the "right people" based on roles, ask yourself who has a stake in your product's success or failure? Who might seem like an untraditional person to gain the support of, but is someone who can still have a major impact on your success?

Finally, outside of the structured titles and roles, there are **influencers** and cheerleaders throughout the organization that won't be so cut and dry to identify.

These influential stakeholders are the people who may have control over resources in unexpected ways or hold clout within your company to help push things forward.

In one product launch I was a part of, I found an unlikely ally hidden within the finance department. Early on, I sat down with this number-cruncher to think through my approved budget. I continued to engage with her throughout my process to ensure we were tracking things properly up to launch day.

By the end of the project, she had become an advisor that went beyond helping me to allocate and spend my budget. She advocated for me during a board meeting and landed additional resources for our team.

To identify your surprise supporters, ask yourself who are the people that have a good understanding of how the company works? Who are the people that others ask for help, advice, or ideas?

Taking time to brainstorm who your stakeholders are within these three categories (title, role, and mentor) will arm you with the right questions to identify the people within your company. The ones you should engage with in pushing your idea forward.

WHAT'S IN IT FOR THEM?

Have you ever tried to get your significant other excited to come to your company's holiday party? For my introverted husband, milling around with strangers and holding small talk is an effort. Each year, I try to sell him on how great the party will be. "Now you'll finally meet Sarah, she's hilarious!" or "It'll be fun to have a reason to get dressed up!"

Year after year, throughout the different companies I have worked and been invited to a holiday party, Ryan puts on his holiday best for me—handsome, but not thrilled.

One year, a startup I was doing product innovation work for planned to hold their end-of-year holiday party at a warehouse. Preparing him for what to expect, I gave him the rundown.

"This year, the holiday party will be in a warehouse. Probably full of people from outside the company more than employees from within the startup. It'll be a live music show with a pay-as-you-go bar in the back." I shrugged. It didn't sound fun to me.

My husband perked up and looked up from working on his laptop, "A bar, good music, and no chitchat? Best holiday party ever."

He was sold when he heard he could order whatever drink he wanted, and with the music as the focus, he wouldn't have the pressure of having to hold superficial conversations. Plus, he enjoys music.

When I was trying to get him excited about the holiday parties, I often highlighted the things that I enjoyed. While he is happy to do things that make me happy, it wasn't intrinsically motivating for him to go to them.

Getting buy-in is always more effective when we're able to connect to what internally drives the other person. If I had thought about what intrinsically drives my husband sooner—I would have realized this kind of party was much more up his alley. But how do we get our bosses and managers to be interested in our ideas in the same way? If we're working towards intrinsically motivating them and finding reasons they would get behind our project we need to start asking questions.

- *What are they focused on accomplishing this quarter?*
- *What do they think about what I'm trying to do?*
- *Do they think the problem I'm solving is worth the investment?*
- *How can I frame my idea as something they care about?*

In 2010, when working at MyEdu, the educational technology startup I co-founded, my two co-founders and I hired a CEO to help our company scale and grow. No longer the heads of our company, we had a new executive to report to which meant we would need to get his buy-in to make big things happen. Gone were the days we could experiment on an idea autonomously or through the buy-in of three. Now we had to get disciplined and focused to get approval for big ideas.

I was focused on growing our usage numbers. To increase the number of college students using our site, I wanted to invest in a program that would harness the on-campus student groups at the universities we served; leverage them for marketing to the greater student body and help increase our usage.

I went right to our CEO with my brilliant idea. "All we need to do is follow this playbook and we will see 10 times the number of students using our site. And we have the team in place to make this happen. We just need to ask them to shift their efforts to this initiative."

He listened to my idea and asked me to hold onto it. "That's great. Maybe this is something we can attempt later. Right now we need them focusing on customer support."

I felt deflated. Why wouldn't he jump at the chance to grow our user base? Maybe I hadn't sufficiently sold my ability to execute the idea. Or maybe he didn't trust that the idea would be worth a try.

I continued on my existing projects and kept my eyes and ears open for an opportunity to test my idea. It still bothered me though... why wouldn't he want to increase our user base?

A month later, we had a board meeting and in it one of the investing partners beat us up over our engagement metrics. Apparently, via emails and meetings I wasn't a part of, my CEO had already heard about this and that was why he had brushed off my idea to increase the number of users.

What I failed to recognize was the problem he was focusing on: increasing the engagement of our current users.

Had I been clued in, I would have rethought my pitch. Either by holding it for another time, or thinking more deeply about how it could increase our user base AND increase engagement.

My idea was all about finding the users that would get the most out of our new services, the ones that would keep them on the site longer, increasing engagement levels.

While we went forward with my idea eventually, I would have seen it take off sooner, and with less friction, if I had done my homework in advance and aligned with the problem my CEO was focused on.

Before waltzing in with your full-color, well-researched, 20-page presentation deck outlining your three-point solution, take a step back and learn where your manager is focused.

Hold on to your *solution* for later. Instead, focus on your manager's perspective on the *problem*.

It will help you learn where they stand on the work you are trying to do. You will step away from your idea, and see the problem from your manager's eyes, giving you a leg up when it comes to the final pitch for your solution.

ASK THE RIGHT QUESTIONS

One way to get more informed is to start by understanding how your boss and other important people think about the problem you're trying to solve. Do they even notice it? Do they think it is worth solving? Have they tried to solve it in the past and failed? Or do they see the issue in a completely different light?

By going to my CEO and sharing my idea before understanding his perspective, I had to do more work later to get buy-in. Having framed my idea as a solution to growing our user base, I had to go back and set it up to solve a different problem, increasing our engagement. Both were valuable problems to solve, but only one gave my idea permission to launch.

The key to really understanding your boss's (and anyone else's) perspective is to start with an open mind, ask lots of questions, and listen. It's critical to ask open-ended, exploratory questions. Get as curious as you can about your problem space.

Try to avoid questions that point the other person toward an expected outcome. Instead of asking, "Do you think we need solution X to increase revenue?" start with something more open-ended, like, "Can you tell me about the problems we're experiencing as a team?" In the first question, at best you will bias your stakeholder without getting any insight into what he/she really believes.

At worst, you will have shared your idea too early in the process, risking an unforeseen landmine that puts an end to your exploration.

Always keep in mind that your goal is to explore someone else's perspective on the problem, reflect on what you learn, and look for ways to fold the learnings back into your idea—and how you pitch it.

Ask questions like:

- *What happens when ____?*
- *Who is most affected by ____?*
- *Can you describe to me how ____?*
- *Can you tell me about your thoughts around ____?*

When you hear the responses, don't follow up with your solution. This is hard. You're excited about your idea. And when you hear something that points to your idea being a clear solution, you will be tempted to share it when it seems like a perfect answer to the described problem.

There will be a time for this, but early on probe deeper to learn more. This will give you more insight into what people are thinking and all the different components that may be considered when weighing your solution later.

If you can't think of more specific or custom questions, simply ask why?

Here's a scenario where a product manager had an idea that would help bring in more customers and create more engagement. But rather than going to leadership with the solution, she used questions to gather more intel and insights.

Product Manager: *Can you describe to me how you think about our customer's experience in using our product?*

Leadership: *Yeah, to start, we need to address how we can make our product more sticky. How will we keep people on our website longer and encourage them to come back again and again?*

Product Manager: (Holding back on fabulous idea) *Hmmmm. Why?*

Leadership: *Well, we are currently going after another round of funding. The founder wants us to really focus on engagement. He's happy with our growth in signups but he's really putting on the pressure for increasing the user's time on our product.*

Good thing the product manager didn't jump straight to the solution of investing in obtaining new users. Now he has more insight into what initiatives will motivate his boss and which ones may quickly be dismissed.

At the end of this phase, you want to have further defined the problem space and the frame of reference from the other person's perspective.

This will likely take multiple conversations. Additionally, asking these questions to others on your team and across your organization will help give you a fuller picture. Ask others about their thoughts around the problem, or ask for their perspective on what problems they know your boss may be facing.

After collecting your intel, take note of themes and overlaps. What differences did you hear between your stakeholder's thoughts on the problem and yours?

STOP STARING AT THE PROBLEM

After you understand the different perspectives on the problem, the next phase is to lean in and learn more about perceived solutions. That is, does the person you're trying to share your idea with already have their own solution to the problem? Can their solution be incorporated into your idea? Or might your solution be perceived as opposition to theirs?

Most problems will have multiple solutions and some may be a radically different approach than the idea you want to implement.

Ask questions like:

- *What's a way we might address the problem of ____?*
- *What does success look like for the problem of ____?*
- *If we don't solve the problem of ____, what happens?*

When you hear their responses, keep an open mind. Don't point out the flaws in the solution or where your idea would be better. Don't focus on the "what" of the solution, instead, focus on what you are hearing. This can help you later, as you shape your idea to fit into their thinking.

A creative director I was coaching worked for a midsized North American advertising agency and was trying to get buy-in from his CEO to open a new office in London. He wanted to expand the company's services into the European market. He knew that the new CEO wanted to increase sales and revenue and believed the best way to achieve this was through new markets. Here's how he went deeper into understanding the CEO's perspective on potential solutions.

Creative Director: *What's a way we might address our problem of stagnating sales?*

CEO: *I want creative, out-of-the-box solutions. Sure, we could expand into new markets, but I want to know what innovative ideas we could try that will make a bigger, long-term impact.*

Creative Director: (discouraged to hear the negativity toward an expansion idea) *That's interesting. Why focus on nontraditional ideas?*

CEO: *Expansion is a no-brainer. What else can we be doing to move the needle? What will make us a relevant company in five years? Ten years?*

While it wasn't the solution the creative director wanted to hear, understanding his CEO's perspective gave him the insight he needed to tweak his thinking. An expansion may still work... but how would it play into the bigger picture of keeping the company relevant in five or ten years?

When you are in this phase of asking questions about your solution, you are hoping to learn more about the other person's current thinking and their investment in solutions. Is the company pretty far down the track toward investing in something? Or are these early days where new ideas are welcome? Listen, learn, and make time to reflect.

This phase will take time. You will need to go beyond your boss and ask questions to different stakeholders. Consider gaining perspectives across the organization. The solutions from a sales team member and an engineer may look very different, but the common throughline may just be the insight you need to support your solution over time.

TIMING IS EVERYTHING

Timing can be everything when you're getting support for your idea.

In 2018, Liberty Mutual hired Voltage Control to run a sprint with a potential business partner. Their goal was to evaluate the possibility of a project that could unlock a lot of revenue through the combination of both companies' data. The sprint gave them the confidence that their companies' cultures aligned well enough to make the project a huge success. Shortly after the sprint, they had to hit the pause button. Their partner seemed to disengage and Bob Taylor, of Liberty Mutual, was savvy enough to realize not to press too hard because clearly, this other company was focused on other things. He knew the partnership had mutual benefits and alignment and believed nothing had been done to compromise that.

And from years of experience, he figured there had to be something at play that would make sense of the other company's behavior. He knew he had the buy-in and that if Liberty Mutual waited until the partner was ready then things would move forward with ease.

Think about a time when you were slammed with work projects and personal obligations and someone sent you an email about a simple ask like, "Want to meet up for lunch soon?" It would've taken a second to respond, but you put it off to get to later when you would have more time for a thoughtful response. Then, months later, when cleaning up your inbox, you realize you never responded.

This happens all the time, even for the big stuff. When it comes to understanding timing it requires that you give people, and your idea, the benefit of the doubt. Your stakeholders have their own lives and stresses going on behind the scenes. Pay attention to their moods and level of engagement.

Go outside of work and think about their day-to-day life. Humanize your boss. Is your boss getting married or having a baby soon? Has your boss been juggling work with family obligations like a sick parent in the hospital?

These issues outside of work are helpful in identifying the right "timing" for a conversation. Don't ask for a meeting at 4:30 p.m. when your boss may need to run out the door to pick up their kids from school.

Internal and external pressures should be considered when you approach your boss to start the conversation. It doesn't mean that you pause altogether, but instead give space to allow for your boss to be an imperfect, juggling-a-million-things human.

Early in my professional career, I wanted to restructure the teams that reported to me and needed to get my CEO to approve the reorganization. I scheduled the conversation in advance and prepared to have a sit-down, outlining my idea. But when I popped my head into his office for our scheduled meeting, his executive assistant, a very lovely and friendly person, didn't look up from her computer screen to say hi. And my boss? He looked exhausted and stressed. I quickly assessed the situation and told him that the conversation could wait. I mentioned that he looked busy and that we could reschedule if that was helpful. Yes, he agreed he needed to recover that time and informed me that he had something come up with the contractors that were building his new home.

My boss was grateful to reschedule, and I saved my idea for a time when he would be in a better, more open-minded state to brainstorm with me.

Instead of trying to harvest too early, I tended to my garden, waiting for better conditions that would give my idea a better chance to flourish.

RETHINK THE PITCH

Wayne, a bidding supervisor at a visual effects company, had a great idea to create a new innovation department that would allow the company to test new ideas outside of the visual effects work they did for movies. At the time, his company was focusing on creating content for movies and video games. But he envisioned a team that would test new markets and technologies, like taking on VR projects.

Early on, Wayne went straight to his boss with his solution. He felt confident in his idea and knew it was one his boss would buy in on. But he didn't have the full picture or buy-in that he needed. By jumping straight to the solution, and not first gaining perspective from his boss, he didn't bring his boss "along" in the thinking. His boss confronted him with other issues and behind the scenes problems he had not considered.

He went back to the drawing board. Going back through the three phases of understanding the people, solutions, and timing, Wayne was better able to bring his boss and the other executives along. Early on, he learned about new problems he was unaware of, like the company's upcoming investments in other initiatives. Wayne's original approach would've required more investment upfront. Upon learning that the company was looking to experiment but unable to invest in ideas, it gave him the perspective he needed to tweak his idea.

Over time, gathering insights and getting buy-in along the way, Wayne was able to shape a solution that fit for the company. They identified a client partner that wanted to work with the company and would pay to do a project together in the VR space. This would allow the new team Wayne was pitching to experiment in this new space. And rather than costing the company a big upfront investment, the majority of the costs would be recovered through the client fees.

By going back and thinking through who, what, and when to talk about his idea, Wayne crafted a story by tying in the people, the problems, and the potential solutions. Wayne took the insights he had learned and rethought his pitch. Rather than selling a new department, he needed to sell the new service. His new story highlighted that they had a client ready to pay for this service and that the market was ripe for someone to disrupt the industry. It wasn't about a new innovation department, it was an opportunity to expand their services.

WATER, WEED & TEND

Identifying the right stakeholders, understanding their perceptions, and gauging the right timing are all important steps. But even with all these components in place, a conversation or idea will fall short when you don't keep people in the loop.

It's not enough to plant the seeds and wait for nature to take over. You have to water, weed, and tend to your garden. For your stakeholders, you will need to continuously check in, share progress, collect feedback, and tweak your idea along the way.

Have you ever worked hard on a project and then somewhere along the line got blindsided when a powerful manager or influencer slowed things down or brought them to a complete halt? This can be incredibly frustrating. Especially when you believe you've been doing your best to communicate frequently, with all the right players.

How and when you engage with stakeholders matters.

Send too much information to a stakeholder who isn't that interested, and they ignore everything, missing key details for your product launch. Send too little to the stakeholder that needs to be more engaged, and risk having them in the dark later, when you need them most.

People want to know that you care about what they have to say. That they are valued and their work is seen and heard. The same goes for plants. The plant can't thrive without the right mix of water and sunshine. You can hope for the best, letting your garden grow like it would in the wild, but with thoughtful planning and tending, you will find you can control your harvest.

ACTIVITY

IDENTIFY THE RIGHT LEVEL OF STAKEHOLDER COMMUNICATION

Step one in getting buy-in for your idea is to make a list of all the people you'll actually need to get buy-in from. As you read this chapter, the names of different stakeholders and influencers should have come to mind. Go through each of the three categories of people: role, title, and influence and create a list of people under each who can have an impact on your project. Think outside the box and always err on the side of adding more than not enough.

Once you identify the right people, you must create a deliberate and strategic communication strategy that balances the stakeholders' needs with your own time and resources.

Take your list of people you thought were influencers and put them on the grid and decide how often is appropriate and realistic to communicate with them.

A great way to map your communication efforts is to use the Mendelow's Matrix to make your launch run more smoothly, and garner the right level of stakeholder engagement.

In the matrix, you'll find the stakeholder groups broken into four quadrants, based on two factors: power (the stakeholder's ability to influence your product strategy and resources) and interest (the stakeholder's level of desire in seeing your product succeed).

It may feel like everyone has power and interest in your product launch. But in reality, people are busy with other initiatives and some stakeholders will have more power or interest than others. Identifying where your stakeholders fit will allow you to understand the frequency of communicating your product launch activities.

Your boss, for example, will likely fit in the key player quadrant. She will be high in power, and high in interest. For stakeholders here, you'll

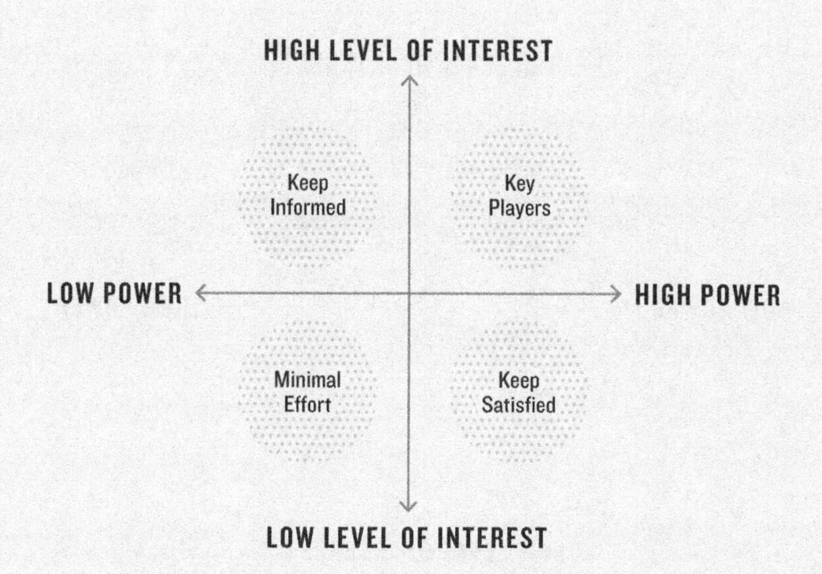

want to manage communications closely and engage in frequent updates and conversations along the way.

You could create weekly meetings to share progress updates or ask for advice in areas where you feel stuck.

Looking to the opposite side, someone like a system administrator may be a stakeholder that you put within the minimal effort quadrant. They will hold less interest in your product and less power within the organization.

Keep this stakeholder satisfied by sharing monthly updates on the launch date and any other details that are required for their work. Minimal effort should go into the communication strategy with this group.

Other stakeholders will have low power and high interest and fit within the keep informed quadrant. An example may include a developer or someone that's testing the product.

For this stakeholder, share a biweekly email with product launch details to keep them informed and engaged, but without creating too much effort on your end. You might also be able to create a sort of "home page" for your interested stakeholders where you can keep an ongoing update of the project and ways they can support you. Whatever you create—the idea is to keep these people engaged so they'll feel like they're a part of the project.

Finally, a stakeholder may fit in the keep satisfied quadrant when they have a lot of power at your company, but little interest in your product. An example may be a busy executive at your organization.

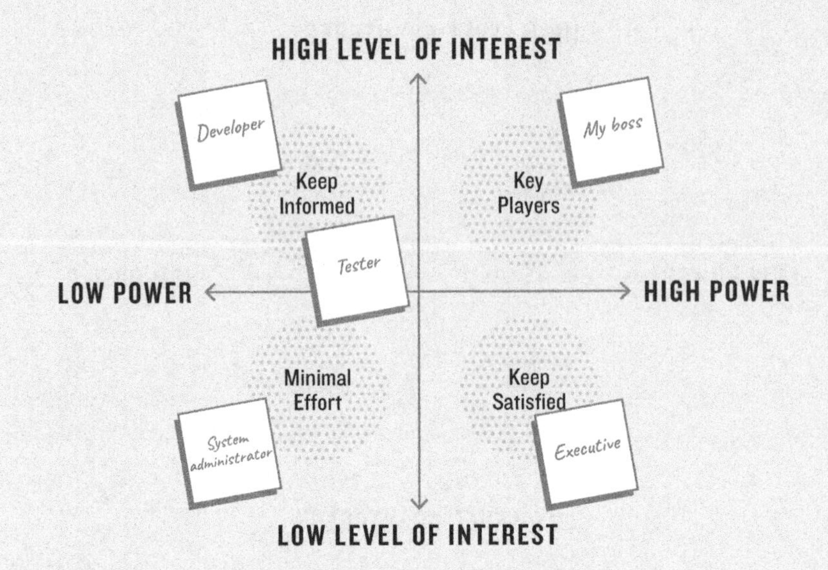

These people will be great for testing new ideas and checking in once a month to bounce ideas off them. Though they may influence the decision, they are not good for communicating throughout the process because of their lack of interest and, likely, time for your project.

There are many stakeholders that can bring your vision to life or, conversely, bring your work to a discouraging standstill. It's your job to identify what level of engagement works for your stakeholders and create a strategy to keep everyone informed on your efforts.

G

GET STARTED

Prototypes

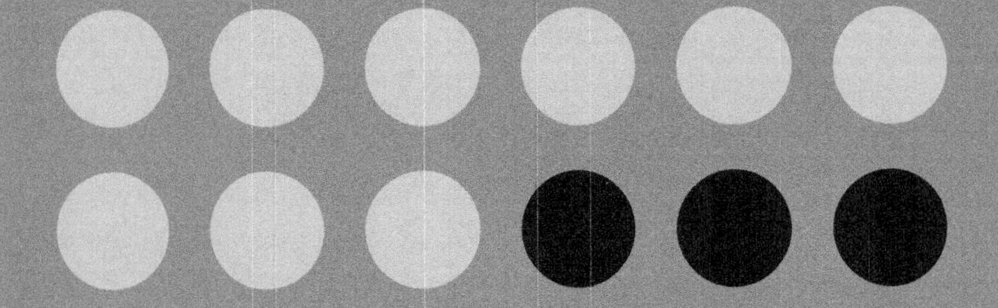

When it comes to launching new ideas, we can get stuck in the first phase of conception—the ideating. We research, think, and talk about our idea, but it's hard to take the leap from idea to action. Most people bounce from idea to idea, or tell everyone how great it would be in theory, but only few do the work. The rest are stuck swirling in the idea soup.

- *Wouldn't it be great if we...?*
- *How would you envision...?*
- *Can I pull this off if...?*
- *Would this fail if...?*
- *Do you think people actually want...?*
- *How would people behave differently if we...?*
- *What would happen if we didn't...?*
- *What if...?*

Eventually, there comes a time where the majority of questions are answered and there is wind in your sails—you're starting to build momentum. At this point, you should be organized enough, understand the process forward enough, and have buy-in from enough of the right people. It's a big jump from preparing to actually prototyping the idea, but at this point, it's time. Enough is enough. You're ready for action.

It all starts small, with a prototype. A prototype is your idea built out just enough for other people to interact with it. It's how you can get people to look at it, use it, and participate with it, all to evaluate and react to it.

At first, it will be a quick, inexpensive, scaled-down version of your idea. The product, service, or process can be refined and perfected as you continue to test it and extract insights from your intended "users" and stakeholders.

Testing a prototype is more than simply giving someone the elevator pitch but it's not yet a fully formed version of the real thing. It's something in between. To prototype a book we might create an outline or print a proof. To prototype an app we could design something as simple as a wireframe on paper or as advanced as a quick version of the app itself. The goal is to create something simple and easy yet allows you to answer critical questions.

When it comes to launching your idea within your company, you need to think about this phase as your opportunity to not just build a mockup of your idea, but to build a "prototype." In fact, don't call it a "prototype." Call it what it is, a "learning prototype."

It's your opportunity to consider what you need to think through, communicate to stakeholders, or test and evaluate. Your "learning prototype" should start out less refined and then, through lessons and learning, move to more defined versions. It is an iterative process.

The intent behind the learning prototype is to practice before the performance. Just like musicians, performers, and athletes require hundreds of practice hours before their big recital, show, or game, your idea needs a safe place to work out the kinks, test out the acoustics, and see how the audience responds.

As a marathon runner, our coach taught us how to use our practice runs as prototypes for the race day. Early on in training, Coach Bobby highlighted that we needed to be running our practice runs in the same shoes we planned to wear on race day. His advice for our clothes was the same.

"The worst thing that can happen to you on race day is the unexpected blister or painful chafing all because you didn't break in your shoes or test out your gear," Coach Bobby would say.

Practice runs helped me realize that maybe I needed thicker socks, or to cut the tag off my shirt after getting annoyed and chafed by mile three. These are kinks you want to work out before you start the long 26.2 race-day miles.

As I got closer to the race, my practice runs started looking more like the race itself. I spent more time creating prototype race days where I trained on the same course and terrain as the race. My tired body knew at mile 16 that I still had a massive incline to tackle at mile 18. I trained in the Texas heat and humidity so I was ready for the climate's effect on my body for race day.

From the logistics of what I would eat and drink during the race to the mental mantras that I was going to repeat to myself when I wanted to quit—the practice runs and training were each part of the prototype to prepare for my best performance, race day itself.

Your idea needs the same level of practice and prototyping. It's your mini-opportunity to test, fail, and find out where you need to apply the chafing cream.

A PROTOTYPE IS WORTH 1,000 MEETINGS

As Tom and David Kelley, founders of design firm IDEO, beautifully stated it, "If a picture is worth a thousand words, a prototype is worth a thousand meetings."

Think about how a single picture can convey a complex story. In the same way, a prototype is the artifact that makes it easier to convey your concept. Instead of struggling over words trying to explain exactly what something looks or feels like, you can just show them.

A few years ago when I was working for a big tech company, we wanted to create a global summit as a way for people across the department to discuss the 10-year vision. The idea was to give people who worked in the product group an opportunity to think about the future and how our work day-to-day could help shape and build that future.

What should the summit look like? I sat through many meetings talking about the outcomes we wanted and the constraints our event would be built within, but we weren't landing on a consensus around what the event should actually look like.

So I took a leap and did a learning prototype of what I thought the agenda would look like. Over a glass of wine with my husband, I talked through my plan. While he wouldn't be attending the summit, he's been to plenty of conferences so he had ideas that gave my agenda some more shape. I synthesized some of what I'd heard my coworkers say and took an hour to write everything down and organize the days in a way that made sense based on past conferences. (Really not rocket science.)

I took my prototype and shared it with the team that was helping to create the event. People immediately reacted with ideas to make it better.

"We should have more time for networking and conversations. This agenda is too jam-packed."

"What about people who are traveling from out of town? We need to plan evening events for them."

I wasn't trying to create the perfect agenda. I just knew that people had been talking about it for so long that ideas were getting lost in our heads and we needed a way to "feel" the agenda. Creating my learning prototype helped people imagine what the experience would feel like.

Then they could react to it.

I presented the agenda with the same sentiment that I created it. "This isn't perfect, I want to know what you think can be moved and where things are too compact." I knew the way I presented a prototype like this was important. People should feel like they are needed to shape and build on what I'm showing them. A lot of times when we present something we care deeply about and ask for feedback, it can come across as defensive. We might say that we want input, but our attitude implies that we really don't.

After that conversation, my agenda evolved. With a place to jump off from, we quickly created a second, third, and fourth version of the agenda that were light-years better than the one I drew up in an hour over a glass of wine.

After we had a pretty solid idea for what the agenda was going to look like, I created another learning prototype—a mock summit to test out the agenda with more details shared. I invited a small group of people who weren't part of the planning.

In the space where we would be holding the summit, I showed visuals of different components that we were thinking of using. From chair setups to lunch buffets, worksheets for participants to gift bags, we went through everything. Then I walked through the agenda with them and asked questions.

"What do you think about this experience?"

"Do you feel like after this event you would better connect with the 10-year vision?"

Getting closer to understanding what the event will look and feel like, people shared deeper insights to help shape the event.

On one slide I shared with the group, I had an image of a buffet table with stacked sodas and water bottles from the food vendor we would be hiring for one of the evening events.

One colleague, Patrick, saw the image and asked, "Can we set up a water station and ask employees to bring their company water bottle rather than using bottled waters throughout the week? Seems like we would be going through a lot of plastic."

"That's a great idea!" I replied, taking note.

Then Patrick continued, "What else will we be doing to reduce waste and offset our carbon footprint?"

This got the group to start brainstorming.

"We could wear our company ID tags on lanyards to display our name, rather than creating and wearing new name tags," I shared.

"I know headquarters has a plan in place to cover expenses related to carbon offset for events, I can reach out to a contact there to see what we could do!" Another team member shared.

As the mini-brainstorm came to an end, I asked Patrick if he could lead a brainstorm session with others around the company to come up with eco-friendly solutions to propose for us to implement for this event. He later held a two-hour brainstorm session with others passionate about this topic and they came up with fantastic solutions we were able to implement.

An idea like Patrick's was a great insight and something our team hadn't considered yet. It took him participating in my mock summit and seeing the water bottles in my image to be able to imagine what the event will feel like to come up with his important feedback.

Like my marathon training, these learning prototypes helped align people and further define the final event. And even helped us avoid a few roadblocks and potential mishaps.

When you're launching something new, or trying to get a grasp on what something will look or feel like—there's no substitution for creating a prototype. In a place where there's no template for how things are done or the right way forward, a prototype allows you to practice something with much lower stakes. You'll very quickly see if you're accomplishing what you'd hoped to or not when you get other people to react to a real version of what you're trying to do.

PROTOTYPING BRAD PITT

Here's the thing about learning prototypes: you'll know you have one when you see how other people react to it. When it's still in the idea form, people may nod and add feedback, but it's much harder to get input and insights until you have the learning prototype to share.

Sometimes we *think* we have a learning prototype, but when we share it with colleagues or stakeholders, we find they still don't see or *understand* it. The learning prototype didn't capture the essence of the idea in a way that would help people connect to it.

Let's say your idea is to improve a process at work. You are interested in trying to implement a new way of innovating at your company. Prototyping this idea is not explaining it to the other members of the team. But it could look like identifying steps you want to test, finding a project with lower stakes, and using that project to follow the proposed steps of your new process. The act of going through the process with a project is the learning prototype.

Or let's say your idea is new software you want to launch at your company. You see an opportunity to bring a new solution that your customers need. It wouldn't be enough to simply show the software's website to your team. A great learning prototype would emulate the experience starting with drawings or mockups of how the customer would interact with the software. Before you write a line of code, the mockup of the software's experience will be the prototype.

You'll know you have a good learning prototype when people are able to connect to it, and react.

Whether it's an excited, positive reaction highlighting the things you need to avoid in the future, or an outright negative reaction, the transformation of your idea into a learning prototype is the moment it looks, feels, and acts real. The learning prototype should be realistic enough that someone thinks it exists. Or, as they say in the film business, you suspend their disbelief.

My husband is in the visual effects industry. As a supervisor on films and big-budget TV shows, he's part of the creative team that transforms Brad Pitt from ducking and driving around on a go-cart in the desert into astronaut Roy McBride, deftly dodging bullets and trekking on the surface of the moon in *Ad Astra*.

I've watched some of the early screenings of the movies he's worked on and from day one up until the final version we see on the big screen (or in the comfort of our living room), they are creating learning prototypes along the way.

To mock the look and feel of Brad Pitt driving on the moon, they will share a few shots of how the environment looks without atmosphere or haze. Or simulations of how the dust is kicked up by tires at 1/6th gravity. They won't do the whole scene, and frankly they aren't able to due to how complex the process is. Instead they share elements or steps along the way to provide a taste, so the director has enough to see a prototype and react to it.

The director may share that he wants the dust to be less bright and distracting. Or that the environment needs to look more rugged with larger craters to increase the audience's sense of danger. Perhaps he thinks that 1/6th gravity might be correct, but it doesn't work as well as 1/4th gravity to tell the story.

When working to move your idea to prototype, it will be messy. It doesn't have to be perfect, and the sooner you can get a reaction from your "audience," the more chances you'll have to refine.

DON'T SKIP THE LEARNING PROTOTYPE

When you've reached this point—you've probably put a LOT of work into your idea. It's tempting to want to skip the learning prototype. You may think your idea has been researched, talked through, and shown to enough people to serve as its own prototype. People get it and seem to like it, so why bother?

Or you believe it's too difficult to prototype your idea, and just easier to build the final *thing* rather than spending the effort to build an imperfect version.

Or, you don't think you have the time to create a prototype, you just need to move quickly and go right to the final output.

But when you skip this phase, you miss the opportunity of making something better, that's more likely to actually succeed. The learning prototype requires people to start different conversations than when it was an idea, discussions around what is working or not.

Imagine going on a first date and popping the question to get married. While there are cultures that arrange marriages, and even reality shows around marriage-at-first-sight, most people date as a way to get to know what it's like to be in a relationship with someone, before committing to a lifetime of marriage. Dating tests the relationship and if it can weather the ups and downs of life together. It's the prototype before the matrimony.

In our work, getting your idea to a prototype allows you and your stakeholders to do real work together. A place to talk about it and move forward from.

I've seen projects go from idea to final product too fast. Building the final thing can get expensive, fast. Recently I watched a group of developers skip the prototyping and come to realize they were building the wrong app, with too many features, that was costing them a lot of time and resources. The entire project was canceled and one developer lost their job.

Want to know what will happen when you skip the learning prototype? Assumptions will cloud reality. Later down the line, they'll bite you, creating more problems and slowing you down. You cannot successfully jump from a locked-up-in-a-brain-idea to a fully-built-and-finalized-product without prototyping along the way.

A simple example is sending an agenda for an important meeting, in advance of the meeting.

If you are going into a meeting to discuss an important topic, trying to get feedback and buy-in around your idea, a solid agenda upfront will ensure that the meeting is more meaningful and reaches its goals. You would share it with team members in advance and ask, "Does this agenda cover everything?"

It won't be enough to copy/paste an old meeting agenda, you will have to build a new one around the needs and goals of this particular meeting. And when you've tweaked your first prototype of the agenda, you'll get closer to an end result that you can use to guide the meeting.

A good learning prototype will get people thinking about your idea. A great learning prototype will get people actively sharing ways to improve it.

THE EARLY PROTOTYPE

The early bird gets the worm and the early prototype gets to uncover roadblocks, problems, and assumptions sooner.

The sooner you get your prototypes built, the faster you can get quality feedback. It will give you a glimpse into the potential future. A future where your idea is possible. And knowing how people react to that possibility sooner rather than later means you have more time to adjust and avoid the list of things that could go wrong.

I remember asking my 3-year-old what he wanted to be for Halloween. Without hesitation, he told me he wanted to be an airbag. Okay, I thought, what might that mean in his little toddler brain?

We talked about the costume and how it could be a poofy bag made out of cloth, where he would have a horn he could beep on his tummy. For a few days I thought I knew what we were doing to make the costume and I started to enlist my sew-savvy friends for tips on making something like this.

I drew a mockup of what the costume would look like and upon looking at the drawing, my son turned up his nose in distaste. He wanted to be stuffed into a steering wheel of some sort, and pop out like an airbag would to say, "Trick or treat" door-to-door.

Over our family's spaghetti dinner, I tried to explain how we could pretend he would pop out. Or perhaps make it look like he had already popped out. It didn't matter what I said, he had his heart set on a design that wasn't possible for execution at his level of expectations.

Despite all the talking we had gone through, it was my drawing that helped us realize the costume wouldn't work. I assumed he knew he wouldn't really be popping out. He assumed he would.

In the end, he decided on Batman. The store-bought costume fit his requirements and with another drawing, I showed him how we could add his requested "fly" and "stop" buttons onto the sleeve. It took some convincing but he finally agreed that it would be safer if they were pretend buttons.

Learning prototypes allow everyone to get beyond assumptions and to understand what the idea will actually look, feel, and act like.

Architects create learning prototypes all the time. They wouldn't be able to convince someone to build a skyscraper without starting with blueprints and later making a realistic model. The same goes for your idea. Whether using software to test real-world behavior and construction, or creating an architectural model as a physical representation, prototypes are meant to communicate the design's ideas.

Some people want to wait to prototype until they have all the data in their hands to prove the idea. Sure, it's great in theory to be data-driven, but the problem with relying on data is that it is used to quantify a hunch. And that leads to waiting around for the perfect data. The data that will *prove* your idea instead of test it.

Waiting for perfect data often requires you to run on hunches. Your hunch is telling you that you need more data. But what you should be doing is experimenting and prototyping to help you get to the data that is most useful—that is, is your idea viable?

UNEXPECTED OUTCOMES

A few weeks before I was supposed to present a new workshop, Quick Wins to Gain Trust and Scale Innovation, that I had created for an Innov8rs Summit I was leading in Los Angeles, I invited four friends to come over and go through it with me. I had practiced out loud, but I hadn't presented the workshop with others participating.

The first part, the actual presentation piece, went great. After I presented, I confidently moved on to the exercises that were built to help participants understand the material.

"Now turn to your table-mates and talk through the questions on the paper in front of you. Try drawing out your own innovation chart as a group."

My friends were around one table in my living room and I sat by and watched them interact with each other and the questions in front of them. It became quite obvious that there were too many people trying to talk through the questions, the activity was taking too long, and some people weren't getting a chance to speak and share their ideas.

I asked my friends to shift gears and to pair up instead. They had better results almost immediately. They were able to cover more in pairs and surprisingly even reach a new level of comfort in sharing when it was just one other person. (An outcome I hadn't expected.)

It took simulating the workshop with real people to realize that my exercises were better suited for one-on-one conversations instead of big table groups. If I hadn't gone to the effort to prototype the workshop fully, and instead just relied on practicing my speaking parts out loud, the people attending my workshop would've had a hard time getting as much value from it.

To get beyond assumptions and really test your idea, you have to make your prototype go beyond something locked up in your head and into something tangible.

Note: We're just scratching the surface of testing your prototype. Depending on the size of your idea and the investment for your company, you'll need to do your research around customer interviews, user feedback, and how you collect the insights.

LEARN & ITERATE

With prototypes ranging from simpler drawings to extensive mocked up features in an app—there are varying levels of what a prototype can look like. What will serve you best?

A low-fidelity, basic prototype, or a high-fidelity, closer-to-finished prototype?

It all depends on what you're looking to get from the people you're showing your learning prototype to. When I created my agenda, it didn't need to be detailed or color-coded or have visuals like our final version did. It was low-fidelity—I just needed people to start talking about it.

But when you're trying to get feedback from external customers on a new product, you're probably building something a little more high-fidelity, like a 3D printed plastic model of a product with movable pieces that can simulate the actual experience of using it. Building something out like this can give you a better idea of how someone will really interact with your product.

When starting to prototype, it's helpful to start with low-fidelity learning prototypes first, to allow you to make changes on the fly. Then after you have gathered as much feedback as possible with low-fidelity prototypes, you can move to high-fidelity learning prototypes, getting more refined in the design and the feedback you are seeking to collect.

PAPER, LEGOS & THE WIZARD OF OZ

Prototypes can be made from all sorts of materials and there are dozens of options to try. Here are seven different types of prototypes. Consider which one might make your idea come alive:

- *Paper*
- *Storyboard*
- *Lego*
- *Role-Play*
- *Physical*
- *Wizard of Oz*
- *User-Driven*

Paper Prototypes

One of the most cost-effective and easy-to-create learning prototypes is the paper prototype. With as little as a piece of paper and a pen, you can sketch up what you visualize your idea to look like and show it to others to get feedback early on.

A while ago I was sharing an app idea with a friend over coffee. I explained how it was a mix of an old social media app, and it would integrate with Amazon, and had features of a food delivery service, too. He quickly scratched his head and replied, "Huh?"

"Hold on," I said and pulled out a piece of paper. "I'll show you."

And in a matter of minutes I'd drawn out the home screen and two other screens. All of a sudden, he was completely bought in. He grabbed the pen from me and started offering ideas and designing the look of certain items.

He quickly crossed out one feature. "This won't work, we've tried it at my company and you won't be able to use it to start. Maybe try something like this," he said as he drew a new option for my social media component.

The paper prototype is your go-to in the early phase of prototyping. It serves as a fantastic way to brainstorm with a team. Even before you write code or begin developing the product or idea, you can co-design your paper prototype to include all stakeholders in the design process.

Consider creating a paper prototype as a way to test your idea. People will feel more comfortable being critical and sharing insights because the mockup won't have a polished look and will feel more "open" to learning.

Storyboard Prototypes

As a kid I loved reading *Archie Comics*. Like a movie, the story would unfold through the pictures and dialogue and I was immersed in the antics of Archie and the gang. I was transported into their world and could feel what it must be like to live in Riverdale.

Tap into the process of visual thinking and planning and consider a storyboard prototype for your idea.

Movies are complex projects and require coordinating lots of people and expensive locations and equipment. In order to make sure they've got everything right, they start with a simple storyboard. My husband interacts with storyboards when the team describes what kinds of special effects are going to be needed for the movie. When they first showed him the scene of Brad Pitt on the moon, it looked like a cartoon sketch but it was enough for Ryan to get the picture.

To create your storyboard, try to imagine the complete user experience. Start with a piece of paper with pre-drawn boxes for you to create and draw a story into.

Perhaps your storyboard depicts a situation where your customer interacts with your product or service. Highlight the frustrations they feel before using your solution and then depict the relief they feel when they do use it.

Storyboard prototypes are great in allowing you to combine elements identified in steps one and two, highlighting tasks and goals of your users or customers. With a storyboard prototype in hand, you can share with others to spark new ideas through discussion and brainstorming, or use it as a way to generate consensus from stakeholders. It's a great learning prototype to help better understand the day in the life of your customers and create the world of your customers for others to learn from as well.

Lego Prototypes

We have a huge bucket of Legos in the center of our living room. Most days of the week you will find various phases of buildings and inventions from the "just starting" foundational green lego plank with some bricks around the perimeter all the way to the "destruction" zone of a once-built skyscraper laying in a heap of multicolored bricks.

Legos aren't just a fun toy for our toddler, they are a fantastic way to prototype your idea.

Legos are not only powerful because they are pre-formed modular symbols and shapes that can save you time in depicting your idea, there is also neuroscience that shows that using your hands can unlock creativity. So you may just find that constructing a prototype with Legos leads you to ideas you had never conceived before.

I've seen them used in everything from architectural prototypes to science experiments. Think about your idea, can a lego prototype be used to try to tell the story of your product or user journey? It's a fun way to engage with a team and is super easy to just rip off a brick and replace to tweak the look based on feedback.

Role-Play Prototypes

When pilots learn how to fly a plane, they get in the simulator and act it all out. The same thing works for your idea.

The role-play prototype is a fantastic way to engage a team into physically acting out what your user or customer may feel. You may need props or it may be enough to pantomime the different components of your interaction.

Not only will your team be involved in creating the prototype, when you all physically experience your prototype in action, you will remember the experience more vividly than when it is drawn out.

To create your role-play prototype create storylines and experiences that you want to script beforehand. Convene your stakeholders and co-designers into a room to help re-enact the scenes and allow team members to add new feelings, frustrations, and motivations as the role-playing unfolds.

Physical Prototypes

Similar to the lego prototype, a physical prototype is a mockup of your physical product that can be used for testing. These learning prototypes can be made up of any kind of material—from paper cut and folded together to depict a new board game to play-doh molded to prototype a new shape of candy.

Back in the day when we were upgrading our office space and designing the new headquarters of my startup—we got scrappy and creative in our physical prototype. Using the supplies strewn across my co-founder's often messy desk, we were able to hobble together a visual representation of the kitchen, common area, and cubicles with an Altoid tin for the reception desk and Altoid candies as the people moving about.

Seeing our space in a scaled-down, interactive 3D physical prototype allowed me and my co-founders to test different purposes for the space and think through how we might thoughtfully design our new office digs.

Consider a physical prototype for your work as a way to spark discussions and be able to react to something that you can literally hold in your hand.

Wizard of Oz Prototypes

Like the mystical, mighty Oz hiding behind the curtain, the Wizard of Oz prototype is one where a function is faked. This learning prototype allows you to mimic or fake the function of the item you are prototyping.

The story of the Mechanical Turk is unintentionally a great example of the Wizard of Oz prototype. In the late 18th century, Hungarian Wolfgang von Kempelen created an automated chess-playing machine as a gift to impress the Empress Maria Theresa of Austria. The machine appeared able to play a competitive game of chess against human opponents and defeated many challengers including Napoleon Bonaparte and Benjamin Franklin. Years later, it was revealed to be an elaborate hoax. Rather than being a machine, it actually had a chess master hiding inside, operating the machine.

Look at your idea, is there an opportunity to fake a functionality or interaction to learn from your customers or users?

User-Driven Prototypes

The user-driven prototype is where you flip the model, allowing the user to create something and by doing so, you learn more about the user's needs. In this learning prototype, you can uncover the desires of the user and also discover assumptions that they may hold.

Let's say you work at a coffee shop and you want to prototype an idea you have to improve the coffee lineup experience. You could ask a potential customer to draw out what they think is the ideal way to line up, order, and wait for their coffee order.

For the user-driven prototype to be the most valuable to your learning, you will have to balance how much prompting you give with how much you allow your potential user to be creative. Give too little direction and you risk the users feeling lost or confused. Or too much direction will stifle their ideas and defeat the whole purpose of your learning prototype.

ACTIVITY

GO FORTH & PROTOTYPE

It's time to get beyond the what-if dream of your idea and prototype it. Unlock the concept and move into a tangible learning prototype to gather feedback.

Start with either the low- or high-fidelity prototype and gather feedback before investing your time and effort into the big idea. It's like building out a set of nesting dolls—start with the smallest version first before you build out for the larger one.

To turn your idea into a learning prototype, follow these 6 steps to help you along.

1. **List Out the Components**
2. **Identify the Lessons to Learn**
3. **Determine the Right Fidelity**
4. **Decide on the Type of Learning Prototype**
5. **Gather Insights**
6. **Rinse & Repeat**

STEP 1: LIST OUT THE COMPONENTS

When you finally get to see your idea launch, it will be tested by the users, employees, or stakeholders you built it for. And if this is the first-ever test, you're likely to encounter some negative feedback on where there is need for changes or improvement. The success of your product's launch lies squarely on your ability to test and learn from your learning prototype.

But what *exactly* is your prototype testing?

Prototypes are the first time all the parts of your idea are tested together. It's like a band practicing for the first time. The drummer and guitarist may have learned their parts separately, but together they make (hopefully) beautiful music.

Start planning your learning prototype by identifying all the different components that make it up. For this step, write down the key elements of your idea with each element captured on a post-it.

Let's say I want to prototype a survival backpack idea as a new product for my outdoor and survival company.

Key elements of my idea that I capture might include:

Flame, heat, & water-resistant fabric

Multi-functional tool stored in right, side pocket

Flashlight & matches stored in left, side pocket

Think about your idea. What elements make up your idea? Take a moment to write down on post-its as many as come to mind.

As you find your writing slowing down, take a moment to pause and look at what you have put on your post-its. To help you in building out your list further, use the four components of prototyping (people, objects, location, and interactions) outlined below to further build out your idea's elements.

People

When you think about the "people" involved in your idea, this not only includes the users or customers you are building your learning prototype to test on, but also the stakeholders from whom you need buy-in.

For the backpack idea, I might add the following "people" components:

Customers are survival enthusiasts seeking an emergency go-bag

Stakeholders include senior product leader responsible for new product development

Take a moment to capture your "people" components. Ask yourself, "Who will be the users or customers of my idea?" and, "Who will be testing or observing the findings from my learning prototype?"

Objects

Consider the "objects" of your idea. This includes the prototype itself and the other artifacts that your people or prototype will interact with. These are the items external to the prototype—it's the product, service, or experience around your idea.

If I think about creating the new backpack, "objects" may include additional items the bag needs to hold. So someone looking to use an emergency go-bag will want my learning prototype to be able to store other personal emergency items in the bag. With this in mind, you could add the following "object" components:

Interior storage space for custom emergency gear

List of items that people should have in their emergency go-bag

Think about your idea and ask, "What objects will my learning prototype interact with? What objects does my learning prototype need to be a more fully-built example of my idea?" Write down the "objects" of your idea onto post-its.

Location

The "location" component of your prototype includes the places and environments that need to be considered for your idea. It's the "where" of your idea.

Considering the idea of creating a new emergency backpack, I may list out the different geo-locations that the customers may live in or various emergency situations they may face based on location. Or I might think about where the backpack would be stored and worn. Here I would add the following "location" components:

Customers in Great Plains, U.S. will need backpack to survive tornado emergencies

Customers may store backpack in garage or trunk of their car

Customers may wear and use the backpack during heavy rain

For your idea, start to write down your "location" elements. Ask yourself, "Where will my idea take place and where will it be used?"

Interactions

The final component to consider are the "interactions" that will occur between the people, objects, and location. Whether digital interactions for software or physical interactions for hardware, it requires the prototype to work between other components.

Again for the backpack idea, I might consider that the user will be making the purchase online. This requires a decision point from interacting with a website and, later, receiving the backpack via postal shipping. Thinking about these "interactions," I would create the list below:

Buyer will make a choice based on online images, product descriptions, & reviews

Buyer will input credit card to make purchase

Buyer will receive backpack via postal delivery

Take the time to start capturing your "interactions" needed for your prototype. Ask yourself, "How will my idea interact across different elements?" Think about your digital and physical interactions and capture each on a post-it.

When writing down the key elements of your idea, think practically about what needs to be tested. What are all the puzzle pieces that make up your prototype, including people, objects, location, and interactions? With these details in hand, you will be ready to move to the next step, determining the lessons and questions you need answered for each of these elements.

STEP 2: IDENTIFY THE LESSONS TO LEARN

Create your prototype to answer the outstanding questions and lessons you want to learn from the identified key components in step one. Taking a look at your list, where do you need to learn, collect feedback, and prototype again?

Let's go back to my backpack idea and some of the components identified and start adding questions.

Under the "people" component, I captured, "Customers are survival enthusiasts seeking an emergency go-bag." What do I need to learn from this as it relates to my learning prototype? When I build my idea out, what lesson do I hope to gain insights on?

Here's where I start to add post-its with different lessons I want to learn:

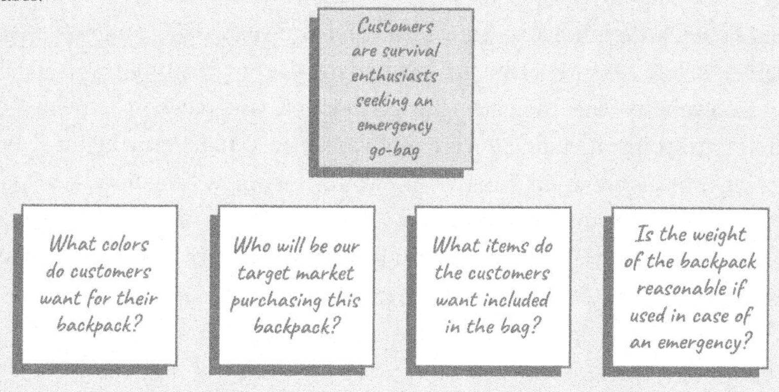

There's a lot more I could add. Here I'm thinking about my customers, but I would need to think about my stakeholders too.

As you start to write out the lessons you want to learn for each element captured, you will find that some could be lessons from an early-stage learning prototype while others a lesson from a later-stage learning prototype.

The way to figure out which type of prototype to build (high-fidelity or low-fidelity) is to prioritize which questions are the most important to learn from. You're going to come up with a lot of questions and won't have infinite time to answer them, so how will you know which ones are most important? There are two factors to consider: risk and knowability.

To map out risk and knowability, we'll use the chart below:

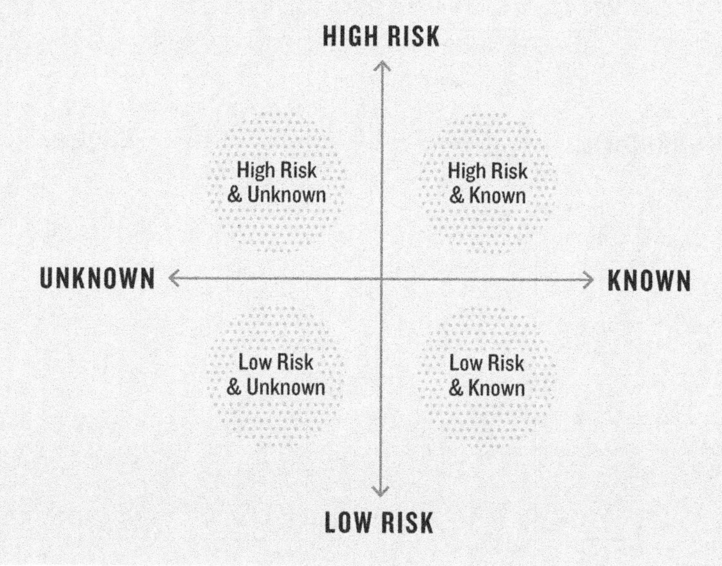

The risk will measure the impact of your assumptions around the questions can have on your idea. Questions you identify as "low risk" would have little impact on your idea whereas "high risk" could create big problems, like your idea causing harm to the user or customer.

Knowability will measure the confidence you have in knowing the answers to your questions. A "known" would be a question you have some insight into whereas an "unknown" would highlight questions you need more information to understand.

Weighing risk and knowability together will ensure that you prototype the highest priority issues and get to the important lessons earlier.

Now we go back to our list of "lessons I want to learn." There are a lot of options for questions to ask users. Let's map some of them out.

I'll pull out one to start with, "Is the weight of the backpack reasonable if used in case of an emergency?" This is an important question. One that if I get wrong, could result in major problems, especially if the customers are using it in an emergency. It's also a question I don't know much about. That goes into the upper left, "High Risk & Unknown" quadrant. This category is the one to pay attention to the most and the questions in it should be of the highest priority.

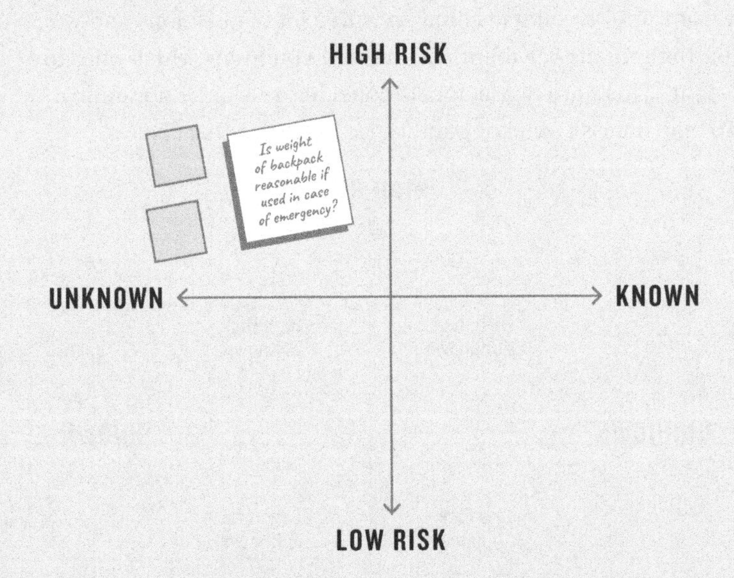

Another question from our list: "What colors do customers want for their backpack?"

This question immediately feels less significant. One with low risk, and most emergency backpacks and equipment have common colors, so this is known. We'll map this into the lower right "Low Risk & Known" quadrant—the category we need to pay attention to the least. These can be back-burner questions to prototype for later.

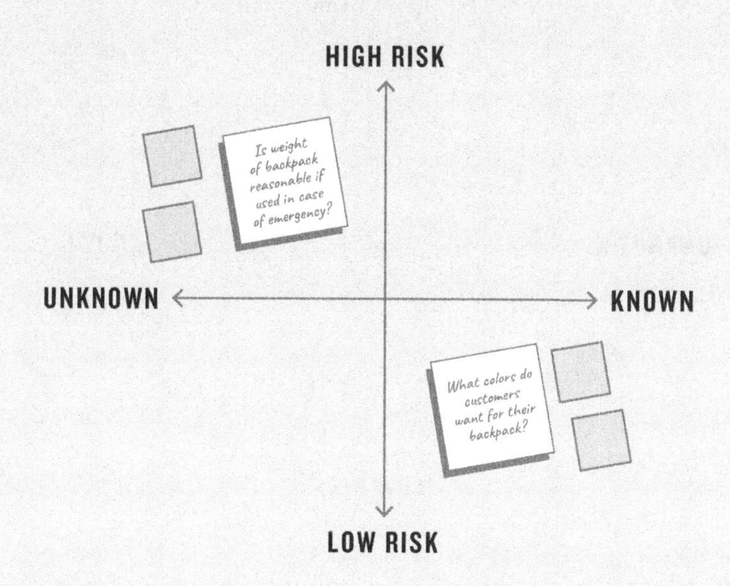
HIGH RISK
Is weight of backpack reasonable if used in case of emergency?
UNKNOWN
KNOWN
What colors do customers want for their backpack?
LOW RISK

The two other categories, "Low Risk & Unknown" and "High Risk & Known," fall somewhere in the middle of the prioritization spectrum. "High Risk & Known" would look something like our question, "What size must the backpack be to conveniently store in the trunk of a car?" Important, yes, but do we know what size most car trunks are? Also, yes. With the information known, we don't need to make it a priority to solve this lesson. The initial design of the prototype should take this into consideration.

The "Low Risk & Unknown" category is filled with questions like, "How many zippers does the bag need?" While we may not know how many zippers the customer ideally would like, the risk isn't high. No one's going to get hurt if there aren't enough zippers. It's still something to consider later on but won't make or break the prototype.

After having prioritized your questions, you'll have a sense of where to focus your energies first. Keep an eye on the "High Risk" categories and prioritize your questions to get a focused answer, concentrating on the riskiest and least known.

With these findings in hand, you are ready for the next step, figuring out the right level of detail and finish for your prototype.

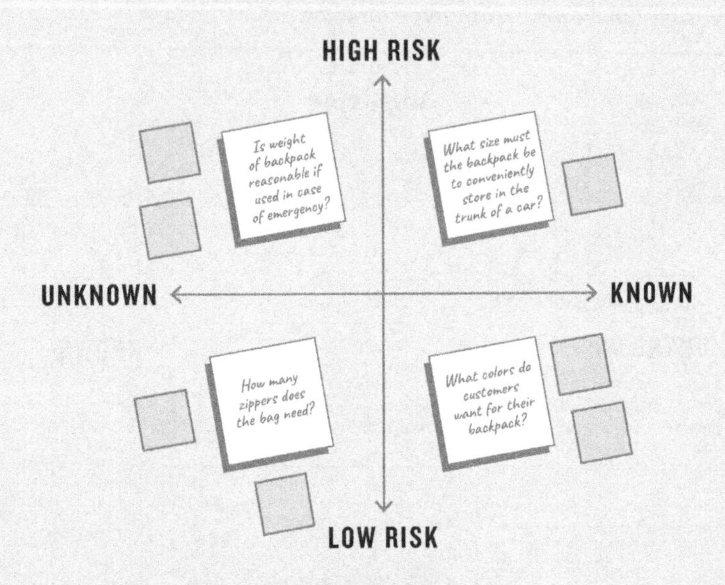
HIGH RISK
Is weight of backpack reasonable if used in case of emergency?
What size must the backpack be to conveniently store in the trunk of a car?
UNKNOWN
KNOWN
How many zippers does the bag need?
What colors do customers want for their backpack?
LOW RISK

STEP 3: DETERMINE THE RIGHT FIDELITY

Your prototypes won't necessarily look like the final product, service, or idea you are building toward. Before that final version, you will need to create multiple prototypes to test the various questions along the way. Typically, with each new prototype you'll get closer and closer to the real thing. This will ensure that you are able to stay true to your concept while also building something that people want.

But how much time and resources should you spend on creating the prototype? Before you embark on creating your prototypes, you need to identify the fidelity required. That is to say, what is the level of detail, realism, and functionality you need built into your prototype to learn from it?

You will need to identify whether you need to build a low-fidelity or high-fidelity prototype.

A low-fidelity prototype is most often in paper form, ranging from a series of hand-drawn mockups to more sophisticated printouts. These can be useful in the early-stage learning prototypes to get people to visualize the solution to provoke ideas and improvements. It's easy to create these prototypes. They will cost less time and resources to execute on and will get the audience to focus on the concept. Because it's early-phase and not completely built out, people providing feedback may be more comfortable suggesting changes.

Conversely, the high-fidelity learning prototype allows for a more realistic experience or user interaction. These prototypes will take more time and resources to create but are better at collecting performance data, such as how long it takes the user to complete the task. A high-fidelity prototype can be more useful later in your idea process to understand more about behaviors and feelings.

To land on what type of prototype you need to build, consider what you are trying to solve. What are you trying to communicate through your prototype and how should the prototype allow for you to test and evaluate whether it achieves that?

To identify the fidelity required of your prototype, answer the following questions with a simple "yes" or "no."

- *Is there clarity on what questions need to be answered? Y/N*
- *Can my audience understand and follow a series of hand-sketched visuals to share what stands out to them? Y/N*
- *Could I create a prototype that answers my doubts with little or no resources? Y/N*
- *Would my stakeholders be happy with only basic findings and lessons from the prototype? Y/N*

If you answered mostly "yes" to the above questions, you should create a low-fidelity prototype. This will allow you to focus on learning from the design and concept of your idea, gathering inspiration rather than focusing on specifics or technical aspects of your prototype.

If you answered mostly "no," you are ready to create a high-fidelity prototype. This requires you to pinpoint the components you want to test and gives you the ability to get detailed feedback on certain elements surrounding your idea.

An equal mix of "yes" and "no" suggests you start with a low-fidelity prototype, which will answer the questions that will get you from a mix of "yes" and "no" to a full list of "no." Then you can move to a high-fidelity prototype.

Jennifer, a partner at a law firm, wanted to prototype a new service to offer her clients. When she went through the questions listed above, she had a mix of "yes" and "no" answers.

Sitting in her brightly lit conference room, she answered the prototype questions with me. I could tell from her answers that she needed to start with a low-fidelity prototype. She was unsure of how many customers would be interested in the new service and how much she could help them. She wanted to learn the best way to move forward, and instead of investing a lot of time or money into an idea she wasn't sure of, she started small.

When you are approaching your prototypes, make sure to identify what you want to learn, the needs of your user audience, expectations of your stakeholders, and resources available. With these factors evaluated, you can identify the right fidelity of your prototype and go to the final step—deciding what type of learning prototype to create.

STEP 4: DECIDE ON THE TYPE OF LEARNING PROTOTYPE

With steps 1 through 3 completed, you are ready to figure out what type of prototype best fits your idea. You have identified the components to your idea, the lessons you need to learn, and the best level of fidelity, giving you the information to help inform what type of prototype to consider.

As described above, there are seven common types of prototypes to consider: paper, storyboard, Lego, role-play, physical, Wizard of Oz, and user-driven prototypes. Each has a different strategy and opportunity to test different aspects of the intended design. Understanding the different types of prototypes, you will then be able to identify the one that can best serve you through each phase of your prototyping.

Go back through the different kinds of prototypes and reflect on which one will be the most helpful in revealing insights. Which type will help you learn more about what does and doesn't work for your big idea? Throughout the process of prototyping, be diligent to capture your findings and lessons learned. This will enable you to continue to iterate, prototyping again and again as you draw nearer to creating your finished version for launch.

STEP 5: GATHER INSIGHTS

Finally, you've built your prototype and are ready to gather insights. Now you have the opportunity to show your prototype to others and get feedback. At this stage you'll need to do a few things.

First, frame what you're looking for.

When you sit down with people, make sure they know exactly what you want feedback on. You don't have to tell them everything you *don't* want feedback on, but make sure you set expectations.

Some good things to tell users:

- *"I just want to see how you interact with this feature. Use it like you would naturally and let me know if there's anything confusing or surprising about it."*
- *"I'm worried this will be too heavy for people to use daily and concerned that they won't use it regularly. How does it feel to you?"*
- *"Would you mind going through the purchasing process and let me know what sticks out to you?"*

Use the prototype to have a conversation. Let the prototype speak for itself and see how users react to it.

Remind them to explore the prototype in an open and curious way. Avoid pointing things out to them—instead ask broad questions. This way, you might learn more about their motivations and how they really feel.

Then, listen to what people are saying.

If you're showing someone your prototype and all they're saying is, "This is awesome!" That's not really what you want to hear. It means you aren't learning and that's either because they aren't the right audience to test with or you don't have the right prototype for them to share valuable insights on.

Choose your users and audience well. If you're creating a tool for doctors, make sure you're testing it with doctors, not nurses. It's important that the people giving you insights have the experience and knowledge about how your idea needs to work in order for them to use it.

Remember that people believe what they want to believe about something, a type of confirmation bias. If it sounds like they're trying to be too positive, prompt them with questions about what could be improved.

Take notes, record their insights, and ask probing questions. Don't get defensive and stay open to all their feedback on the prototype—you're here to learn, not be right.

Lastly, choose how to use insights.

The great thing about insights is that they're insightful. Sometimes they'll show you you're right on track, other times they'll illuminate a problem area or confusing piece of your idea. With these insights, you'll have a better understanding of what to do and where to go. Adapt what needs adapting and use the insights to build a better offering.

Remember, you don't need to test it with 100 people. Just start with five. If you're testing out a new walkway and the first five people trip over the steps—you don't need to send 95 more people down to validate that something needs to be changed.

Test early and often. Use your insights to keep prototyping and learning as you go.

STEP 6: RINSE & REPEAT

Once you have a learning prototype completed, take your insights and make changes and improvements on your idea to prototype again. As time goes on, the fidelity of your prototype will increase.

You can go back through steps 1 through 5 to help you on the journey of learning from each prototype that you create. You'll get closer and closer to landing on the best product, service, or form of your idea.

How will you know when to stop prototyping? Well, usually you will have time constraints. A timeline that you have to "launch by" and the prototyping will have to come to an end then. If you find yourself in a situation where you have an endless amount of time to prototype, you will have to be disciplined enough to ensure you do enough prototyping, but not too much.

The more you prototype, you will start to see a diminishing return on the lessons learned. You'll be making small, incremental improvements to your idea and the prototypes won't have the same payoff of insights and aha moments.

When this starts happening, it may be time to launch your idea. Time to actually execute on your idea outside of the petri dish in the lab.

As you go through the process of creating the learning prototypes, you are not only learning how to make your idea better, but you are learning what it takes to create within your company and one step closer to bringing your idea into the world.

Getting to this point won't be easy, but it's the payoff you have been working toward. The "see, we can do this" moment that will feel like completing Magellan's voyage circumnavigating the globe, proving that the world is indeed not flat.

TURN A *NO* INTO A *YES*

The Art of Co-Creation

When I was a kid and wanted something, I mean really wanted something, I would strategize how to get my parents to say "yes."

Yes, we can get the slip 'n' slide you saw on TV for the front yard. Yes, you can have brown sugar sprinkled on top of your spaghetti, just this once.

And as I got older, the requests got bigger and with that, the strategizing became more complex.

When I was 16, I wanted to drive two hours to where my favorite bands would be playing. The Butthole Surfers would be opening for the Toadies in San Antonio—two bands I loved and despite the names, still rock out to on occasion.

I had been driving to and from school and work for some time but I knew that driving out of town in the evening would be a big ask. I also knew there was no way we wanted one of our parents to drive us.

Despite these challenges, I started to lay the groundwork for how to get to a "yes" from my parents.

"Whoa, the Toadies are going to be in San Antonio soon, I wonder if tickets are sold out?" I casually mentioned it to my mom.

She didn't pay much attention to my question, but I considered the seed planted. Later I shared the great news, "They do have tickets! It's March 9th, can I go?"

"What time? In San Antonio?" my mom asked, full attention on my big ask.

"Doors open at 8 p.m., so I'll probably leave here around 6 p.m. and be home by 2 a.m.," I shared as straight-faced as an excited teenager could.

"Not a chance. You aren't driving with your friends, at night, out of town," my mom replied.

I started to come up with rebuttals but she wasn't having it and told me to quit asking. It wasn't going to happen.

Back to the drawing board. If I wanted to get my mom to say "yes," I needed a better strategy.

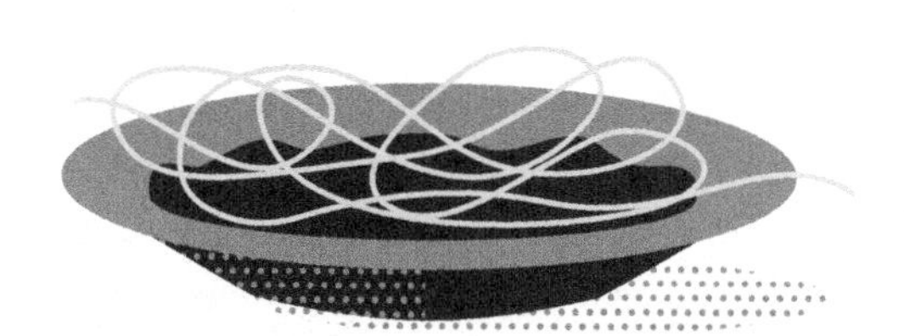

How could I prove that we'd be safe? What plan would she say "yes" to?

I went to my room, determined to make it happen and started making a list of arguments and points that would help:

- *I already drive to/from work waiting tables at these late hours. Why is that okay but this isn't?*
- *I could get the car's oil changed, gas up, and make sure it's safe to drive the long distance.*
- *One of my friends had family that lived in San Antonio, we could crash there and come back the next day.*

I went back to my mom in the kitchen and shared some of my thoughts. I knew better than to whine. Instead, I shared that I understood why she might be concerned and that I may have come up with some things for her to consider.

We talked through my list and she said she'd think about it.

A couple days later, after I got my car tuned up and inspected, and she talked to my friend's family, she felt comfortable with my idea. We could go in my car if we didn't drive after we arrived in San Antonio and returned the next morning.

As an adult, it's pretty easy to see why my mom would say no. Anything could have gone wrong. The other drivers, the driving at night, the concert itself.

As a 16-year-old, I was upset but knew that by seeing things from her perspective, I would be able to work out an agreement with my mom that made sense for both of us.

When we really want something and are passionate about it, it can take time to get to the "yes." But if we're willing to see the "no" as an opportunity to problem-solve and build trust, we might just get the keys to the car after all.

WHY "NO"

While we're not trying to get the car keys from our parents anymore, there are a lot of reasons you'll hear a "no" when trying to launch your big idea. Sometimes you'll get a "no" from someone just because they want to say "no." They might perceive you as a threat or stepping on their toes.

Having launched 25 different initiatives in big companies over the last 20 years, I've heard "no" hundreds of times. There's an opportunity to hear "no" almost every day, especially if you include the minutia. In those hundreds of times I've heard the word "no," I've rarely stopped pursuing my project. I view a "no" as an opportunity to solve the problem differently.

When you're solving a puzzle and one piece doesn't fit into another, we don't throw the whole thing away. We enter problem-solving mode. "Okay, maybe I need to turn the piece, or try a different piece, or wait until later to use this piece." In the puzzle of launching an idea, every "no" is a sign that the pieces aren't working that way and there's an invitation to try something different.

Last summer I took my son, Bear, to a cornfield maze. We wandered around the big corn stalks looking for our way to the other side. Bear trudged forward and when given the chance to go left or right at a fork, he pointed his small finger left, "This way!"

He confidently marched forward until he turned the next corner only to find a dead end. He stared up at the big wall or corn stalks and turned back to me, pouting and said, "I don't like this anymore. I want to play a different game!"

Now Bear is only 3 and a half, but his first reaction isn't that different from those of us launching our ideas. We're wired to take a "no" as a roadblock or barrier and feel discouraged at our perceived failure.

"Bear," I explained, "It's okay. We're actually even closer than we were before. Now we can go back and know the right way to go. We just have to find another way!"

It took a little convincing, but soon he was running in the opposite direction yelling, "We're getting closer!"

You'll hit these same sorts of barriers as you launch your idea. If everyone who tried to launch something big or create something new turned away at their first "no," the world would look a lot different.

Edison's light bulb was initially mocked by the British Parliament Committee, who said his ideas were "good enough for our Transatlantic friends... but unworthy of the attention of practical or scientific men." Similarly, the beloved Harry Potter books received 12 rejections in a row, until the daughter of a Bloomsbury editor demanded to read the rest of the book. They reluctantly published the book and advised JK Rowling to get a day job.

A "no" is always a chance to learn how to move forward differently. By being curious and asking more questions you'll learn ways to make your idea more likely to succeed. For the most part, these "nos" have reasons behind them. Someone knows something about how this thing might not work, you might as well choose to learn from them.

There's a lot of insight buried in a "no." Maybe you learn more about the process behind getting an idea passed, or more about your company's budget, or about the best timing to launch. The more you learn, the closer you'll be to finding a different way around, or maybe turning that "n"o into a "yes."

This isn't about being manipulative and tricking people to get what you want to support your idea. It's about working together to create something that's really going to work.

After hearing hundreds of nos, I've codified a few of the top reasons you'll get a no and ways to move past them. We'll dive into each one:

1. *But the Data Says...*
2. *Get Past the Troll, Pay the Toll*
3. *Your Performance*
4. *You Aren't the Right Person*
5. *We've Already Tried It*

Reason 1: But The Data Says...

Data is important, no doubt about it. Most companies make decisions based on data and with good reason. Data shows market trends, customer insights, and bottom-line projections. At this stage in your idea, you should know the data, and the data should support your idea. (If not, you need to look for more data or tweak your idea to fit the data.)

You can prove that customers want what you have to offer through data. You can show how much time and money the company will save by implementing your idea. You might even be able to use the data to demonstrate how many millions of dollars will be made.

What happens when, despite the data, you still get a "no"?

The problem with using data to turn a "no" into a "yes" is that numbers, percentages, and bar charts don't always change minds. Oftentimes, people make decisions based on their gut or experience despite the data. There's an art to combining the data with a human component. It takes intentional practice.

There's an internal practice that Amazon employees use when they're presenting a new idea or initiative. They are required to write an internal press release and a six-page narrative detailing their idea and why the company should pursue it. The press release quickly identifies the problem, the value this new idea will bring to the customer, and how customers would react. This exercise ensures that ideas are data-driven and human-driven, providing both reasons why an idea will succeed.

Brittain Ladd wrote about this process for *Forbes* and shared, "I wrote multiple press releases when I worked for Amazon, I read numerous press releases, and I taught others how to write press releases. I never witnessed a product or service become a reality if the press release didn't effectively identify the value of the product or service to the customer. Ever."

"The rule of thumb I used at Amazon was this: If it was hard to write a press release or understand why a product or service would add value to customers, the product or service wasn't worth the effort. Move on."

The value in the press release was done right alongside a six-page narrative that contained the data to support what the press release promised. "Just like the press release, I never witnessed a product or service become a reality at Amazon unless the six-pager contained the required data and was able to clearly articulate the value to customers and to Amazon."[1]

Changing minds, or even getting someone to understand your perspective, means appealing to their values over your own. Some people claim to be "data people" but most others aren't moved or motivated by that. They might care about employee retention or customer engagement but if the numbers you're showing them are focused on revenue, it's not going to get them excited. Instead ask yourself: What data matters to them? And how do I display that in a way that makes sense?

And if you're still getting a "no," try a different approach. Be vulnerable. Ask, "What am I missing?" Their answer will tell you volumes. If they give you advice on your data, segmentation, and numbers, they're probably a data person but you don't have the data that's convincing them. If they bring up something else unrelated to the data, you'll realize they're not a data person and will need to appeal to them in another way.

Proceed with caution and present data without your own emotions taking over. It's normal to be excited about the idea and even more excited when the data backs it up, but people will probably poke holes and resist the sources. Don't get caught up in, "But I'm right! The data proves it! They're all idiots!" At the end of the day, it's your job to sell the story behind your idea, not just *present* data.

[1]Ladd, B. (2018, August 28). These Tools Are Why Amazon Is Successful. Retrieved March 25, 2020, from https://www.forbes.com/sites/brittainladd/2018/08/27/these-two-things-are-what-make-amazon-amazon/#44499fb35fd5

Craft a narrative with the data. Answer the question: What will this allow us to do? Connect the dots between the numbers and what that means for the people standing in front of you.

"This decrease in wasted time will save us 5,000 man-hours per month, giving us $75,000 on the bottom line every month which finally gives us the buffer to create the charitable fund we've been talking about."

When you understand what's important to the people in front of you, you can frame your message to connect to the value others are looking for. Use this opportunity to either find more data, or make your data mean something.

Reason 2: Get Past the Troll, Pay the Toll

There's an old nursery rhyme called *The Three Billy Goats Gruff*, where three billy goats are trying to cross a bridge over a river to eat some grass on the other side. They're stopped by an angry troll who lives beneath the bridge. "You can't pass the bridge! I want to eat you up," says the troll.

Understandably, the goats tell the troll, "No, we don't want to be eaten," and in that moment, the troll and the billy goats are at a standstill (not for long—but I won't give away the ending).

Sometimes, when you get a "no" from someone, it can feel a lot like this. The other side seems totally ridiculous (like a troll with no good reason to say no to your simple request. All you're trying to do is cross a bridge, after all).

But when you encounter someone like this, their "no" still matters, they still present a very real barrier to your idea's success.

A friend of mine, Daniel, used to work in a secret lab in The American Museum of Natural History. He ran experiments that required a chemical he often got shipped to the museum. This chemical was testy—it had to be kept at a very specific temperature and if it fell below that, the chemical was ruined and the experiment at risk.

One day he was waiting for his shipment to arrive and kept himself busy with other work. He lost track of time and realized the package was scheduled to be delivered hours before. He checked the status and it was marked "Delivered 2 hours ago."

Worried about his temperature-sensitive chemical, he ran out of the office and hurried down the hall to the mail cart. Nothing—no package there. He continued around the building, checking stranded boxes on desks. He made his way to the mailroom where a few of the mail delivery people were sorting through envelopes.

"Have you seen a box marked for the lab? Name on it Daniel? It's a temperature controlled package."

One of the mail delivery guys, Tom, stopped sorting mail and replied, "Oh yeah, I think we got something a couple hours ago. We're behind here so we didn't have a chance to bring it up yet. It's in the back over there." He pointed to a stack of boxes on the counter.

Daniel could see the box dripping with condensation. He picked it up and it was warm—the chemical was definitely ruined. He explained to the mail guys what had happened.

"Ah man, we had no idea. Didn't even notice it was temperature-sensitive," Tom said.

Daniel took total responsibility, "It's not your fault. I'm sorry I wasn't paying more attention. I should have told you I was expecting something. It's totally my fault. You guys are super busy down here. I had no idea it was this crazy!"

And just like that—Daniel had created allies. He didn't get upset, there was no point now. He was kind to the mailmen, and in response, they started to look out for one another.

Daniel started to check in on the mailroom more regularly and always let them know when he was expecting something (and even once he brought them brownies). The mailroom guys always looked out for Daniel's packages. They'd run them up to him if they could and if they were busy, they'd always call him immediately. (They didn't do this for anyone else in the building.)

Sometimes, getting past a "no" or a barrier looks like paying the toll to get past the troll. In this case, it was simply treating other people like they were human and developing allies instead of creating enemies when something went wrong.

We're not saying that you work with trolls. But there are surely gatekeepers that stand between you and where you want to go—and these people are important. Treat them like they're on your team (because they are) and you'll get a lot further.

Innovation work takes a lot of people and a lot of support. You'll get closer to a "yes" the more you can build coalitions and allies. Show up, give your time, have thoughtful conversations, and you might just turn a troll's "no" into an ally's "yes."

Reason 3: Your Performance

"I'm sorry, but we don't think you're ready for this sort of role."

When trying to launch your big idea, hearing that you won't be able to lead it can be tough. And you will probably be told a version of this at some point in your career. Instead of getting defensive, acknowledge that you are always looking to grow professionally. Ask what things this person sees as places you fall short on and take note. Don't get defensive and point out where they are wrong but instead listen. Recognize that whether the person's reasons seem valid or not, their perception is their reality and one that you need to overcome.

Imagine you were invited to a Thanksgiving dinner hosted by your friend and fifteen other people are coming. You graciously offered to bring the turkey. You've never made a turkey before, but after a spiral down YouTube videos you're feeling ready to conquer the task.

The big day finally comes and you wake up early to get started. You're pulling the turkey out of the freezer and start to preheat the oven while you glance over the directions one more time.

"Remove your thawed turkey from the refrigerator..." Uh oh.

Your turkey is fully frozen—and big. You don't totally panic. A quick Google search reveals that you can still make it work, you just need a few more hours. You put the turkey in right away but as you count the hours you need for the turkey and the hours you have until you have to leave, it's not adding up. By the looks of it you're going to be late—very late for the Thanksgiving lunch your friend has planned.

You spend the next few hours watching the turkey cook, trying to will it to cook faster. No luck. You do the best you can but end up bringing the turkey two hours late. The sides are cold, the people are hungry, and you feel awful.

Realizing your mistake, you try to explain the story but the hungry guests are louder than you. It was your first time cooking a turkey, you still got it there, and everyone enjoyed it. Next year, though, your friend will definitely not ask you to bring the turkey.

It was your inexperience in turkey cooking that ended up costing you two hours and your reputation to cook one in the future. This same thing happens at work and in our companies. Someone might tell you you're not ready to lead an innovation effort because of your lack of experience.

Maybe you sent out a report with numbers that weren't right, or an important email with typos. Or maybe you're just new to the team and they're afraid to support your idea without having seen enough of your experience and performance.

Remember, whatever the reason for this "no," don't get defensive. Ask questions about what parts of your performance haven't been up to speed and take note of how you might be able to showcase your abilities next time.

And if you're new and made a Thanksgiving-style mistake—that's okay. Experience comes with time. Accept that you've made a mistake and learn from it.

Once you've had a candid conversation with the person you're getting the "no" from, thank them for their insights and take time to self-reflect.

What have you learned from others to help you improve upon your idea? With time, you will start to exhibit your growth.

In the meantime, find out where you do qualify, and take steps to help on that front. Maybe you don't have enough experience in leading a massive project, but how might you break down the project into something smaller, and drive that first?

Take time to understand where there are viewed shortcomings and identify where you can still carve out a place to create impact. Consider joining forces with someone who can fill the "experience gap" or create some buy-in with higher level leadership to build more trust. Keep working towards your "yes."

When you approach these missteps and lack of experience as an opportunity to learn, you show the people around you that you can grow, handle feedback, and implement changes. In the long term, these qualities are instrumental in innovation and will get you a lot further than an angry, defensive response to their "no." Remember, it's not necessarily a "no" forever, it's a "no" for now with a lot of opportunity to change it to a "yes".

Reason 4: It's Not You, It's Someone Else

"Sorry, you're not the right person to lead this. We think someone else is a better fit."

When it comes to doing the work of our idea, no one likes to hear that someone else can do it better—even if it's the other person's job. But if you hear something like this, there are still options to move forward. First, don't consider that your work on this idea is done. You might not be the person to lead, but maybe you're the best person to add new ideas to the conversation, or perhaps you're one of the people who are most passionate about the problem and understand the issue you're trying to solve. A supporting role in this case is almost always an option.

If your team is trying to push forward a front-facing, UX-centered idea and you're a back-end developer—you might not be the best person to lead the solution. You might be a great project manager, but the new initiative might call for someone who's closer to the marketing team.

Acknowledging that there is a supporting role for you will give you the chance to be at the table when the "right person" who's leading can open doors for you down the line. Ask if you can be part of the conversation or included in meetings. Approach the person who is the right fit, and ask if you can help them make the idea happen. Your contribution at these early entry points can lead to a more formal role and increase the level of participation later.

Other times, an experiment or idea will fall into someone else's job description. Maybe this person doesn't have time for the project. Perhaps this person isn't interested. Or the person has tried in the past and failed.

When you ask your boss or manager for buy-in on a project that falls under someone else's paycheck, you're likely to stir up a response like, "Well, why aren't they doing that?"

And if you suggest it to those people, they're likely to respond, "Don't tell me how to do my job."

The good news is that there's someone else who you can turn into an ally, and while you might not be responsible, it allows you to help. Is the project something that you could lead together, or could you help create a team of passionate people to assist this person?

It may not be the sole ownership you were planning on, but it can provide an unexpected co-founder. Take this as an opportunity to find a place to collaborate. Express your passion for the project and offer help where you think you can add value.

Focus on impact rather than the formality of who owns what.

Sometimes you might hear, "No, you're not the right person for this" because you have a full time job doing job A. This point can be a difficult one to argue. You were hired to do job A, and you are asking to do job B—how will you ensure that job A has 100% coverage?

Is the concern that your current role or job would fall short? Do you have a big project on your plate or have you had a recent failure in execution?

Both are legitimate reasons for someone to believe you aren't a good fit for taking on one more thing. It is your responsibility to show your ability to perform in your current role and in the capacity you are suggesting for the added idea. (You don't want your idea to be your first failure or lack of experience mishap.)

At a previous company, I worked closely with someone in the HR department. She wanted to implement an idea that revolved around mental and emotional wellness—but the company had already outsourced this space to a wellness agency who offered meditation days and gave out stress balls. They weren't ready to take any other steps and saw the initiative as something the outside agency would take care of—so my friend had to get creative on why she was allowed to start the project. She pitched it as a preventative measure, one that would increase employee retention (her main job focus).

It was easier to push the idea as a measure to increase retention rather than the separate category the executive team had labeled it. She ended up using different language, words that were closer to what she normally did to describe what the project would look like.

It's not easy hearing that you're not the right person for the job. Especially if you're excited and passionate about it. But it will be a long, hard journey if you're trying to jam a square peg into a round hole. Maybe you ARE the right person for the job—but if they're telling you you're not, it's worth it to stop and listen to address their concerns. You'll build more trust that way, and if you really listen to their insights you might even end up with a tweaked idea that's even better suited for you in the long run.

Reason 5: Been There, Done That

"We've already tried that before and it didn't go well. It doesn't work here."

What a deflating response. It doesn't even pretend to be interested in the idea and totally rejects it before you can even share more details. If you're paying attention, though, this can be one of the most insightful responses you can get.

When I joined the California Department of Education, one of the projects I worked on had been tried and failed before I arrived. The idea was wonderful, and had been executed to some extent. They'd curated a repository of curriculum, resources, and a huge database pulled from some of the best content creators for teachers to search through and use to make their lives easier.

I was amazed at how such a beautiful and helpful product hadn't been launched officially, and that educators weren't using it. The team had tried a few things before, but the resounding response I got was, "It's just not something teachers are ever going to use. We've tried. It just doesn't work."

Similar to finding my way through the corn maze with my son, I realized my colleagues were coming up against a lot of dead ends. They were stuck. It had been years of work and they didn't see a way out. I took a similar approach to getting out of the corn maze: enter the problem-solving mode.

Okay, so if that way doesn't work, which way will? Slowly, through getting lunch and coffee with different people who had been part of the project, I collected all the reasons it had failed, all the dead ends, and all of the bitter complaints about the process.

Surely if I knew all the ways it didn't work, I could piece together some ways that might. I created new questions and presented other opportunities and ideas to the team. It took a lot of reframing the solution before I could get to a, "Maybe that could work."

A lot of people on the team were hoping we could come up with a new solution, but many felt too defeated from the failures. I framed the failures as learning opportunities and spent more time digging in with the people behind what "didn't work." This helped to uncover new ways for things that "could work." It also gave people the permission to acknowledge the failure and with time, let go of the bitterness.

Sometimes it's timing, sometimes it's execution, and sometimes it's just dumb luck. Whatever the reason, just because something failed once doesn't mean it's doomed to fail in the future.

In hearing about what didn't work, are you uncovering something that you didn't know about? If it's new information, that's valuable feedback that you can put thought behind to understand better.

Ask questions about timelines, what they tried, and why it didn't work. Show genuine interest in learning and understanding. Leave the conversation with an open-ended comment like, "This was so useful to learn about. I would like to think about these points and see if I can come up with some other ideas. Given your experience and tenure with the company, would you be willing to chat again after I have had some time to put some ideas together?"

Keep in mind the "we've tried it already" objection is not the be-all and end-all. Use this opportunity to try new things and build relationships with the other people you're working with. Leverage their knowledge to find a better way forward, together.

LIFE AFTER "NO"

Getting a "no" is a hard place to be, but take heart, there are so many ways to move forward from a "no." Once you've identified what "no" camp you're in, you'll better understand the underlying reason and how you can work to move through it. Not all "nos" are "no" forever. What can you take from what you've learned to move closer to a "yes" or even a "maybe"?

My friend Rachel started at a large enterprise SaaS company and joined a new group that would help improve the experience of clients. The project had its own team and had a hard time working with sales and marketing, but they needed the constant approval from both departments to implement their new client experience model.

Sales said, "Look if you get in the way of our funnel, clients are going to drop off and then we just lost this big sale. So we're not going to just let you come in here and try this new thing."

Rachel knew there was only one way forward: slowly. She started spending lots of time with the people who were getting in her way. The more "nos" she got, the more she dug in and tried to understand them. Over time, she would find small ways to get closer to her idea, "Can I come and just listen-in on one of your calls with that client?"

Then one step even closer, "Can I send the client that one email that you saw and liked?" And over time as she was chipping away at the group of naysayers, she built allies. Her job was getting done and the marketing and sales teams weren't losing clients. The process evolved to something that worked better for everyone.

She didn't turn the "no" into a "yes" overnight, but she slowly got closer as more people trusted and became comfortable with her. Most "nos" don't change overnight. In reality, the process looks more like turning a "no" into a "well, maybe" and then into an "okay."

ACTIVITY

ONE MAYBE AT A TIME

Turning a "no" into a "yes" is not about manipulating someone to get what you want. It's about co-creation and problem-solving. It's not about *my* idea or *your* idea. It's about the idea and initiative that gets the best result for the business, customer, or client.

When we approach this work thinking more about other people and collaborating to make something amazing, that's when the real magic happens. The sooner you talk to other people, the sooner you ask them what they think, the more the co-creation process grows.

Imagine you're the CEO of a big company and someone comes into your office to schedule a meeting. Which of these feel like they're going to go better?

> *"Alright boss! Buckle your seat belt. I've got an incredible idea and it's going to blow your mind."*
>
> Or
>
> *"I've been thinking about this idea and it's been keeping me up at night that our users can't access what they need. I spent some time researching potential solutions. What do you think?"*

Instead of focusing on how to get a "yes" and blow someone away (which rarely works) think about how to just get a "maybe." One "maybe" at a time, and one conversation at a time, will get you a lot further than trying to bulldoze through a "no".

No Because, Maybe If, Then What

When you're trying for a maybe, you're looking for the ingredients to change. "Maybe" is often followed by "if." The potential agreement is contingent on a change.

To dissect each "no," we're going to move them through the process of *No Because → Maybe If → Then What.*

Start with three columns on a board or wall: *No Because | Maybe If | Then What*

No Because

The far left is your "No Because" column. With your "nos" you always have a "because." If you don't know the reason behind the "no" this is the time to investigate. Take a minute to list out all the "nos" and all the reasons for each one.

"**No**, you can't run this new program **because** your job is to run the office space, not focus on cultivating the culture of the people here."

NO BECAUSE | **MAYBE IF** | **THEN WHAT**

No, you can't run this new program because your job is to run the office space, not focus on cultivating the culture of the people here.

Keep thinking on what reasons you are hearing for why you might not be able to take on the project.

Once you have your "No Because" you can start brainstorming what would move you past into the "Maybe If" column.

Maybe If

"Maybe If" is your opportunity to take the "no" and provide other opportunities that might work instead.

If your boss said "no" to the idea because the work wasn't in your job description, your "Maybe If" might read:

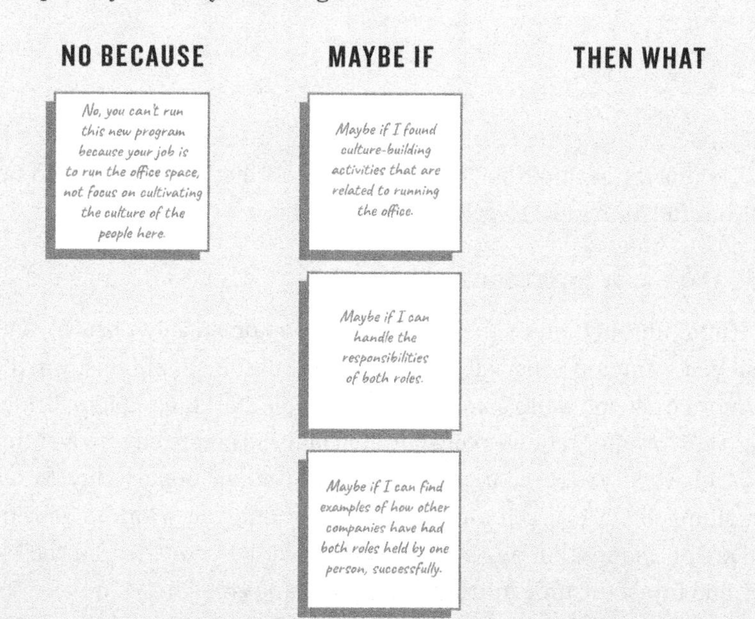
NO BECAUSE
MAYBE IF
THEN WHAT
No, you can't run this new program because your job is to run the office space, not focus on cultivating the culture of the people here.
Maybe if I found culture-building activities that are related to running the office.
Maybe if I can handle the responsibilities of both roles.
Maybe if I can find examples of how other companies have had both roles held by one person, successfully.

After you have potential solutions, you can come up with more concrete actions to input into the "Then What" category.

Then What

Now it's time to take your "Maybe Ifs" and turn them into actions. If you need to find culture-building activities that are related to running an office, where would you start?

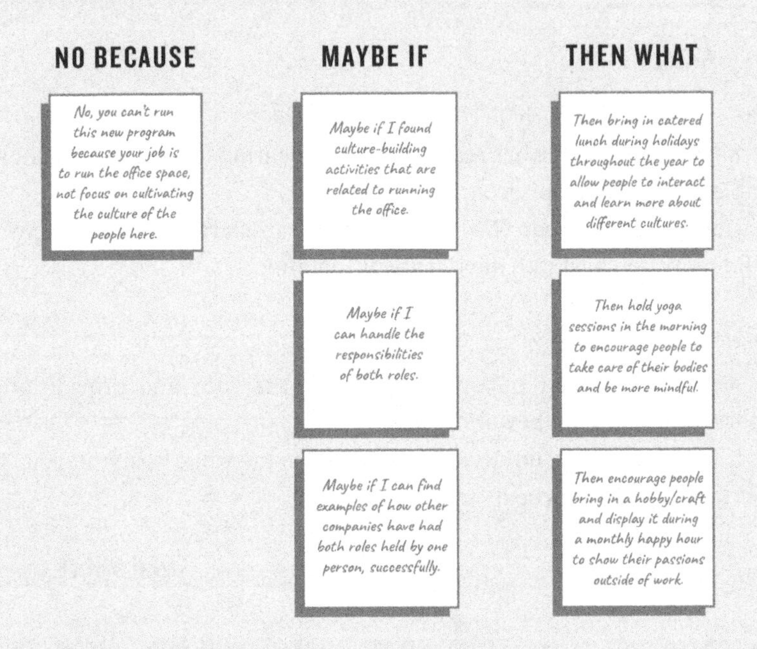

NO BECAUSE
MAYBE IF
THEN WHAT
No, you can't run this new program because your job is to run the office space, not focus on cultivating the culture of the people here.
Maybe if I found culture-building activities that are related to running the office.
Then bring in catered lunch during holidays throughout the year to allow people to interact and learn more about different cultures.
Maybe if I can handle the responsibilities of both roles.
Then hold yoga sessions in the morning to encourage people to take care of their bodies and be more mindful.
Maybe if I can find examples of how other companies have had both roles held by one person, successfully.
Then encourage people bring in a hobby/craft and display it during a monthly happy hour to show their passions outside of work.

Do this for each of the "Maybe Ifs" on your list and continue to build out your full *No Because | Maybe If | Then What* list.

This Isn't a Guaranteed Yes

Going through all of these steps won't automatically ensure you get what you want and especially not right away. But by doing this, you'll create more trust and build something that people start buying into. Bridging to a "yes" together requires collaboration and will create buy-in over time.

And while you're at it, take every "no" as an opportunity to learn something about yourself and the people around you. Work to gain trust and create change. Put on your problem-solver hat, don't let the "no" stop you, and invest the time into creating something great.

ASSEMBLE THE A-TEAM

Form & Lead Your Launch Team

I love Scrabble.

Reaching into the bag of cold, clinking tiles, then feeling around in the hope of drawing the coveted 10-point Q or Z gives me a real thrill. I love the frisson of indecision as I ponder which word to put on the board when my turn comes. Should I hold back some high-scoring letters in the hope of a bigger score later? Or does it make more sense to dump the useless ones to refresh the bench? Perhaps I should toss them all, gambling that my next grab in the bag will produce a seven-letter grand slam?

Sure I can forfeit a turn for a tray of fresh letters, but the real challenge lies in playing the board I have, with the letters I've drawn. I have to make magic with what I've got if I hope to keep the lead.

Like anything else, the highs of a Scrabble game are punctuated by lows. All too often, I find myself at mid-game staring at a rack full of Es plus one Z. Really? After all, there are only 12 E tiles. What are the chances of me having half of them?

I badly want to commiserate with my fellow players: "Man, do I have the worst set of letters to play from, or what?" But, hey, I'm winning, and no one cares about the bum-letter plight of the reigning Scrabble Queen.

And, whaddaya know, grit and patience invariably pay off. I see an opening to play Z-E vertically, appending the E at the end of Q-U-I-T to spell Q-U-I-T-E. With a triple-word score under the Z, the two-word tally comes to 47 points! Not too shabby for the hand I was dealt. (Of note to my fellow word nerds: You don't need to know what "Z-E" means, just that it is in the Official Scrabble Players Dictionary, 5th Edition.)

And so it goes: tough choices... excitement... nervousness... self-doubt... failure... and, ultimately, success.

You don't have to geek out on Scrabble to get the message. Life's most satisfying rewards often come from taking risks when the odds seem stacked against you.

Building the corporate team that will help move your idea forward has much in common with a Scrabble game. Sometimes you are dealt a winning hand, clearly understanding where things go and how to play your hand. But all too often, you have to get creative with a mismatched group to make the magic happen. The good news is that with hard work, patience, and a little imagination, you can build a bench of high-scorers who will get your project off the ground, and make victory possible.

As you move from idea to action, you'll need to build a team of people that will go beyond conversation and buy-in, and help in doing some of the work. Your stakeholders may share with you the names of people who can help, or they may be the people that join your efforts to make things happen.

Your project's success will depend heavily on the team that you attract and recruit to help in launching your idea. Depending on the size and scope of your idea, building your team may be as formal as identifying key roles you need to fill, or as loose as assigning tasks to engaged team members.

At Autodesk, I wanted to create an innovation-focused event that brought team members together from across the globe. With a modest budget and only four months to plan an event that 300 people would attend, I had to get creative to draft a team to help make it happen.

Taking the challenge by the horns, I started to look around the organization and ask, "Who around here is ready and willing to make this happen?" Soon, I assembled my A-Team of creative-thinking problem-solvers. I had Jaz from finance to help me think about my budget and get creative on my spending. And Ajay, an executive administrator, not only knew the systems and processes to get vendors into the company, he was excited to help make the event a success and willing to put in extra hours to make that happen. Nancy joined the team when I interviewed her to learn about her experience in putting together fabulous events for the company, and she said she was interested in helping because of the size and content we would be sharing. I also recruited volunteers who were uniquely talented in different areas, like Tracey, a content manager, who in her spare time was a theater set designer. She rolled up her sleeves and helped us design the space to enable collaborative and inspirational conversations. Or Patrick, a QA analyst who joined our team when he had a fabulous idea to make the event more eco-friendly.

For this project, I didn't have a team assigned to me to make it happen, and rather than listing out the roles I needed, I found individuals who were passionate about the idea and willing to wear many hats to pull it off. None of my teammates were traditional in the way we think about teams at work. When you're pursuing innovation, traditional and "normal" aren't the only way to get things done. Teams can look a lot different than we're used to.

Your team will likely comprise one or more of four types of people. I call these four different groups: "Your Inheritance," "Part-Time Players," "Inhouse Seat Warmers," and "New Hire Moonshots." You can use each as a standalone model or, more often, find an appropriate blend that best suits the needs of your project and your company.

YOUR INHERITANCE

Sometimes, the team charged with helping you bring your idea to fruition will be made up of colleagues—and perhaps a few newcomers— who have already started work on the project. But for one reason or another, they've come to a dead end, not knowing which way to turn. For better or worse, these people are your inheritance.

When I joined California's Department of Education in 2014 as head of educational technology, my job was to come up with new ways of applying the internet, mobile apps, digital tools, and handheld devices to transform teaching and learning in the U.S.'s most populous state.

One of my first tasks was to overhaul a website, known as Brokers of Expertise, which contained a wealth of information for educators. Brokers of Expertise was designed as a resource for teaching, including lesson plans and web activities that could be used in the classroom, as well as a forum for educators to share ideas. Trouble was, the educators it was built for weren't using it.

Before I even started the job, I had a zillion questions about why the existing platform was missing the mark, and twice as many ideas about how to improve it.

About a week into my new role, I learned that many others before me had put a great deal of work and effort into the same project. Despite a splashy launch, it had failed to gain traction in the marketplace. As a result, an idea full of promise was in danger of going nowhere. My boss, State Superintendent of Public Instruction Tom Torlakson, was clearly looking to me to breathe new life into the initiative, and to move it forward without further excuses.

I soon discovered that I had inherited a team of smart but rather jaded individuals. They were immensely talented but didn't share the fresh sense of optimism that I, a newcomer, was able to bring to the table. Sure, they still cared deeply about Brokers of Expertise, but they had an attitude of "been there, done that." Most were skeptical that we could obtain the resources needed to make the site more user-friendly, or persuade educators across California to start using it. There had been little progress on either front since the site was launched four years earlier. The team had put in a lot of work to try to move things forward but because they had seen little payoff, they felt frustrated and burned out.

Multiple factors may have typically contributed to the impasse confronting the "Your Inheritance" group when you join them: scarce resources, internal politics, marketplace dynamics, and decisions by management and the board of directors, among others. Whatever the hold-up, you have little choice but to work, at least initially, with players who are already at the table holding their cards and—chances are— some of yours too. You're the newbie, so playing your hand will require finesse plus an extra dose of empathy.

The "Your Inheritance" team often includes a long-serving leader with a firm vision of what needs to be done. This person is typically a fountain of knowledge, but all too often has a stubborn focus on what won't work, rather than being open to what might. It's not easy to engage with such naysayers, nor to convince them that some fresh thinking may give the project the jolt it needs to move forward.

Yet in many cases, spending a bit of time with "Your Inheritance" team can be well worthwhile. An open discussion will help you understand how you can harness their skills, without allowing them to block progress. If you are able to find that magic formula, "Your Inheritance" will turn out to be helpful and loyal cheerleaders.

The first step is to get together one-on-one with "Your Inheritance" team members, and ask them some probing questions:

- *In looking back at the evolution of our project, what do you think has stalled or slowed it down? (Be careful here, you aren't looking for dirt or gossip, but rather a fuller understanding of how the new product or service will fit into the company's overall business strategy.)*
- *Which members of our group do you think have been pivotal in getting the project where it is today?*
- *Who in the company has voiced concerns about this idea, and what were those concerns?*

- *What still interests you about the idea today, and what role would you like to play in bringing it to fruition?*

Whenever I embark on trying to launch a new idea, I spend time getting to know all the players that may be inherited on the project. From the indifferent engineer to the enthusiastic project manager, I try to listen and learn from them. After all, I reason, they were the experts, and they had already learned valuable lessons from months in the trenches.

True, some wanted to complain and point fingers, but for the most part, they showed an enthusiastic curiosity about how we might move forward, even if it meant revising our strategy.

Even so, stepping into this kind of situation can be a hairy experience. It takes perception and empathy to fully understand all the baggage "Your Inheritance" may be carrying. Be patient as you learn more about your new team. Take care not to fall into the trap of thinking that they have no value simply because they could not implement the idea before you arrived on the scene. Be humble and open to learning. My experience has taught me that you will often be pleasantly surprised when all the facts are brought into the open.

In many cases, the members of "Your Inheritance" may be more senior than you in age or experience, and have more clout in the C-suite and boardroom. Bear in mind that they likely have friends scattered throughout the organization, including right at the top. On one hand, their support can be hugely helpful in moving a project forward. But beware that locking horns with them could be costly in terms not only of your time, but possibly even your career. Taking decisions without consulting and listening to them is likely to cement your reputation as a know-it-all maverick, and bound to lead to problems down the line.

In working with "Your Inheritance," it is important to recognize both their benefits and their weaknesses. Here are some to consider:

Potential Benefits of Your Inheritance:

- *They have a vested interest in the idea.*
- *They have learned from past failures.*
- *They understand the corporate politics involved in moving the idea forward.*

Potential Weaknesses of Your Inheritance:

- *They are stubbornly attached to the original concept.*

- *They are unable to appreciate that new approaches may solve even the most intractable problems.*
- *They have difficulty letting go of their egos and the role they may have played in getting the project bogged down.*

The best way of leveraging the strengths and overcoming the weaknesses is to spend a lot of time listening, learning, and communicating as you move forward. This means keeping tabs of all the people at the table and ensuring each one's concerns are heard and, if possible, addressed.

Most importantly, let go of any bias that they have failed and therefore aren't a good fit for your team. At the same time, you may need to work on winning support from other team members who are passionate and knowledgeable, but have been discouraged by repeated failure.

PART-TIME PLAYERS

One option for building your team is to cast your net throughout the company, looking for colleagues who are sympathetic to your project. With luck, you'll be able to persuade at least a few of them to earmark part of their day for you.

A word of warning is in order. We're talking about employees with their own full-time jobs. While they may have some time to spare for your project, there's always a risk that they will be distracted by their other duties. What's more, you need to understand that they are not undermining you when they give priority to those responsibilities.

I witnessed just such a situation in my role to help launch IDEO U in March 2015. I was one of the project's early outside hires. The founder of IDEO U, Suzanne Gibbs Howard, was already a partner and had 20 years' experience leading teams and projects at IDEO. She had a hunch that the timing for IDEO U was right, and was already working on prototypes when I joined the team.

Suz recruited a terrific team whose members had a passion for the project and brought the skills needed to get IDEO U off the ground. She worked closely with a fellow partner who had experience teaching and leading design thinking workshops. She also recruited an expert in devising business strategies for start-ups. Suz consulted widely with educators, designers, content creators, and other experts to ensure that her team had the right mix of skills. Some of them were "Part-Time Players" who spent a few hours a week with us, while others popped in to help as needed. In some cases, Suz simply bought them lunch and picked their brains as they ate.

Demanding as it was, this collaborative approach worked wonders. Ask Suz now about the early days of IDEO U and she will tell you that it took the hard work of many IDEO employees who already had full-time jobs but were bursting with energy to help her turn an exciting new idea into reality.

The trick to recruiting "Part-Time Players" is to look for passionate individuals who can bring a fresh perspective or deep knowledge to your project. You may be surprised to find that by firing up enthusiasm for your idea, you are helping to motivate and retain employees throughout the company. That's good not only for your project but for the entire organization.

But, as mentioned before, you need to proceed with care. If you're looking for "Part-Time Players" to give up some of their valuable time, make sure they are rocking it in their day jobs. If they are already doing a great job without undue stress, their bosses will surely be more inclined to allow them to take on other assignments. Bear in mind that those bosses can quickly shut down your "Part-Time Players" if your demands are distracting them from their regular duties.

As you size up your target part-timers, ask them these questions to see if they'll make a good fit:

- *What motivates you in the work you do today?*
- *Why are you excited to be part of this project? How do you think you can help to get our idea off the ground?*
- *Considering your current job, how will you find time to take on the extra work? Will your involvement be restricted to certain hours, days of the week, or times of the year?*
- *How would you describe your relationship with your manager?*
- *How can I help you manage both your current job and your involvement in this project?*

Potential Benefits of Part-Time Players:

- *They have a vested interest in the idea.*
- *They are excited to flex their muscles and apply their expertise in a new way.*
- *They understand the internal politics involved in bringing your idea to fruition.*

Potential Weaknesses of Part-Time Players:

- *They require regular check-ins to ensure they aren't dropping the ball on their current role.*
- *The company owns the time shared, and could cause delays if other priorities intervene.*
- *They may suffer burnout if they try to juggle too many responsibilities.*

It can be a tough balancing act to keep "Part-Time Players" engaged without overburdening them or stepping on their reporting managers' toes. Your job is to promote your idea and keep everyone in the loop. You can persuade potential team members over a coffee, and at the same time gain some insights into their thinking and priorities. The same applies to your interactions with senior executives, even if you just bump into them in the kitchen. Lose no opportunity to keep them engaged and informally take the pulse of their commitment to your big idea.

One final point: if you're working with "Part-Time Players," you'll need to spend time managing expectations and keeping in touch with their day-to-day colleagues, especially their managers. Remember at all times to be gracious and grateful for the time and effort they have set aside for your project. Trying to bulldoze your way to success is sure to backfire.

IN-HOUSE SEAT WARMERS

If your idea is showing promise, chances are you will need to go beyond part-time help, and take on some full-time staff. But top management may insist for budgetary or other reasons that you cast your net no further than existing colleagues, even though they may not be the ideal fit for the tasks you have in mind. Some may not share your enthusiasm for the project, others may not have the expertise you need.

Have no fear, there are plenty of tools at your disposal to point these "In-House Seat Warmers" in the right direction, and mold them into productive members of your team.

I found some of those tools really useful after I co-founded Pick-A-Prof in 2000. The business was initially designed as an online platform to help students improve their academic performance, but we branched out in 2008, renaming it MyEdu and setting up a new division to help students land jobs after graduation.

This new project required dedicated marketing brainpower, but on a shoestring budget. To staff the team, we had no choice but to reorganize and bring in colleagues from other parts of the company. For starters, we shifted Jaime, a smart young marketing graduate, from an administrative and operations role into a newly created position to drive our outreach to college students across the U.S.

In a perfect world, we would have hired a more senior marketing executive for this job. But we were still testing the new platform. Before the board would give us a decent budget, we needed to show that we had a receptive audience.

With regular check-ins and clearly defined milestones, Jaime powered her way forward. She found creative ways to make up for her inexperience by enlisting the help of former professors and mentors outside the company. They all wanted to see their recent graduate succeed and were eager to help her. As someone still familiar with campus life, she was able to tap into an army of students to help market our services at universities and colleges. All in all, Jaime proved that "In-House Seat Warmers" can be highly effective additions to your team.

Getting the most out of "In-House Seat Warmers" means allowing yourself to be persuaded that they, like Jaime, can deliver what you want. Identify the tasks that make the best fit for each of them, and focus heavily on those. Understand areas where they may have less expertise or interest, and then give them the tools they need to address those shortcomings. Suitable training should be top of your list.

Also, think long-term about your expectations for specific roles. For example, how long are you willing to cut "In-House Seat Warmers" some slack to adjust to their new jobs? At what point will you need to replace them if they are not up to scratch? Six months? A year? You should set a deadline, and be upfront in communicating it to each individual.

"In-House Seat Warmers" often seem like an inexpensive and quick solution to a staffing shortage. But they can end up doing more harm than good if they can't handle the responsibilities you've set out for them. One way to prevent this from happening is to simultaneously screen both internal and external talent. Understanding how an "In-House Seat Warmer" stacks up against external candidates will both reinforce the argument for hiring outsiders (today or in the future) and identify growth opportunities for an existing colleague.

Remember at all times that you're the team leader, which means—obvious as it may sound—that you need to show leadership. Think about how you might help your new colleagues grow into their new roles. Do they need guidance and coaching to fulfill your expectations of them? Ask them these questions to ensure that their expectations match yours:

- *Are you willing to take on a role beyond your comfort zone?*
- *Would you be comfortable taking responsibility for specific tasks and checking in weekly to update progress?*
- *How do you feel about having a measure of autonomy now, but then reporting directly to someone else later as the project gathers steam?*
- *If there is an opportunity for you to grow into a more senior role, are you willing to put in the necessary time and effort?*

If you need a senior project leader but find yourself saddled with a less seasoned "In-House Seat Warmer," be sure to communicate your concerns to the "In-House Seat Warmer." You need to define roles and responsibilities, and create ample opportunity for team members to check-in and discuss progress along the way. This will provide reassurance that the project is unfolding as planned. Everyone should feel free to call for help if they need it.

Potential Benefits of In-House Seat Warmers:

- *They are dedicated full-time to advancing your project.*
- *They are eager to make a good impression and, by so doing, to climb the corporate ladder.*
- *They can quickly get up to speed, thanks to their knowledge of the company's operations, culture, and customers.*

Potential Weaknesses of In-House Seat Warmers:

- *They may be inexperienced or under-qualified.*
- *They often require frequent monitoring.*
- *Despite their enthusiasm, they may be unable to do the job, even with a heavy investment in coaching.*

Having decided to hire an "In-House Seat Warmer" after taking all these pros and cons into account, it's your duty to provide the tools that will help that person succeed. Those tools may include an investment in coaching and, almost certainly, maintaining open communication about performance. Only after such efforts have been tried and failed should you consider looking elsewhere.

Rather than dwelling on your "In-House Seat Warmers'" shortcomings, focus on flexing your mentoring skills to guide them toward the product or service you're designing. With proper training, a team member who may initially seem like a square peg in a round hole can end up as a perfect fit.

NEW HIRE MOONSHOTS

If you're lucky, you'll be free to scour the world for talent. This usually means that your idea is at an advanced stage of development and you need a person (perhaps more than one) with skills and experience not available within the company.

On the plus side, this is a great opportunity to find exactly the person you're looking for. You can cast your net far and wide. But be warned: it often takes time and effort to secure the approval and resources you need to go ahead with an outside hire. The bean-counters in particular are sure to ask why you can't find the skills in-house, and why an outsider is so crucial for moving your idea forward. More often than not, they may suggest an "In-House Seat Warmer."

I had just such an experience in 2018 when I was hired as an advisor to e180, the Montreal company whose business is to help people learn from each other online. My job was to help e180 identify new sources of revenue for its flagship platform, Braindate, which enables participants either to post topics that they can teach, or send invitations to others from whom they feel they can learn.

Braindate has had huge success since its launch in 2011, but e180's founder, Christine, had even loftier ambitions. While the company already employed some of the smartest and most thoughtful people to create the product, none of them had experience in diversification. Christine brought several of her colleagues together and raised the possibility of bringing in an outsider to help reach their targets. Together the team agreed that they would benefit from the perspective of someone with different experiences. Luckily, they chose me as their "New Hire Moonshot. "

Before hiring a "New Hire Moonshot," evaluate the talent you have in-house. As with building a team of "In-House Seat Warmers," you need to consider insiders and outsiders at the same time, so you have a complete picture of the qualities you need, and where you can find them.

Once you have the go-ahead to recruit an outsider, I recommend setting up a hiring team to see the process through. Its members should be up to speed on your project, and familiar with the jobs you are looking to fill. The recruiting team should be able to answer these questions before you even think of posting a job ad:

- *What experience or knowledge do we need this individual to have?*
- *What personal qualities are best suited for our company?*
- *How will we need to equip this person to drive change, even as an outsider?*
- *Do we need a strategic thinker, a tactical doer, or a balance of both?*

One way of bringing in a "New Hire Moonshot" is to consider him or her a consultant-for-hire. That gives each side an opportunity to feel the other out, and then to decide whether they make a good fit. In particular, hiring for a new, unfamiliar role typically raises plenty of questions.

The "New Hire Moonshot" will be uncertain whether the company is ready for the new role. One way of dealing with this problem is to position the job as a project-based opportunity that can evolve into a full-time position. While not every qualified "New Hire Moonshot" will be attracted by this model, the right person will likely see it as a great opportunity to "feel each other out."

Understanding the pros and cons of hiring a "New Hire Moonshot" will lay the groundwork for a mutually beneficial relationship.

Potential Benefits of New Hire Moonshots:

- *They can draw from their experience in similar industries or companies.*
- *They are not burdened by an attitude of "This is the way we've always done it"; in other words, they are well-equipped to provide creative insights that can give your project a fresh start.*
- *At least initially, senior managers often give "New Hire Moonshot" more credibility than "In-House Seat Warmers" or "Your Inheritance" to put new ideas into practice.*

Potential Weaknesses of New Hire Moonshots:

- *They need time to get up to speed with the company's operations, culture, and customers.*
- *Insiders may resent a newcomer, especially if they were expecting to fill the role themselves.*
- *They often need hand-holding to avoid the pitfalls of office politics or the risks of stepping on valued employees' toes.*

As you consider taking one or more "New Hire Moonshots" on board, you'll need to find a balance between the urgency of filling a key gap, and the time it takes to recruit and acclimate an outside hire. Circumstances sometimes force you to move fast, perhaps too fast to justify hiring a "New Hire Moonshot." Be sure to weigh carefully all the pros and cons of a new hire before you write that LinkedIn ad.

Once you've decided to hire a "New Hire Moonshot," it is your responsibility to bring your team and other colleagues on board. This may require considerable time and effort, involving both top-down and bottom-up consultation. You'll need to convince the C-suite and other senior executives that the newly created role will benefit not only your project, but the company as a whole. At the same time, be sure to hear the views of those who will report and work with the "New Hire Moonshot" so that everyone is on the same page.

TEAMWORK MAKES THE DREAM WORK

Building your A-Team can be a time-consuming process. The group that you eventually assemble may turn out to be quite different from what you expected at the start. The process will depend heavily on your skill in negotiating resources and weighing the balance between speed, efficiency, and expertise.

Most of all, you will be judged on results. Screw up the team-building exercise and your project—and quite possibly your job—will be on the line. If you manage to lead your team in the right direction and move the project forward, your early successes are sure to snowball into more resources, greater responsibility, and growing influence within the company.

ACTIVITY

BUILD & LEAD YOUR A-TEAM

As you're looking at the group of players you've assembled, your team is going to be made up of different people from different backgrounds. It's going to take work to bring your team members together. We're going to go through the various development phases that affect change in how a team works together and think about what shifts and changes in our teams throughout the process. Teams need different things at different times to keep them on track. Use the following exercise to guide your team through the different phases and keep building toward the big idea. You'll learn what phase your team is in and how to move forward.

Each phase presents a question to ask yourself to help the team stay on track and continue the important work required of your idea. Throughout each phase, think about why people are doing this work and how you, as a contributing team member, can help keep people passionate and aligned. Here are the phases ahead: forming, conflict, and peforming.

Phase I: Forming Phase

Since this combination of team members have probably never worked together before, and most likely haven't participated in this kind of innovation work before, they're going to need some help getting off on the right foot. You'll know you're in this phase if your team shows signs of confusion and uncertainty, as they're still testing out the ground rules and feeling each other out.

During this phase, make sure everyone is well-informed and goals are clearly defined. Co-create these goals together and establish a way of working so everyone feels comfortable.

During the early phase of your A-Team, when team members are starting to work on the idea, be sure to keep a very important question in mind:

Why are we doing this work?

Aligning on the purpose of the work you're doing creates an understanding and can be a bonding force for a new team. When everyone knows what they're working toward they're more likely to get on board and you'll be able to connect to their individual purpose in why they're doing the work.

An "Inherited Team" may be anxious to see the idea finally completed. Their "why" may have been borne from inspiration but time has dulled that and the new "why" is to see the finish line.

On the other hand, a "Part-Time Player" may be pumped to share their time to solve a problem they believe in. Their "why" is the core belief that the idea will make a difference.

Connect with the "why" of your team and ensure you are all aligned on the objectives and goals of the idea. A good way to do this is to explore goal- and objective-setting.

SETTING GOALS & OBJECTIVES

Sure, your project has a description and everyone has an idea of their job description but what are you really working toward?

Start by brainstorming your goals. When you invite members of the team to be a part of this process, rather than telling them which goals they should care about, you'll see a much better, more collaborative response.

It's similar to the "IKEA effect" we discussed earlier. The IKEA effect says that something happens when we participate in the building of something. We place a higher value on what we've created, we care about it more, and we feel more ownership of it. This is how we want our team members to feel about the goals and objectives we create together.

Get your team together for a meeting and start by stating the purpose—to identify and articulate your group's goals and objectives to help you see this project to successful completion.

Ask your team questions like:

- *What's our purpose?*
- *What are we trying to accomplish?*
- *What do we want this to look like in three months? Six months?*
- *What does a successful outcome look and feel like?*
- *How should we celebrate successes?*

Ask more questions related to how people want to see themselves as contributors to this idea. Here you may ask questions like:

- *What drives you in this project?*
- *What superpowers can you bring to this work?*
- *Is there anything you want to try to do that's not in your job description?*

Allow each team member to share their thoughts to these questions and capture each on a post-it, shared on the wall for everyone to see.

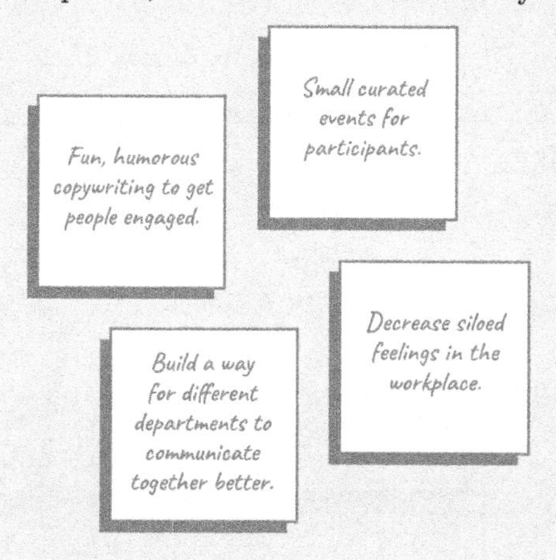

At this moment, you aren't worried about grouping goals or pointing out whether something is "right" or not. It's an opportunity for people to share what's on their mind and start to uncover more understanding about each other's motivations.

MAKE IT ACTIONABLE

When the brainstorm starts to slow down, and everyone has participated, it's time to assemble your important themes, setting clear and simple goals and objectives from them.

Looking at your post-its, what themes rise to the top? Ask the team to help identify groups or categories.

Purpose:

- *Build a way for different departments to communicate together better.*
- *Decrease siloed feelings in the workplace.*

Engagement:

- *Fun, humorous copywriting to get people engaged.*
- *Small curated events for participants.*

With different groups of post-its identified, start to set goals and objectives around them. It is important to follow the SMART model. Setting objectives and goals, make sure what you come up with is Specific, Measurable, Attainable, Relevant, and Time-bound.

Looking back at our example "Small curated events for participants" could become "Once a month events for 10-15 people focused on building community." This makes it fit the SMART model and turns the comment into a living, breathing goal.

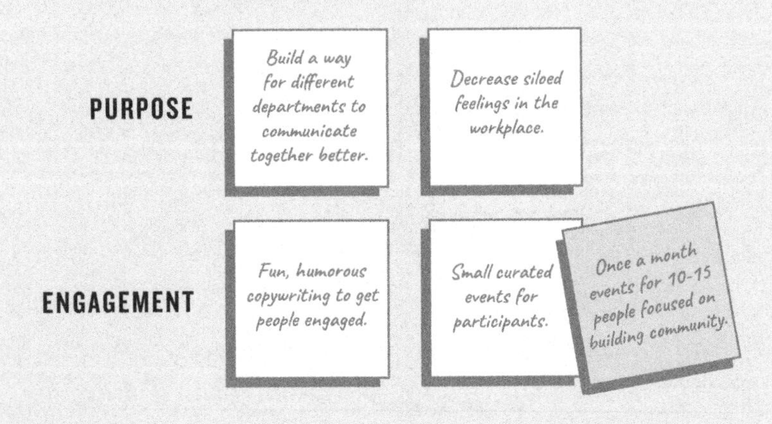

After the group has gone through this exercise, together vote on the two or three most important and relevant goals. These are the ones you will use to guide you in your work.

Doing this goal-setting together as a team will inherently get your group to commit to the goals. The team that sets goals together, crushes and achieves them together. It's an opportunity to clarify what's needed for the idea to succeed and will provoke the team to think about the steps to make the goals happen as well as a way to track progress.

Phase 2: Conflict Phase

Once you get past the honeymoon phase of a new group, you enter into the conflict phase. Every group will eventually reach this phase. It's the moment when tensions inevitably collide and the group disagrees and can't get back on track. There will be tension and frustration among members in this phase.

Here you'll notice disagreements over priorities, and a tendency for small cliques to form. You might encounter a struggle for leadership and power, but don't spend too much time on the tension. Instead, keep the group aligned and motivated.

Throughout this phase, it is important to think about how to help manage the conflicts that arise. Ask yourself:

How might we confront our disagreements or misalignment head-on?

Tension and disagreements are to be expected. They mean your team is evolving and changing. Don't hide your head in the sand, these problems won't disappear on their own. They should be dealt with in a healthy, open way. The best way to do that is through a check-in conversation.

CHECK-IN CONVERSATION

The goal of this kind of conversation is to align with your team and give team members a chance to air their grievances after a period of frustration. Keep in mind that the goal of this conversation is to help them to feel heard while looking for proactive solutions to move forward.

When you invite them into the conversation, frame it in whatever way works to get the team on board. You don't have to call this a "Think/Feel" activity (but it is one). You could call it a "Check-In Conversation"—or whatever you need to do to help people come to the discussion with an open mind. This kind of activity will encourage people to open up and talk about the issues at hand in a facilitated conversation.

Give people a piece of paper with two columns that they can fill out:

FOR OUR PROJECT, I THINK...	FOR OUR PROJECT, I FEEL...
...we'll never be able to hit our deadline.	...stressed and frustrated.
...I'm not a valued member of the team.	...sad and unimportant

Asking team members to fill something like this out when tensions are high is a big ask. Remind them that the only way they'll be able to move forward in a better way is to acknowledge what's really going on.

When team members get stuck, or you notice they're not writing anything down, share more examples of things you think and feel. Lead by example and be vulnerable in your own responses.

Now, with their papers filled out, team members can identify common themes that they are thinking and feeling. Are most people on the team concerned about the deadline? Do they feel like they're not being utilized to their best ability? Take some time and group these themes so you can get to the root of the issue.

Once you have the different themes of ways people are thinking and feeling, open the conversation up for suggestions on how your team can improve their practices. For the deadline stress, you might ask, "How can we reduce stress around our deadline?"

Open up the conversation for participants to share their thoughts and solutions. Note that you may get conflicting solutions. Encourage team members to wait on evaluating the solutions and instead focus on capturing as many different ideas that come to mind. The team will have an opportunity to vote later.

Write out each suggestion on an individual post-it and add it to the corresponding feelings.

FOR OUR PROJECT, I THINK...	FOR OUR PROJECT, I FEEL...
...we'll never be able to hit our deadline.	...stressed and frustrated.
...I'm not a valued member of the team.	...sad and unimportant

We could change the deadline to give us more time.

Add more people to the team to spread out responsibilities.

Can we set up a more detailed plan of action to hit our deadline?

After all team members have each contributed to the brainstorm of potential solutions, talk through them and positively identify the solutions that might work for each issue.

To help the team collaborate in a positive and helpful way, encourage them to use the "Yes, And" method. This is a method used to train improv actors and requires people to collaborate and build solutions together. When used by improv actors, the first actor begins to act something out and when the second actor steps in, they affirm what the first character said or did (**yes**) and then continue to build out the scene (**and**).

The game "Yes, And" forces the actors to avoid rejecting the first actor's ideas; they find a way to collaborate and go with the flow instead. It's the opposite of "No, But," which can lead to people feeling devalued or unheard.

While you guide your team through this part, they don't actually have to say, "Yes, And" (though it's a lot easier to stay on track if you do). Point out that using this technique provides the opportunity to embrace the ideas and solutions presented by fellow team members.

Help the team members to respond with a, "Yes, and..." for the different solutions and capture each on a post-it.

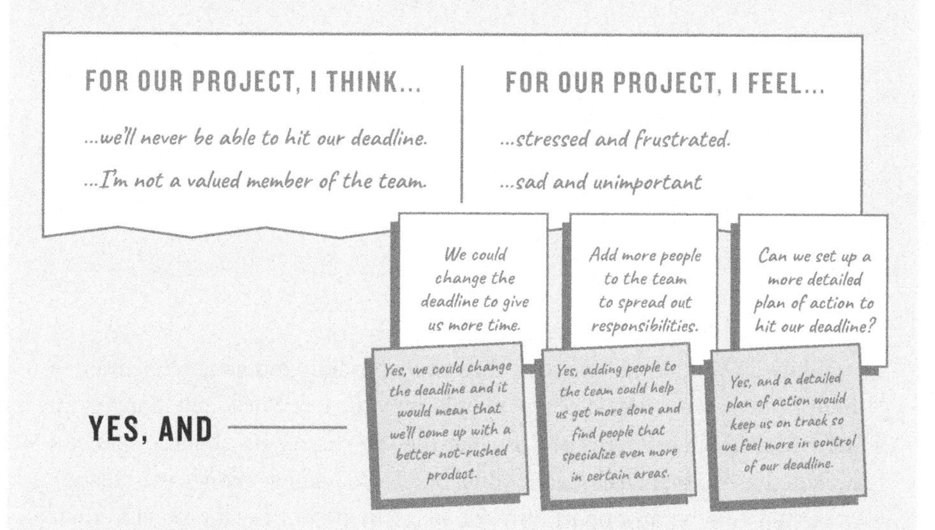

Then, wrap up the conversation by having people vote on their favorite solutions. Depending on how many solutions you can actually act out, give each team member one to two stickers to add to the post-it with their favorite solution. Tally up the votes and chose the solutions with the most votes that you will move forward on.

Before you part ways with your team, ask each person what they learned from the conversation and what was resolved.

"Let's work to make a detailed plan of action and see who else we can bring into the project. We'll talk to the higher-ups about moving the deadline and if we can't we'll make sure everyone feels prepared and supported in their tasks."

Continue to enforce and remind the team members about this conversation and the decisions that were made in the following weeks. You'll find a much more positive outcome when you can co-create these decisions.

Phase 3: Performing Phase

As your group continues to chug along, you'll need to keep them engaged while making sure you stay out of the conflict phase. A great way to do this is to make the work more personal to the members on your team.

During this time, the newness has worn off and the conflicts subsided. You will need to ask yourself:

How might we make this project meaningful to all of the team members?

This is such an important question to tune into. Team members may not feel personally invested. Or they're not able to share their unique abilities. A contagious "clock-in, clock-out" mentality sets in, because once one team member starts to check out, others will follow suit.

Getting your team to purpose and meaning will cut this issue off at the source. You will eradicate this contagious virus by redirecting toward purpose.

TAP INTO PURPOSE & PASSION

How do you get people to realize their passion and strengths and use them in their work? Most of the people on your team probably don't even know what their strengths are or what they're passionate about. If you can awaken these in them as a leader, you'll unleash a fuller version of your team.

Could this be an opportunity for team members to step outside their usual roles and have new job responsibilities? Using a SWOT test helps team members identify their Strengths, Weaknesses, Opportunities, and Threats.

Lead your team members to ask these questions for each of the quadrants. To give them time and space to really consider each one, have them take it home and think about it themselves, outside of the office.

Strengths:

- *What do you do well?*
- *What unique resources can you draw on?*
- *What do others see as your strengths?*

Weaknesses:

- *What could you improve?*
- *Where do you have fewer resources than others?*
- *What are others likely to see as weaknesses?*

Opportunities:

- *What opportunities are open to you?*
- *What trends could you take advantage of?*
- *How can you turn your strengths into opportunities?*

Threats:

- *What threats could harm you?*
- *What is your competition doing?*
- *What threats do your weaknesses expose to you?*

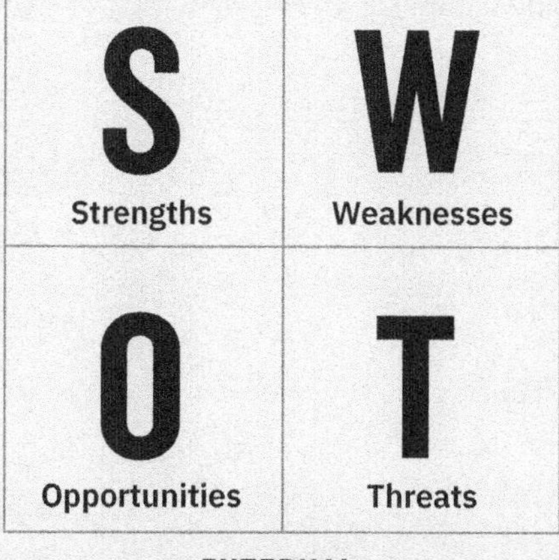

Once team members have filled out their SWOTs, meet with each member individually to talk through their responses. Challenge them to think about how they could integrate some of these revelations into their work. Invite them to take more responsibility for certain tasks. Offer opportunities for advancement to make use of their gifts and to help improve upon their weaknesses. Encourage them to keep growing and to make this work their own.

By empowering team members to learn more about themselves and the way they work, you're showing them that they're a valued member of the team and that they have something unique to offer.

Some team members may find they're gifted in connecting with others and can take a chance to work with more customer-facing opportunities. Let team members explore their strengths and encourage them to use this project as a way to further develop their careers and identify opportunities for growth.

Lead your team through the awkward phase of starting up and getting to know each other by aligning on goals and objectives. When you hit conflicts and tension, stop and have a check-in. It sets the tone to deal with confrontation head-on. When things start to get menial and the day to day takes over, remind your team how important they are by showcasing their strengths in new ways. Invest in them by helping them grow and reach new opportunities.

These phases will change and evolve as people join and transition out of your team. As the project grows, you'll need to revisit different phases to keep everyone motivated. Leading a team to work through your idea is worth it—you can't do it alone.

WHAT'S THE WORST THAT CAN HAPPEN?

Predicting the Future

We see it in movies right before the main character plunges into a booby trap or as the adventurous group runs straight into the bad guys. Luckily for us, we're being somewhat ironic when asking ourselves the question, "What's the worst that can happen?"

When it comes to the work of pushing ideas forward, imagining failure is worse than the failure itself. Our feeling that we might fail keeps us from doing the work. The only way to get past it is to acknowledge that failure is inevitable. (Because it is.)

We envision the worst that could happen: the project falls apart, it looks completely different than we wanted it to, or maybe we even get kicked off the team. We have a feeling that something terrible could happen, but we haven't identified what that really is. At its core, it's the anxiety of failing.

It's why adults have difficulty learning a new language. We want to have perfect accents and an extensive dictionary of words to pull from. What if, gasp, we mispronounce or misuse a word? Wrapped up in trying to be perfect, we forget about the messy middle where we will fail. Without those failures, we're just reading and studying a language. We aren't putting ourselves out there to speak with others. We aren't actually learning the language until we start practicing and learning from our missteps along the way.

When it comes to pushing your idea forward, the truth is you're going to fail. It's inevitable. That's the nature of innovation. It's about trying something new and inviting change. Imagine walking up to a complex math problem on a whiteboard thinking you should be able to solve it perfectly without ever having been taught how to do it.

I speak some conversational Spanish, and to keep it up, some friends and I have a monthly Spanish dinner. We hire a tutor to join us for a private lesson and he listens in as we stumble over our words and look to him for correction. Just when I thought I had gotten back into the hang of it, I confidently blurted out what I was planning on doing next weekend. My tutor quickly responded, "Well, when you talk about something that might happen in the future, you have to use the conditional tense."

Innovation is like learning the nuances and complications of a new language. Along the way, it gets more complex as you put together new tenses and conjugations. With your idea, you might forget to get buy-in from an unforeseen stakeholder or budget approval after a new company policy is introduced, but getting a few things wrong along the way is unavoidable.

While you're figuring it out, you're up against other factors that will slow down your progress. Big companies are often the antithesis of innovation. They're built on following a system of operations, thriving when they can optimize and increase the number of times a process can be repeated. Innovation threatens to change "the way things have always been done" in an effort to make things better. This makes "learning the language" even harder.

If you're going to do this work successfully, you can't use a plug-and-play formula—you'll need to think of it more as an adventure into the unknown wilderness. You've got to be ready and willing to pivot and charge your way forward.

Like any adventure, a lot will come up along the way. Some things will make you want to turn back and give up, while others might force you to find another way forward. But remember: whatever happens and wherever you end up—all outcomes are good.

IT'S ALL GOOD

After doing this work for 20 years, I've discovered that there's a spectrum of what failure on a project looks like. On the low end, you'll hit a roadblock that slows you down, deters your progress, or threatens to change the idea. Somewhere in the middle is where your idea looks different from what you'd planned and imagined, and you might be disappointed. As you get further to the other side of the spectrum you'll cross through graveyards of projects that didn't make it and maybe even situations where the project was a total disaster.

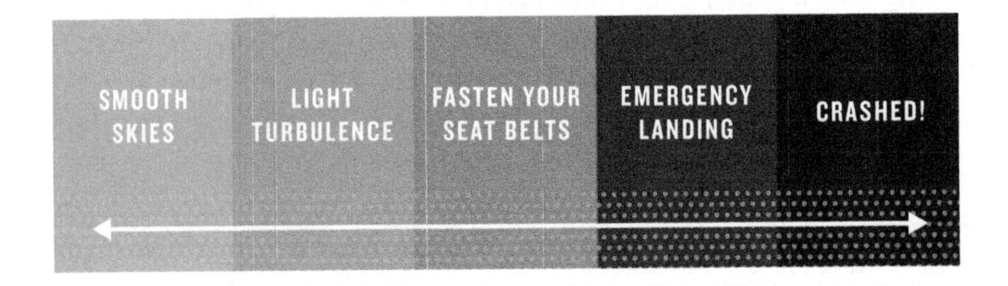

You're likely to run into situations that toggle between the low and middle ends of the spectrum. Hitting a roadblock and having an idea evolve into something different are situations you should prepare for. Accept that these will happen in your work and that the "worst case scenarios" are not as bad as they sound.

Three points on the "failure" spectrum:

One: You'll hit a roadblock/barrier/issue that threatens or slows your idea.

Two: At the end of the process, your idea doesn't look exactly how you'd planned. It's changed and that's frustrating.

Three: You tried and totally failed—the project was scrapped, you were removed from the team, or maybe worst-worst case scenario, it was a total disaster.

You might not launch your idea hoping for one of these outcomes—but they're still incredibly valuable results.

In 1968, researcher Spencer Silver was working in the 3M laboratory trying to develop a super strong, permanent adhesive. After some testing, he realized he had invented almost the opposite: an adhesive that stuck to objects but was easily lifted off. It was neither strong nor permanent.

For years he looked for potential uses of his new, weak glue. He continued to tell his coworkers about the "microspheres" in his glue that allow them to be removed without damage. "I got to be known as 'Mr. Persistent,' because I wouldn't give up," he said.

Twelve years went by before Silver found a use for his new adhesive. He was approached by a coworker, Art Fry, who'd heard about Silver's microspheres. Fry had been in choir practice, struggling with the bookmarks in his hymnbook. Wednesday night he'd bookmarked the appropriate hymns, but by Sunday morning the bookmarks had fallen out and he found himself frantically flipping through his hymnbook. He told Silver that he needed a bookmark that would stick to the paper without damaging the pages.

So the team started writing messages and notes on pieces of paper and using this temporary, removable adhesive to communicate around the office. Thus, the post-it was created. It wasn't long before post-its took off and 40 years later, we're using them in offices around the world and in this book.

Silver's goal and original aim wasn't to create the post-it. It was to create something much different, and for good reason. He had plenty of reasons and uses to create the stronger permanent adhesive. His idea didn't go as planned and he technically failed in what he was originally trying to create.

After the adhesive was created, it took 12 years to figure out what to do with it. Finally, after coming up with what to use it for, it took another six years to get his company to launch the product.

Eighteen years is a long time from conception of an idea to execution and launch. Throughout those 18 years, Spencer Silver spent a lot of time fighting to push his idea forward. Innovating and launching new ideas in a big company like 3M is guaranteed to have some roadblocks, take longer than you initially imagined, and at times feel like a total failure. But if you can approach the process with an open mind, acknowledging there will be failures and that you will learn from them along the way, you might just land on your own version of the post-it.

ROAD BUMPS AHEAD

Sometimes, as you're building and launching your big idea, you'll hit an unexpected road bump. Have you ever been in a car when the driver (maybe you) didn't see a speed bump coming? If you hit it with any amount of speed you're bound to catch some air and potentially bottom out. It can be jarring, surprising, and damage your vehicle if you're not careful.

When you're in the first stages of launching your idea, you're like the people driving in the car, oblivious that a speed bump is coming, singing along to the music and having a great time. You're building up momentum for your idea, and when you do hit the bump everyone goes silent—"what do we do now?"

A road bump can look like:

- *Finding out customers don't love your prototype.*
- *Getting a "no" from your manager.*
- *Not getting the budget for your project approved.*

Big telecommunications company AT&T was working closely with Douglas on his idea Famigo, which provided safety controls on electronics for kids and toddlers. Douglas and his team had built the software and were already preloaded on Android phones.

They were planning a big marketing push with the company when Douglas got a vague but ominous email, "Hey, we're going to put a hold on the marketing campaign. A month or two. No further details at the moment."

This deal was a make-it-or-break-it for Douglas' idea. He started to hear rumors of a merger between DirectTV and AT&T. Almost all other projects were put on pause as the company prepared to acquire DirectTV for over 67 billion dollars. If Douglas wanted to find a way forward, it would have to be without AT&T.

A road bump can feel like the end of the world or the end of the idea as you know it. But like a speed bump, it's a sign to slow down and take time to fix the problem ahead. (And prepare for future speed bumps.)

On a recent trip to Italy, I learned the expression, "Hai voluto la bicicletta? E adesso pedala!" In English, it translates to something like, "You wanted the bike? Now pedal!" It's modeled after something you'd tell a kid learning to ride a bike. You wanted the bike, and yes, it's hard learning how to ride a bike, but you've still got to keep going.

We must adopt the same kind of thinking for our project. Didn't we want this? Weren't you dreaming of the day when the project is launched and it's a success? It's going to take time and problem-solving to get there. Might as well treat each opportunity as one we wanted to solve. Don't be so surprised by the road bumps and barriers that come up along the way—they're part of the process too.

IDEAS EVOLVE

When we first come up with our idea, it's all in our head. It takes a while to get the idea out of our brains and onto paper to share it with others—and eventually the world. A lot can happen in the time between the idea on day one and the eventual launch. When the end product starts to look different than the original concept, it can be frustrating and upsetting for the person whose original idea is changing.

"This wasn't what I wanted. This wasn't worth my time building, it's completely different than I planned."

Maybe that's how Spencer Silver first felt when he didn't meet his goal of creating a permanent, strong adhesive. Just because something doesn't go exactly as planned doesn't mean it isn't a good or useful idea.

Think back: Was there ever a time when you didn't have to make changes to an idea or a project, where other people's ideas for improvement were totally invalid and you built it out exactly as you initially imagined? No project in the world was built in a silo with no changes. And if somehow it was, it means that the person building it wasn't listening to other people, they weren't collaborating with stakeholders and they were completely inflexible. That's the opposite of the work we're doing.

Don't be surprised when your project looks different than it did at the start. Iteration is the way forward. Accept that your process is going to evolve along the way.

A few years ago I spent some time consulting for a technology company that was trying to instill new cultural values around innovation. I was working closely with a woman named Danielle she had an idea to create innovative capacity by training people with the right skills and mindsets. Rather than focus on launching another innovation incubator lab, Danielle believed in empowering people.

Danielle's boss thought the idea had potential and if she could continue her other responsibilities, it was worth it for her to develop the idea. Danielle spent lunch hours interviewing people who had worked on innovative projects in the company, researching about the top innovation programs, and putting together a master class in innovation.

She'd run a BETA version of the class with a couple of colleagues in the company who were interested in the culture behind innovation. She got rave reviews and real results from the people who tried her program. Danielle had evidence for why she believed her new program would help the people in her company and came to her boss with the newly designed initiative.

"I think the Innovation Masterclass is ready to be opened up to everyone across the company. I imagine a number of people from each department will want to do it so I'm estimating we can start capping the class at thirty."

Danielle's boss lowered his head, "I'm really happy that you've been getting such positive results. I noticed and actually already spoke to some people in other departments and our programs manager. Unfortunately, in a company of our size it would take a huge investment to run a program the way you've laid it out. I think it's incredibly valuable, I'm just not sure it's going to work for us. We don't have the resources to open enrollment for everyone."

Danielle had a hundred different solutions floating around in her head almost immediately. She was tempted to respond, "But we could..." or "I know it will work if we..." But instead she responded, "Okay, I understand. I'll do some research to investigate if there's any other kind of implementation that might work better."

Danielle was back to the drawing board. While ruminating over her idea in the company cafe, a manager from a different department approached her. "Hey, I heard about your idea. Really excited about it. I have someone on my team I'd love to nominate when it's up and running! They'd be a great fit. Let me know when you're open for nominations."

The manager's suggestion gave Danielle the idea to fix the problem. She could change the enrollment to be nomination-based and ask managers to nominate someone to go through the program. It wouldn't look exactly like the open source material she'd hoped could be easily shared and implemented more rapidly throughout the company, but it was a start.

She outlined how much time the program would take, what the outcomes would be for the participants upon completion, and a voting criteria for selecting the handful of people that would be in the first iteration of the program. The company said that something of this size scale would be fine to continue to run and test. Perhaps the final product was not as she had imagined it—but the flexibility in her implementation allowed her to move forward with the idea.

An idea is going to be better the more you can get feedback from others and the more it doesn't look exactly like you planned. Most everything you use today has evolved from something else. Our laptops, smartphones, cars, and even the houses we live in. They all look drastically different from their first iterations and from the first idea that popped into the inventor's head.

A HAPPYBOT ENDING

The worst has happened: you've tried and failed. The project was canceled, deemed a failure, or maybe you even got kicked off the team. These are a big deal. They can be incredibly discouraging and hard to cope with. No one wants to run a project into the ground—but in most cases, that's probably not what happened.

There are a lot of reasons for an idea to fail. It might have meant timing, resources, or circumstances completely outside of your control. Or maybe you had a big launch and customers didn't respond to it—whatever the reason for the perceived "failure," there's actually exponentially more to be gained than you think.

A friend of mine, Charlie, had an idea to improve employee happiness at his company. The financial services company was experiencing high turnover rates and it seemed happiness was a big factor.

He created a slackbot that made people happier at work. The automated solution was called Happybot, it gave anonymous feedback to management, as well as nudged employees to do things that were scientifically proven to make you happier.

Charlie brought everyone together and shared the goals for the new program, "I want to make people on this team happier. This program will give you the opportunity to share honest and anonymous feedback with me. I really think we'll benefit from this."

They started a two-month trial of using the bot. Initially, they had positive reactions from the team, but as they got busier, a chatbot was the last thing they were paying attention to.

The Happybot team started to add too many features and the employees lost interest. It wasn't solving the problem they set out to solve and turned into just another notification. The interface was nice, the content was good, but the actual connection between human and bot wasn't working.

"We learned a lot," Charlie said. "The bot sent a lot of scientifically proven things that would definitely work if we had the time and commitment to use them. It was a good reminder but just didn't stick."

After their two-month trial they didn't keep using Happybot. Charlie said, "There were a million reasons the idea failed, but the big one was that we focused on the wrong thing, and in the end didn't create a user-experience that actually helped people. And it turns out—people don't like doing things a robot tells them to do."

So from the outside, it looks like Charlie spent two years working on something that eventually failed. But when you talk to him about his experience, he says it was far from a failure.

"I met some amazing people I never would have if I hadn't run Happybot, including one of my best friends to this day. I learned how to pitch to executives and lead a team. The opportunities that I had simply because I started doing this work were incredible. I was invited to conferences and had speaking gigs. I wouldn't trade it."

The worst thing that can happen is that you try something new and it doesn't work out—but the benefits outweigh perceived failure.

The *real* worst thing that can happen? That you don't learn from your experience.

THE TRUSTED INNOVATOR

Every time I catch up with my friend Charlie and ask him what he's been up to he says, "Oh, well, earlier today I had coffee with so-and-so, who wanted some advice about launching their business idea. I don't have enough time on my calendar for all the people who are reaching out!" Charlie has launched more companies than the failed Happybot, but more than that he's become known as someone who innovates.

That's the risk you run when you start to do this work. You're going to become known as someone who launches ideas, someone who tries new things, someone to talk to when others have an idea.

As we've mentioned throughout this book, when you start to launch your idea, you have to get buy-in from others, create relationships, and build a team. There's a lot of collaborating with others. You'll create a reputation and other people who want to do that work will come to you for advice, help, or in some cases a new job.

I've worked with and coached people who have launched ideas and failed, but quickly become known for doing this type of work. Soon their boss understands that they can be trusted with launching new initiatives or managing a big project. They're known as someone willing to take risks and try new ideas.

When I first started launching ideas in big companies 20 years ago, I took a lot of time building trust and learning from my failures. Some days I had to face a failure head-on, to fix things and get my work back on track. But with my team of collaborators and cheerleaders at my side, I had a full bench to call on for help. After we got to the other side of our failure—fixing, changing, and iterating, along the way—I was seen as a leader who makes things happen. Someone that is persistent, willing and able to come up with creative solutions even in the most challenging of times.

FAIL BETTER

Failure is inevitable, but not the end of the world (or the end of your idea). As soon as you name the "failure" and call it out, the sooner you'll be able to recognize the value you got from the "failure" to grow and learn from it.

Didn't get to launch your idea because no one bought into the problem? Maybe you've gotten better at pitching your ideas.

Your company didn't want to go in that direction? Maybe you've learned how to adapt your idea or find a new home for it.

There's no failure we can't learn from. And success isn't always what it looks like. The notion that any of us comes up with one idea and retires off of it is a myth. You'll try and maybe fail, and then try again and get better along the way. Maybe you'll launch a brand-new, big successful idea and maybe other times you'll launch a great small feature on a product that makes people's lives easier. You'll learn and get better every time.

So if you've failed and are worried about putting yourself back out there, get up and dust yourself off. You've learned some invaluable lessons and it's time to pedal that bike.

Along the way, take time to acknowledge these failures and mourn them as needed. You're a human and spending years working on something and the emotional energy to push it forward is going to take a toll, no matter the outcome.

ACTIVITY

TURN FAILURES INTO LESSONS

Every project has some elements of failure. Creating space to talk about those failures and reminding ourselves of the lessons associated with them aren't something that most people talk about. We usually try to brush our mistakes under the rug or try to move on from them quickly. But giving space to talk about what happened and how you feel is scientifically proven to help you move on.

When Charlie from Happybot closed the doors to his idea officially, he called his mom and cried. When startup Famigo shut down, Douglas took six months off, pursuing his own ideas. And they both spent the time to reflect on what lessons could be learned from it all.

When you are at the end of any project, whether a success or a failure, take the time to uncover lessons using the *Rose, Thorn, Bud* method.

Rose, Thorn, Bud

What exactly is *Rose, Thorn, Bud*? A concept popularized by design thinking, it's a method that guides a conversation to talk about the good, the bad, and what has potential to grow. Using it to hold a discussion at the end of a project allows us to analyze what happened. The purpose of making space for this is to ask, "What happened? What went well and how can we do better next time?" and then deciding, "How do we move forward?"

Create space to learn, grow, and process with your team by following the three steps to using *Rose, Thorn, Bud*:

STEP 1: SET EXPECTATIONS

Everyone involved in the conversation about the project should walk into the room with a good understanding of what to expect. These meetings are meant to share insights and talk about aspects of the project that didn't go as planned—the best way to do that is to give people ample time to think and prepare for that conversation beforehand.

After consulting on a recent project, Douglas helped an engineering team organize a *Rose, Thorn, Bud* conversation after their company decided to go a different direction with the app they had been working on. Before the meeting, they sent out questions to consider.

"What went well?"

"What could have gone better?"

"What didn't go well?"

Participants came to the meeting knowing they were going to be talking about potential improvements, not in fear that they'd be talking about their individual performance. For best results, set expectations and ask your team to come with honest and thoughtful considerations.

STEP 2: HAVE THE CONVERSATION

There are a lot of different frameworks you can use to have a conversation like this. Once you get people together it's all about having a chance to talk about every facet of what happened during the project: the good, the bad, and what could have been better. The opportunity to gain insights could make a huge difference for what you take into future endeavors.

In the meeting with the team, pass out colored post-its: pink (rose), green (bud), and blue (thorn). If colored post-its aren't available, use red, green, and blue markers on plain post-it's or on a white board.

With post-its in hand, introduce *Rose, Thorn, Bud* to the team. The rose symbolizes "what went well" in a project. It's the pretty parts that you want to talk about, the successes, and things you would keep if you had to do the project all over again.

Thorn is the other side of the coin, it symbolizes "what didn't go well." Like a thorn, these are sharp pieces that might be difficult to admit or discuss within a team, but being able to pinpoint these are essential for moving on in the future.

And a bud symbolizes an unrealized or potential opportunity. You may discover an insight that's worth exploring, or an idea that has potential.

By brainstorming with the team through each of these categories, you can get a fuller picture of what went wrong, where you can improve next time, and opportunities to grow.

When Charlie's idea for Happybot didn't work out, he held a retrospective with his team and used *Rose, Thorn, Bud* to facilitate the conversation.

Charlie's insights were valuable in being able to take a step back and understand what had happened. He realized that the problem he had was spot-on but the solution needed to be different. By reflecting on these questions, a team can better prepare themselves for the future and up their chances of success.

When you finish a project or launch an idea, use something like *Rose, Thorn, Bud* to talk about how it went. When given the chance, team members may be able to voice what they saw happening and how they thought it could have gone better.

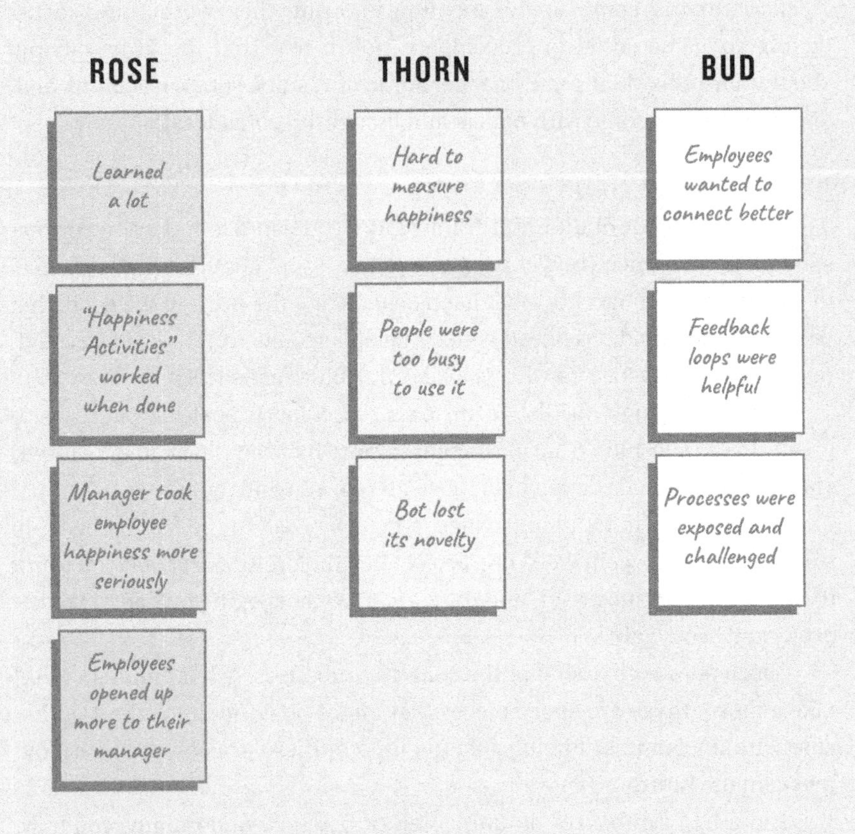
ROSE
THORN
BUD
Learned a lot
"Happiness Activities" worked when done
Manager took employee happiness more seriously
Employees opened up more to their manager
Hard to measure happiness
People were too busy to use it
Bot lost its novelty
Employees wanted to connect better
Feedback loops were helpful
Processes were exposed and challenged

STEP 3: ACTIONABLE TAKEAWAYS

After having the conversation and rounding up insights, you'll be able to move on to create actionable takeaways. From what you talked about with your team, what should you share with the rest of your organization?

It's important to share back with your boss and greater team so they also understand what good, bad, and potential came out of the project you worked on. There's a way to synthesize these learnings without "finger pointing" and instead, embracing lessons. It's tempting, especially when talking to higher-ups at a company, to want to shift blame and make yourself look good. Instead, when you can, accept responsibility and show that you're a leader who can handle all types of situations, good and bad. You're more likely to build trust with those leaders.

Think about the difference:

"We failed because we couldn't get enough resources from corporate headquarters. Our team was understaffed and our developer got sick a week during crunch time."

Vs.

"We learned a lot from the experience. Ultimately our solution wasn't the right fit for this audience. While we got a lot of positive feedback around the idea and branding, we learned that we need to find a different approach. We may need to revisit how we organize our team in the future and how we secure the appropriate resources."

The first response sounds defensive and immature. By only pointing out the problems there are no visions for future solutions. The second response shows leadership potential, that you're embracing lessons learned and can carry a team.

Once you've shared the takeaways, make a plan to implement them for future projects. It's one thing to write the lessons down, but it's more important that you utilize the lessons learned.

The worst that can happen is that we don't learn from our mistakes. Understanding everything that can go wrong, it's not that bad. Take the risk, believe in your idea, and start the process now.

THE ROAD AHEAD

A Letter to the Idea Pioneer

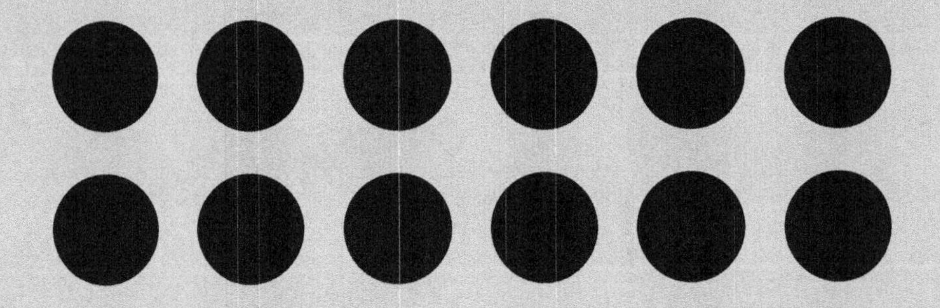

DEAR IDEA PIONEER,

You've reached the end of this book, but the work has really just begun. The journey ahead is one of the most challenging but rewarding ones you'll ever take. Following your idea will allow you to take on new challenges and own the work.

You're leaving behind the stale, predictable to-do list, and trading it for an empty map into uncharted territory. You'll fight your way forward for the pursuit of something more fulfilling. Others might tell you it'd be easier to stick with the status quo (and they're probably right) but easier isn't the only thing you're after. You're committed. You're not going to give up.

You started this journey with a bunch of mismatched puzzle pieces and were attempting to create a masterpiece. Staring fear in the face, you're taking on the problem and believing it's your time to fix it. You're finally taking the big leap from dreaming to doing. You're ready.

Quickly after taking the leap, you're going to be confronted by your own assumptions. You're coming to the harsh reality that maybe you don't know what's always best for everyone—we're better off asking. By creating a space in between decisions, you're challenging the way things have always been done. You start to answer the question, "How do I know what I don't know?" But for the most part, you're learning what it means to listen to the people around you (even the naysayers who don't believe in what you're doing). Because everyone's voice matters.

You've even wrestled through some of the less glamorous parts of launching an idea like organizational readiness and assessing the environment. When we think about launching the idea, we imagine the flashy, inspiring moments like pressing "go" on a new product or getting the applause for solving the company-wide problem, but in reality, most of launching an initiative isn't sexy. It's asking questions like, "Can my organization support what needs to happen for my idea to flourish?" or, "Where will I find capital and resources?" You've got to prove that your organization is ready for your idea and do the work to build the gap when it's not.

At this point, you probably have your very own "crazy wall" with PowerPoint slides, post-its, and emails outlining your plan ahead—everything is organized in it's own way. You've learned to explain it and perfect your pitch. Your idea has its own container and a place for each piece so nothing gets lost in the shuffle of corporate systems. Even if you hate the idea of organization, you're finding what works for you because your idea is worth it.

All along the way you're learning how to operate in your organization's specific world. From policies to regulations to office politics, there's a process for just about everything. It can be frustrating—especially when you don't know the rules you're playing by. While so much in an organization is done by the book, there's so much you've found is unwritten and must be uncovered by asking the veterans. By blending the formal process with the informal, you're coming up with your own understanding of "The Way Things Get Done." And while it's frustrating as hell, you've constrained yourself from trying to rehaul the entire system. You're getting closer—the map is getting clearer. You've got where you are now and where you want to go and you're finally filling in how it's done.

You're finding there's a delicate balance between going off on your own to pursue your idea and working with the people in your organization to co-create something even better. You're the clever artist painting a picture that everyone understands. It might take some modification to make it fit—but more often than not, accomplishing the goals of everyone involved leaves you better off.

With your idea taking shape, you'll begin to create buy-in with your story. Getting other people on board can be hard—and the consequences of not getting them on board can be big. When the boss says, "no" it can stop a project in its tracks. But you've learned how to find the right people, whether they've got the right title, role, or influence. By partnering with them, you'll discover how to tie together the problem you're solving with the people in your company you need to solve it. Ask and include others, you'll be surprised how much they'll want to help.

Finally, once you've laid the groundwork, tended the soil, and prepared in every way possible—it's time to start building. You start building the prototype, something small to test the idea. Prototypes are one of the best ways to test something without having to build out an expensive, time-consuming idea that no one might want. Prototypes finally answered your questions like, "Will people really use this?" and "Will this accomplish what we want it to?" They let other people touch and feel the idea for the first time and open up a conversation that can't be had without it. You're finally starting to see your idea come to life when you prototype.

Along this journey, you've been working to blaze a trail through the unknown for your idea to flourish. With each new step, you're likely running into some roadblocks or people that have told you, "no." Some people just like to tell others "no" and others have a good reason for their hesitance. But if you've gotten this far—that means you haven't given up or listened to everyone who told you it couldn't be done. Instead, you took the innovator's mindset and switched into problem-solving mode. A "no" is always an opportunity to lean in, learn, and find a different way forward. It's not about manipulating people to get what you want but instead, it's about gaining trust and co-creating something that everyone wants.

When you get into the business of really building the idea, you'll realize that you can't do it alone. Assembling your team will be an interesting mix, but it will be your job to lead them. You'll bring them through the awkward phase of learning how to work together through conflict that may arise all to build something great. You will be a leader that brings out their strengths, offers them new opportunities as they grow, and encourages them to make the idea their own.

Whether you're going through everything outlined in this book or you're just thinking of starting—it's a big undertaking. It can be scary and there's a potential for failure. Sometimes you're going to feel like you're working your ass off and no one is paying attention or listening. You know they should believe in your idea—and it's your job to convince them.

You'll get through it by remembering why you started. Remember that you're going to miss 100% of the shots you don't take. You can always choose to sit back in your cubicle and check the next item off your to-do list—but you want more than that.

With full knowledge of the challenges ahead, you're pressing forward. You're building something new. You're solving a problem that needs to be fixed. It's time.

Start Within,

Karen & Douglas

ACKNOWLEDGMENTS

To Douglas Ferguson—thank you for joining me as an author and thought partner on this adventure. You have a gift for toggling between the analytical and philosophical, bridging the science and reasoning with humor and stories that pull the reader in.

I owe a debt of gratitude for my co-collaborators, colleagues, bosses, and mentors that I have had the privilege of working alongside and learning from over the last 20 years, helping to shape this book. To Chris Chilek and John Cunningham, my dear friends and co-founders, you both take building great products and enjoying great beer seriously, and for both lessons, I salute you - cheers.

To Lenny Mendonca and Peter Sims, co-founders of FUSE Corps, your work in designing the executive fellowship program allowed me to learn the early lessons of *Start Within*. And to Cindy Kazanis and former California State Superintendent of Public Instruction, Tom Torlakson, I will forever be grateful to you both for the opportunity to create technology with a broader impact.

To Suzanne Gibbs Howard, I am in awe of your ability to empower others to think big and build an organization that is exciting, fulfilling, and fun. Thank you for bringing me into the IDEO U family and teaching me so much. To Katie Alba, Madeline Armstrong, Divya Balakrishnan, Hillary Braseth, Erin Bogar, Kat Chanover, Em Havens, Dawn Riordan, Coe Leta Stafford, Olivia Vagelos, and Kaleigh Walls. You are fierce women, creating beautiful experiences for humans. You push me to be the best version of myself. To Christopher Ancheta, David Good, Austin Harshberger, Danoosh Kapadia, Mark Magellan, Geoff Schwarten, and Zack Terrill, each a superhero in your field of work, you have taught me so much about the power of diversity in thinking and collaboration—thank you. To Tim Brown, Rochael Adranly, David Aycan, Katie Clark, Tom Eich, Margaret Kessler, and Diego Rodriguez, thank you for living, breathing, and teaching the values and behaviors that make IDEO such a special place. Your generosity in mentoring me has followed me through every role since and plays a part in my approach to solving problems.

Thank you to Megan Leatham, Amy Sell, Dianne Starke, Carlos Alfaro, and the team at LinkedIn Learning. It has been an honor and pleasure to work with everyone and learn more from you about what it means to create engaging content.

Kudos to our editor, Kellie McGann. I enjoyed collaborating with you, and thank you for your ability to keep us on track and help synthesize some of the more complicated parts of this book. And to our copy editor, Traci Parks, thank you for turning our draft into the completed piece it is today. A huge shout out to our designer, Shawn Bueche, for your work in illustrating the book. You took the idea and made it more visual, friendly, and accessible to readers.

To my mentor, Stacy Holland, thank you for always ending our calls with, "And how can I help you?" Your unwavering support and mentorship throughout the years have meant the world to me. And thank you to my early-career mentor, Dr. Isabella Cunningham. You have mentored and advised more people than I could count but have always been generous with your time and knowledge.

Thank you to the Voltage Control crew for your guidance as we worked on this book. Tara Weghorst for being the master wrangler, John Fitch for your relentless optimism, Lilly Davis for ground cover, Jamie Lafrenier for behind the scenes support, and Frankie Francis for the clever creative. And many thanks to Mark Peterson and Dawn Szombathy for sharing your master facilitation and design skills to assist with the book's activities.

I am eternally grateful to our early, test readers Angela Arnold, Lee Duncan, Ajay Dwivedi, Leila Kayali, Pat Henneberry, Kristina Paider, Steve Rader, and Shirley Tudhope. Your feedback and questions helped push us to make this book better. A special thank you to Jaime Sutton Wells for not only sharing the most feedback but being spot on for where the readers may be hungry for more. And Jamie Gardner, for your insights and work you do in advising others on the power of courage, connection, and community.

Thank you to my brother, Jeff Holst, and sister-in-law, Jana Holst. Your strength and resilience in launching the nonprofit Colin's Hope will always be a source of inspiration to me and countless others. You have created a community of doers that are passionate about creating solutions to childhood drowning prevention.

To my father, who still teaches me the power of curiosity and supports my wild ideas and in honor of my late mother, who would've bought the first copy of this book, you taught me how to be generous with others and to always look on the bright side of things.

Finally, to my husband, Ryan, my son, Bear, and my many dear friends (you know who you are!) that have supported me through life. I am grateful for every lesson you have provided me and the endless support and inspiration I draw from each of you.

ABOUT THE AUTHORS

Karen Holst is a product leader with deep expertise in human-centered design strategies, creative problem-solving, and product innovation. Boiling down her 20 years of experience into disciplines, her work has covered the gamut from business strategy and entrepreneurship to strategic partnerships and marketing communications. Karen loves to create technology with broader impact. Karen's work proves she thrives in the unknown. From co-founding a startup to launching new technology within a government agency, her secret sauce is the ability to take complex information, fragmented across disciplines, and make sense of it all. In the projects and roles she has taken on, the playbook was undefined, but the mission was clear. Karen rolls up her sleeves to get work done "in the weeds" and rises above it to bring teams along, seeing the "big picture." She is a natural observer and dot-connector, bringing together intersectional ideas to make an impact.

Douglas is an entrepreneur and human-centered technologist with over 20 years of experience. He is president of Voltage Control, an Austin-based workshop agency that specializes in Design Sprints and innovation workshops. Prior to Voltage Control, Douglas held CTO positions at numerous Austin startups where he led product and engineering teams using agile, lean, and human-centered design principles. While CTO at Twyla, Douglas worked directly with Google Ventures running Design Sprints and now brings this experience and process to companies everywhere. He recently published his first book, Beyond the Prototype, which offers a six-step plan for companies struggling with the shift from discovery to launch. Douglas is active in the Austin startup community where he serves on the board of several non-profits, mentors startups, and advises early-stage ventures. He spends his free time patching up modular synthesizers, playing guitar, and taking photographs. He graduated from Virginia Polytechnic Institute and State University.

Authors Douglas and Karen can be reached at info@start-within.com or visit
start-within.com/resources for book-related resources.

Made in the USA
Coppell, TX
08 September 2021